A Call to Care

THE WOMEN WHO BUILT CATHOLIC HEALTHCARE IN AMERICA

by SUZY FARREN

The Catholic Health Association of the United States

St. Louis, Missouri • *Washington, DC*

ACKNOWLEDGMENTS

Many people helped make this book possible. Here are a few of them. Martha Slover, whose diligence, ingenuity, organizational skills, and patience made this project possible. Ed Giganti, whose "integral involvement" and artistic inspiration shaped the project. Sandy Gilfillan for excellent editing. Renée Duenow for a beautiful design. Jack Curley for believing in this project from the beginning and supporting it during the tough times. Bill Cox, who said, "go for it" in the very beginning. Sr. Maureen Lowry and Brian Elderton for constant encouragement and fund development help. Josephine Mandeville and Emily Riley of The Connelly Foundation, with deep gratitude for the idea of writing a book. Steve Hilton of the Conrad N. Hilton Foundation and Gerard Garey of the Raskob Foundation for Catholic Activities. Sr. Maryanna Coyle for a great job in Philadelphia. Sr. Bernice Coreil for suggesting that it can't hurt to ask.   SF

Writer: Suzy Farren
Project Coordinator: Martha Slover
Editor: Sandy Gilfillan
Design/Production: Hawthorne/Wolfe, Inc., St. Louis, Missouri
    Renée Duenow and Vicky Nappier
Indexer: Linda Caravelli
Printing: Scholin Brothers Printing Company, Inc., St. Louis, Missouri

Copyright © 1996 The Catholic Health Association of the United States

Printed in the United States of America

ISBN 0-87125-234-1

The Catholic Health Association of the United States is the national leadership organization of more than 1,200 Catholic healthcare sponsors, systems, hospitals, nursing homes, and related organizations and services. CHA enables its members to accomplish collectively what they could not achieve individually. The association participates in the life of the Church by advancing the healthcare ministry and by asserting leadership within the Church and the rest of society through programs of education, advocacy, and collaboration.

National Headquarters: 4455 Woodson Road, St. Louis, MO 63134-3797, (314) 427-2500. Washington Office: 1875 Eye Street, NW, Suite 1000, Washington, DC 20006-2213, (202) 296-3993.

FRONT COVER:
SR. SABINA, CIRCA 1916, MATERNITY NURSE, ST. ALEXIUS HOSPITAL, BISMARCK, NORTH DAKOTA.

INSIDE FRONT COVER:
IN 1917, ST. JOHN'S HOSPITAL, FARGO, NORTH DAKOTA, ESTABLISHED THE CITY'S FIRST RED CROSS CHAPTER. THE HOSPITAL WAS OPENED BY THE SISTERS OF ST. JOSEPH OF CARONDELET IN 1900.

BACK COVER:
THE FIRST SISTERS OF MARY OF THE PRESENTATION IN AMERICA, 1902.

Foreword

When the first sisters arrived in what is now the United States, they came to nurse. Like so many of the tens of thousands of courageous women who would follow in their footsteps, those twelve French Ursulines set off for a new place and a new form of ministry, uncertain as to what would await them, but willing—even eager—to undertake the challenges of the unknown.

Today, it is difficult to fathom what these formerly cloistered nuns had agreed to do. Although they had no training or experience in healthcare, for their order was devoted to teaching, Mother St. Augustin Tranchepain and her companions responded to the pleas of a handful of New World colonists, arriving in New Orleans after a five-and-a-half month sea voyage on August 7, 1727. It took seven years for their hospital to be built but, by New Year's Day, 1728, the small band of sisters was nursing those who came to them, running classes for both boarding and day students, teaching a number of African American and Native American women and girls, assuming responsibility for orphans of both sexes, and agreeing to "take care of the girls and women of evil life." Thus, as Sr. St. Stanislaus Hachard—only a novice, but still actively engaged in all these works—could write home, with understandable pride: "You see, my dear father, that we are not useless in this country.... We are determined not to spare ourselves in anything that will be for the greater glory of God." As teachers, nurses, servants of the poor and orphans, and benefactors of "fallen women," she declared, the small band of sisters "discharge at the same time the functions of four different communities, that of the Ursulines, which is our first and principal one; that of Hospital Sisters; of St. Joseph; and of the Refuge." [1]

In many ways, these New Orleans Ursulines set the pattern for those who would follow. Like members of countless other communities, they assumed responsibility for ministries that were completely new to them—because those were what was needed in the setting in which they found themselves. They adjusted to unforeseen changes in plans and made themselves useful in whatever ways that they could. In their desire to make themselves useful, they made themselves indispensable. When, within a few years of their arrival, an interfering cleric threatened the Ursulines' autonomy, Mother Tranchepain declared that she would relocate her congregation to the West Indies unless the sisters were allowed to follow their rule without interference. The protests of both seculars and other clerics were unanimous on the women's behalf; no one could imagine New Orleans without the sisters' ministry. As a result, the disruptive priest backed down—and the Ursulines have enjoyed nearly 270 years of uninterrupted service to both Catholics and others throughout Louisiana.

These sisters may have been the first to arrive in this country, but they would not remain alone for long. By as early as 1820, women religious could outnumber priests in the United States— a fact that is still very much true today. What this means, really, is that for nearly all of this nation's history, women have comprised the majority of those serving in professional Catholic ministry here. And this has played a tremendous part in shaping and stretching what the American Church has been all about.

Stated simply, sisters have broadened our understanding of what it means to be Catholic—to "be Church." They are the heirs of those in the Book of Acts who fed the poor and who cared for the

---

[1] Sr. St. Stanislaus to her father, Jan. 1, 1728, in [Sister Therese Wolfe, OSU], *The Ursulines in New Orleans and Our Lady of Prompt Succor: A Record of Two Centuries, 1727-1925* (New York: P J. Kenedy & Sons, 1925), pp. 199-200.

abandoned. If priests have been entrusted with the sacramental legacy of the Last Supper, it has been nuns who, like Jesus on that same occasion, have washed the feet of their brothers and sisters—who have, in other words, adopted as their own Christ's mandate to serve others, whatever and wherever the need may be.

In this compendium of stories from the history of American Catholic healthcare, Suzy Farren has provided stunning evidence of the commitment of women religious to Jesus's mandate. In the accounts that follow, we discover the variety of ways in which healthcare has been provided: on the battlefield, through home visits, in hospices and rural clinics, as well as in hospitals both primitive and modern. We meet young girls who begin to nurse within days of entering their communities' novitiates, and mature women who, with hardly a moment's notice, leave classrooms or other workplaces to tend the sick in times of emergency. We find pioneer nursing educators, pharmacists, physicians, and technicians. Some of them enjoy the finest and most advanced training available; others acquire most of their eventual expertise on the job—from sister-colleagues who mentor and nurture them both as professionals and as religious.

Few of the nuns whose lives are presented here are "famous." Most lived and died obscurely, their names unknown even to most of those they served. As such, they typify thousands of "ordinary" sisters whose collective ministry has contributed mightily to both the social and religious history of the United States. Yet as the distinctive personalities we learn about in this book should remind us, these women were and are individuals, not interchangeable cogs in interchangeable caps and veils. Some were shy; others extraordinarily assertive. Some incited controversy, often finding themselves in hot water with secular and church authorities. Some left their original religious communities to found new ones; a few even left religious life. No stereotypes or plastic statues these! But, together, they reflect the range of very human personalities who, as sisters, have been the mainstays both of their congregations and of their congregations' ministries.

As the twentieth century draws to a close, the number of women religious communities is in decline. One reason for a book like *A Call to Care,* then, might be that it records a saga that, in its traditional guise, appears to be approaching its end. But the work of legions of sisters, forming the backbone of extensive healthcare institutions, is only part of the story that is told here. Another lesson, at least as important, is that what is recorded in this book began with one or two individuals, or with small groups—bands like those pioneer New Orleans Ursulines. The significance of sisters' contributions to American healthcare has never been solely dependent on number; it must be measured at least as much in qualitative as in quantitative terms. In that respect, the "call to care" will continue—in forms as unforeseen to us today as they were to Mother Tranchepain and her companions nearly three centuries ago, as they left the shores of France for a New World they could envision only in hope, and in faith.

Margaret Susan Thompson

Margaret Susan Thompson is Associate Professor, History, Syracuse University, Syracuse, New York.

Preface

This is a book of stories. It does not aspire to be a history of Catholic healthcare in the United States. Such histories have been very competently compiled by historians.

The idea for this book and the accompanying video took shape gradually. Talking to members of the Catholic Health Association, we uncovered one story after another about the foundings of hospitals by Catholic women religious. The stories were rich with drama. The women overcame tremendous obstacles, not the least of which was the fact that they were operating in a man's world.

Story after story added up to a saga. In fact, this saga is a piece of American culture that has been largely overlooked in the history books. In the telling of the stories, we came to realize that Catholic sisters shaped the American healthcare system.

These were women of vision. They were courageous too. And enormously creative. They had to be. How else do you start a hospital in the United States with $5 in your pocket and not knowing English? And while some of them went begging for money or built hospitals, others served quietly, day after day, year after year in a multitude of ways. For each sister, it added up to a lifetime. All told, hundreds of thousands of lives given to caring for people.

In some instances, sisters were invited to a town specifically to open a school, only to be told on their arrival, "What we really need, sister, is a hospital." So they opened a hospital. These were flexible women. They were about meeting needs.

When nurses were needed during the Civil War, the sisters served. The horrors they saw on battlefields, in hospitals, and on Naval vessels defy description. Their courageous service, their willingness to care for any soldier who needed them—black or white, Northern or Southern—did more to improve the image of the Catholic Church in this country than any other act before or since. And when the war ended, they quietly went back to their lives of service.

The idea for this project was inspired by a comment from a Sister of Mercy: "By the end of this century," Sr. Virginia said, "women religious will no longer have the influence they have had in healthcare in this country." It seemed a good time to tell the stories.

But make no mistake. Just because there will be fewer women religious does not mean their story is over. Far from it. Catholic women religious will continue to meet the needs of the times far into the future, with characteristic boldness and creativity.

It is our hope that their works, their courage, and their willingness to give their lives to meet the needs of people will inspire others in our society to give selflessly. The world needs more of that.

"What we have to give is our lives," a friend, Sr. Betsy, once said. "That's something anyone can do." But it's not something everyone does, and it is a truly remarkable gift.

Suzy Farren

In this year of beginning we ask ourself where are we going? What does it mean? It was all so casual in its happening, so unlooked for, so unexpected... we pray that with a quiet mind and firmness of will all shall meet the challenge, as year follows year.

FROM A LETTER WRITTEN BY MOTHER BERNARD, THE FOUNDER OF THE SISTERS OF ST. JOSEPH OF WICHITA, ON THE SISTERS' FIRST CHRISTMAS AS AN INDEPENDENT CONGREGATION.

This book is a celebration. Its text and photos tell the stories of the women who have fashioned Catholic healthcare in America.

One need not be Catholic to appreciate the legacy of these women. By their dedication, and through their example, they make God's love visible while showing a nation how to care for its people.

Their stories are more than entertainment; they are an encouragement. It should be reassuring to each of us that ordinary people still make extraordinary choices. And, in the process, grace is made visible.

John E. Curley, Jr.
President
The Catholic Health Association
of the United States

Contents

BELOW:
FOR THE SISTERS OF
PROVIDENCE, DOOR-TO-
DOOR SOLICITING AND
BEGGING TOURS TO OTHER
AREAS WERE WAYS OF
ACQUIRING MUCH-NEEDED
FUNDS TO KEEP THEIR
HOSPITALS OPERATING.

ABOVE:
SISTERS OF SAINT JOSEPH
OF CARONDELET AT CAMP
HAMILTON, KENTUCKY,
DURING THE SPANISH-
AMERICAN WAR.

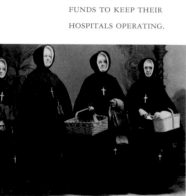

ABOVE:
THE LAUNDRY AT SAINT
MARY OF NAZARETH
HOSPITAL CENTER,
CHICAGO, ILLINOIS, 1924.

ABOVE:
THE OPERATING ROOM
OF MERCY HOSPITAL,
HAMILTON, OHIO, AS IT
APPEARED IN 1903.

RIGHT:
SR. IGNATIA GAVIN,
A CO-FOUNDER OF
ALCOHOLICS ANONYMOUS,
WAS A TALENTED
MUSICIAN.

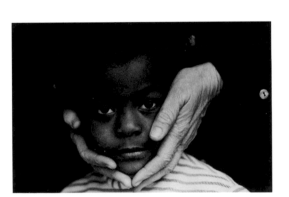

ABOVE:
SR. MARY STELLA SIMPSON
HOLDS THE FACE OF
A YOUNG BOY IN MOUND
BAYOU, MISSISSIPPI, IN THE
LATE 1970S (PHOTO, ALEN
MACWEENEY).

Courage

*O*ur hearts made our hands willing,
and with God's help, we did much
toward alleviating the suffering…

MOTHER AUGUSTA ANDERSON, A HOLY CROSS SISTER

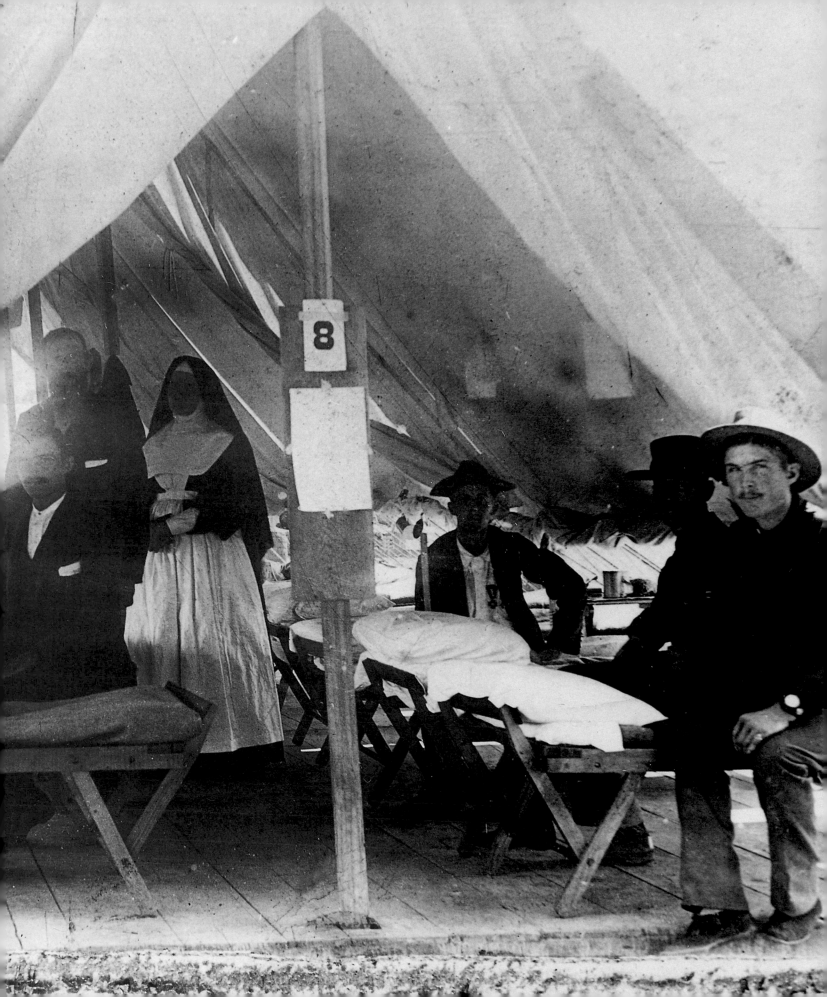

From caring for wounded soldiers on the battlefields of the Civil War to speaking out on behalf of justice the world over, women religious do not flinch in the face of need.

THE CIVIL WAR

Six hundred and seventeen sisters from 12 religious communities were nurses during the Civil War. They served on battlefields, in military hospitals, on transport ships, in tent hospitals, on the first naval hospitals, in prisons, and in isolation hospitals.

The sisters responded immediately, often within hours of being summoned to service. The discipline of religious life helped them adapt to the rigors of war. They willingly took orders, and they worked tirelessly to care for all who needed their help. When urged to leave their wounded charges because of danger to themselves, the sisters refused—time after time.

At the onset of the war, anti-Catholic sentiment ran high. The sisters' habits and accents seemed truly Old World and even frightening. At times, the very soldiers they attempted to care for rebuffed them. Dorothea Dix, Union superintendent of nurses during the Civil War, was decidedly anti-Catholic and made a point to avoid using Catholic sisters.

Bringing Order to the Chaos of Battle

But the sisters won the respect of soldiers everywhere. They seemed not to see whether a soldier was from the North or the South. Nor was the color of a man's skin or his religious preference a determinant of the care he got. The sisters who were nurses in the Civil War brought order and cleanliness to the most chaotic and abominable situations.

They nursed, they cooked, they cleaned, they mopped up blood and removed maggots from wounds, they assisted in surgery, they wrote letters to the loved ones of wounded or sick soldiers, they consoled, they spread cheer, they dressed wounds, they soothed the suffering, and they eased the final moments of the dying. They seldom slept and never complained.

And when the war ended, they quietly went back home to pick up where they had left off: meeting the needs of the times.

SISTERS OF ST. JOSEPH
Wheeling, West Virginia

Wheeling Hospital was the first hospital between Pittsburgh and Cincinnati, and the bishop of Wheeling wanted it run by the Sisters of St. Joseph.

During the Civil War, the sisters felt it was their duty to protect wounded men from both armies. When one of the sisters died of smallpox, Mother de Chantal did not notify authorities for fear that a search of the hospital would reveal the whereabouts of hideaways. She and another sister wrapped the dead woman in her habit and buried her one night in the garden.

Space was so tight at the hospital that the sisters gave their sleeping quarters to the wounded soldiers and slept on the floor of the chapel. Sr. Ignatius Farley, one of the Civil War nurses, recalled, "One autumn night, it was necessary that I remain in the surgical ward long after schedule time, and it was therefore very late when I was relieved from duty. Going toward the chapel… I opened the sacristy door with the utmost care and closing it softly behind me I stood fascinated by the unusual picture of seven professed sisters, worn out from severe hospital duty, who were lying fast asleep on the floor, and soldier fashion, each sister was enfolded in a blanket, while each weary head was resting upon a pillow made of leaves gathered on the campus…"

On July 26, 1864, the hospital was at its capacity when 200 additional wounded men were brought to its doors. Mother de Chantal calmly ordered the orphans who lived in one hospital wing evacuated to an emergency building and had the sisters place blankets on the floors of the wards and corridors to receive the wounded soldiers.

Mother de Chantal died in 1917. In 1918, she was remembered in the House of Representatives:

"For four years during the war, with other members of her community, she rendered aid and comfort to many distressed and afflicted soldiers… She and her devoted companions tenderly nursed the soldiers who were brought in from prisons and neighboring battlefields, never failing to render them ready and sympathetic attention…"

SISTERS OF CHARITY OF CINCINNATI
Mount St. Joseph, Ohio

*T*he first call for sister volunteers came on June 1, 1861. Six Sisters of Charity of Cincinnati reported for duty at Camp Dennison, about 15 miles away.

On June 8, 1861, *The Catholic Telegraph* reported: "There are about 12,000 men in the encampment. The Sisters have to walk in mud and water over their shoe-tops in heavy rains to attend to their no sinecure duties…"

Commented the *Cincinnati Commercial*: "Sr. Anthony and a number of Sisters of Charity are acting as nurses and do much of the cooking for the sick… The services of these good women cannot be estimated. They are the Florence Nightingales of America."

Besides nursing in camps and hospitals, the Sisters of Charity of Cincinnati

ABOVE:
SISTERS OF CHARITY NURSE THE WOUNDED ON A CIVIL WAR BATTLEFIELD.

served on floating hospitals, where they cared for wounded men who were being transported from battle sites to hospitals.

The Battle of Shiloh, in April 1862, was among the bloodiest of the entire war, with 23,000 casualties. Sr. Anthony O'Connell was among 38 Sisters of Charity of Cincinnati who served. "At Shiloh," wrote Sr. Anthony, "we ministered to the men on board what were popularly known as the floating hospitals. We were often obliged to move farther up the river, being unable to bear the terrific stench from the bodies of the dead on the battlefield. This was bad enough, but what we endured on the field of battle while gathering up the wounded is beyond description.... Day often dawned on us only to renew the work of the preceding day without a moment's rest."

A soldier's diary offers the following comments about Sr. Anthony: "Amid this sea of blood she performed the most revolting duties for those poor soldiers. She seemed like a ministering angel, and many a young soldier owes his life to her care and charity.

Happy was the soldier who, wounded and bleeding, had her near him to whisper words of consolation and courage...."

Sr. Anthony was a friend of many Civil War generals and Jefferson Davis. On one occasion she saved the life of a young Southern boy who had ventured across Union lines. When Sr. Anthony learned that he had been sentenced to death, she pleaded for his life before General Rosecrans. The general told her it would be impossible to spare the boy, but Sr. Anthony begged the general to think of his own young son. Finally General Rosecrans relented and placed the boy in the care of Sr. Anthony, who sent him home to his mother.

Sr. Anthony served throughout the Civil War. She died at age 86 on December 8, 1897.

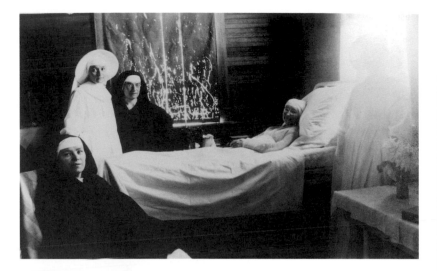

SISTERS OF THE HOLY CROSS
Notre Dame, Indiana

A pounding at the door of Saint Mary's Academy in Notre Dame intruded on the peaceful night of October 21, 1861. When they opened the door, the Sisters of the Holy Cross saw in the lantern light a priest and a brother they knew well. The men had come to discuss a request from Indiana Governor Oliver P. Morton. He was looking for 12 sisters to serve as nurses in Union hospitals. The sisters agreed to send six to war.

Within hours, they were on their way. The first group of sisters was dispatched to the Military Hospital in Paducah, Kentucky. In November, a second group was sent to Mound City, Illinois, to manage a hospital. The following month, a third group of Holy Cross Sisters went to manage a hospital in Cairo, Illinois.

Trained as a dressmaker, Mother Augusta Anderson knew nothing of nursing when she was dispatched in 1861 to Cairo to care for sick and wounded soldiers in the Civil War. Of the experience, she wrote: "Many wounded men whose limbs had been amputated were there with little or no care. We pinned up our habits, got brooms and buckets of water, and washed the blood-stained walls. We were not prepared as nurses, but our hearts made our hands willing, and with God's help, we did much toward alleviating the suffering."

At age 93, Sr. de Sales O'Neill, who nursed in the Civil War, recalled watching Mother Angela assist the chief surgeon during an operation: "It was a deliberate and difficult operation and the life of the soldier depended largely upon the accuracy of the surgeon, whose head and that of Mother Angela, on opposite sides, were bent over the poor lad… Suddenly from above a heavy liquid drop fell upon the white coif of Mother Angela who, true to her Celtic strain, did not quiver. Another, and still another, drop after drop came faster and faster. At last, the final stitch had been taken and the two heads, that of the surgeon and of the sister, rose simultaneously, and not till then did the doctor know that a stream of blood, trickling through the open chinks of the upper floor, had fallen steadily upon the devoted head of Mother Angela, who stood before the surgeon with head, and face, and shoulders, and back bathed in the blood of some unknown soldier."

SISTERS OF THE HOLY CROSS, NOTRE DAME, INDIANA.

ABOVE, TOP:
HOLY CROSS SISTERS ALSO SERVED IN THE SPANISH AMERICAN WAR.
BOTTOM:
HOLY CROSS SISTERS AND SPANISH AMERICAN WAR SOLDIERS.

LEFT:
THE RED ROVER, A U.S. NAVY HOSPITAL SHIP.

A letter written by another sister described what they saw upon their arrival in Cairo:

"The apartments on the first floor had been used as receiving and operating rooms, and amputated arms and legs and pieces of human flesh were strewn around, while here and there a mound of decaying flesh and bones sent forth a sickening odor throughout the entire hospital. To add to the horrors of the gruesome sight, the walls and even the window-panes were blood spattered."

Another sister wrote:

"As we stepped into each room on the first floor, what a fearful sight stared us in the face.... Some of the wards...resembled a slaughterhouse the walls were so spattered with blood.... Sister M. Isidore and I cried with horror until we were tired.... We never knew what war was until that 7 day of Dec. 1861.... Mother {Augusta} looked at us both a kind, pitying look and said now stop, you are here and must put your heart and soul to work. Pin up your habits, we will get three brooms, three buckets of water and we will begin by washing the walls and then the floors."

The Holy Cross Sisters were the first Naval nurses in U.S. military history, serving on the Union transport and hospital ship *Red Rover*.

After the war, Mother Augusta became the first American-born superior general of the congregation.

SISTERS OF CHARITY OF NAZARETH
Nazareth, Kentucky

"After the Battle of Shiloh, the hospitals could scarcely accommodate the victims of bullet, powder and disease. Wherever and whenever it was possible to give succor, the sisters did so—thus immortally enrolling themselves in their country's and Nazareth's roll of honor. Unostentatiously, as they passed from one field to another, dispensing charity and mercy to men of the Blue or the Gray, these humble nurses were making some of the greatest history of the tragic epoch, and because of their humility, many of their noble deeds failed to be chronicled..." ANNA McGILL, IN A HISTORY OF THE CONGREGATION.

Sr. Lucy Dosh, a Sister of Charity of Nazareth, Kentucky, was 22 years old in 1861 when she nursed the sick and dying at a makeshift hospital in Paducah, Kentucky. In addition to war wounds,

dysentery, diarrhea, pneumonia, and typhoid were common ailments. While she cared for the men, Sr. Lucy sang in a beautiful soprano voice.

She nursed for less than a year. On December 29, 1861, suffering from exhaustion and typhus, Sr. Lucy died. Leaders of both sides called a truce so her body could be transported up the Ohio River accompanied by an honor guard of Union and Confederate soldiers. Its final resting place was St. Vincent's Academy near Louisville, where the sisters had opened a convent in 1819.

SISTERS OF MERCY
Chicago, Illinois

Not long after the Civil War started, the Sisters of Mercy in Chicago volunteered their services. They journeyed to St. Louis, where they boarded a troop boat bound for Lexington, Kentucky. During the journey, the boat was ambushed and riddled with bullets. Unable to continue, the ship returned to Jefferson City, Missouri, where the sisters took charge of a military hospital. They worked there for about seven months until orders came to close the hospital in April 1862.

Although they assumed they would return to Chicago, the Sisters of Mercy were ordered by the government to take charge of the *Empress*, a troop boat headed for Shiloh. When they arrived, the sisters stared at the devastation. Death was everywhere. Sick, mangled dead and dying men and horses were strewn over the battlefield. By lantern light the sisters searched for soldiers who were still alive and had them taken on board the *Empress*. The sisters fed the soldiers and tended their wounds.

Years later, Mother Austin Carroll and other Sisters of Mercy encountered Jefferson Davis en route to New Orleans. The former head of the Confederacy asked to speak with them. "I will never forget your kindness to the sick and wounded in our darkest days, and I do not know how to testify my gratitude and respect for every member of your noble order," he said.

At one point during the war, when the Sisters of Mercy had been refused supplies by the War Office, President Abraham Lincoln wrote: "To Whom It May Concern: On application of the Sisters of Mercy of Chicago, furnish such provisions as they desire to purchase and charge the same to the War Department."

SISTERS OF MERCY
Vicksburg, Mississippi

*T*he Sisters of Mercy went to Vicksburg from Baltimore in 1859 to open a Catholic school. The siege of Vicksburg began in May 1862. Townspeople who could leave took shelter in caves in the hills. The sisters left the city too, but when they learned the Confederates had converted their school into a hospital, they returned to nurse the sick and wounded. During the bombardment, the bishop urged the sisters to return to their motherhouse in Baltimore, but they refused. The siege ended on July 4.

Meanwhile, the Confederate government established a primitive, makeshift hospital in a dilapidated house in Mississippi Springs, and two sisters and a postulant moved there to nurse. The wounded poured in: 400 at the end of the first week, 700 at the end of the second. The sisters worked there throughout the summer.

Following the Battle of Shiloh, the sisters went to Oxford, Mississippi, to nurse at a military hospital. As with most situations the Civil War nursing sisters encountered, conditions upon their arrival were deplorable. The Sisters of Mercy managed to clean things up and establish order, but they could do nothing about the food shortage. According to the journal of Sr. Ignatia Sumner, the sisters ate unsalted cornbread and drank sage tea or sweet potato coffee. When the Union forces neared Oxford, the sisters loaded all but the 60 most severely wounded soldiers onto boxcars to flee south.

BELOW:
A SISTER OF MERCY
COMFORTS A CIVIL WAR
SOLDIER.

The Sisters of Mercy and their charges ended up in Jackson. When Vicksburg fell on July 4, 1863, the Union Army headed toward Jackson. Food and medical supplies all but disappeared, and hours before Jackson fell, the sisters again boarded a train. Traveling in open cars, they spread a tent over themselves during the day for protection from the sun. They eventually arrived in Shelby Springs, Alabama, where the Confederates had opened a hospital.

By the end of the Civil War, the Sisters of Mercy were unrecognizable: their habits and veils in tatters, their feet bound in strips of cloth, their health shattered. They were near starvation. They returned to Vicksburg, only to find that their convent had become the headquarters of General Henry Warner Slocum. After contacting Secretary of War Edwin Stanton, the sisters were eventually able to return to their home.

SISTERS OF CHARITY
Bronx, New York

*F*rom a September 9, 1862, letter to Secretary of War Edwin Stanton:

"The commissioners of the Central Park of this city have given a very large building for a government hospital for the reception of wounded soldiers....

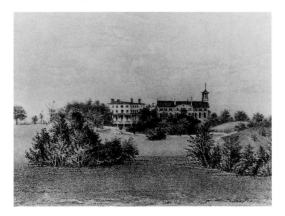

The point is this: we want the nurses of this hospital to be the Sisters of Charity, the most faithful nurses in the world. Their tenderness, their knowledge, and religious convictions of duty render them by far the best nurses around the sick bed which have ever been found on the earth. All that is asked is that they be permitted to be nurses under the direction of the War Department and its physicians...."

The letter was signed by Edwards Pierpont. Two days later, the surgeon general of the United States agreed that the Sisters of Charity be selected to nurse wounded soldiers in New York City.

The St. Joseph Military Hospital was open from October 28, 1862, until August 1865. Fifteen Sisters of Charity served there.

One grateful soldier wanted to thank the sister who had taken care of him during a long convalescence. Looking at her worn habit, he said, "Madam, I'd like to buy you a nice black satin dress."

Of all the forms of charity and benevolence seen in the crowded wards of the hospitals, those of some Catholic sisters were among the most efficient.... More lovely than anything I had ever seen in art, so long devoted to illustrations of love, mercy, and charity, are the pictures that remain of these modest sisters going on their errands of mercy among the suffering and the dying.... How many times have I seen them exorcise pain by their presence or their words! How often has he been refreshed, encouraged, and assisted along the road to convalescence when he would otherwise have fallen by the way, by some home memories with which these unpaid nurses filled the heart.

ABRAHAM LINCOLN, ON THE SISTERS OF MERCY, STANTON HOSPITAL, WASHINGTON, D.C. (NATIONAL ARCHIVES).

SISTERS OF MERCY
Pittsburgh, Pennsylvania

*O*n November 26, 1862, a group of sisters from Mercy Hospital, Pittsburgh, took charge of Stanton Hospital in Washington, D.C. A total of 26 sisters from the Pittsburgh Sisters of Mercy volunteered their services during the war.

In September 1863, a young soldier with beautiful rust-colored curly hair lay dying in a ward at the hospital. When he saw a sister, he asked her to find a sister from Pittsburgh. It turned out that the woman, Sr. Mary Regina Cosgrave, was a teaching sister from Pittsburgh, serving as a nurse at Stanton. As she held the hand of the dying young man, he told her his wife Mary lived in Pittsburgh with their infant son, a baby born with six fingers on his left hand. He begged the sister to tell his wife not to hurt the baby, not to cut his finger off. And then he died.

Twelve years later, Sr. Regina was teaching a class of boys in the convent classroom in Pittsburgh. Two latecomers appeared, dragging a tiny feisty boy, who broke loose and ran away. Sr. Regina asked about the child's family and learned that his mother and father were dead. She encouraged the

boys to find the lad and bring him to her. When "Wooden Will"
was brought to her, Sr. Regina fed him and learned that he lived on
the streets. She invited him to stay with the sisters and offered to
teach him in their school.

When she asked Will if he could bless himself, the lad raised his
hand to try. She noticed that his left hand had six fingers. She looked
closely at the boy and noticed his rust-colored curls. She asked about
his father, only to learn that the man had died during the Civil War
at Stanton Hospital in Washington. Will knew that, he told her,
because it said so in a book that had been his mother's. In the front
of the book was the inscription that had been written years before by
his father: "To my wife, Mary." From that day on, "Wooden Will"
was known as Sr. Regina's boy.

BELOW:
A PAINTING OF THE
DAUGHTERS OF CHARITY
ON A CIVIL WAR
BATTLEFIELD.

DAUGHTERS OF CHARITY
Emmitsburg, Maryland

Daughters of Charity made up more
than a third of all sisters who nursed
during the war. Two hundred and thirty-two
Daughters served in tent hospitals, on battlefields, in military prisons, and in isolated

camps reserved for contagious cases. Within days after war was
declared, they had taken charge of two military hospitals in
Richmond, Virginia.

Emmitsburg, Maryland, where the Daughters' convent is located, is just 10 miles from Gettysburg, site of the bloodiest battle of
the Civil War. On the evening of June 27, 1863, the sisters were
preparing for bed, unaware that the Union Army was nearly at their
door. Gradually they began to hear strange sounds outside.

The sisters did what sisters do. They fed the Union Army. And
when the men marched on to Gettysburg, the Confederate troops
arrived. When the grounds were at last free of troops, Sr. Camilla
O'Keefe, wrote in her diary: "Glad we were to get rid of them."

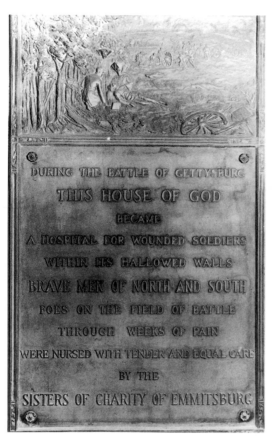

RIGHT:
MONUMENT TO THE
DAUGHTERS OF CHARITY
OF EMMITSBURG.

BELOW:
DAUGHTERS OF CHARITY
AT SATTERLEE MILITARY
HOSPITAL.

Never did human eyes behold such a spectacle! Soldiers, slain or half dead, lay before them, groaning in ghastly heaps, some calling for aid and others gasping alongside hundreds of breathless steeds, whose nostrils no longer scented the grimy smoke of battle. Here, among these ruins of life, thousands of guns, sidearms, wheels, projectiles, and all sorts of military accouterments were promiscuously scattered. Into the midst of these grim ravages of war went these noble messengers of peace and charity, with hardly an inch of ground to step on, and helped to pick up the wounded and carry them to farm wagons which had been requisitioned as ambulances.

A TRIBUTE TO THE SISTERS BY REPRESENTATIVE
AMBROSE KENNEDY OF RHODE ISLAND, MARCH 1918.

From July 1 to 3, the battle raged at Gettysburg. The rain started in the evening on July 3 and fell all through the night. On Sunday morning, July 4, twelve Daughters of Charity arrived at the battlefield to assess the situation and care for the wounded.

"The rains had filled the roads with water, and here it was red with blood. Our carriage wheels rolling thro' blood. Our horses could hardly be made to proceed from the horrid objects before them. Dead men & horses here & there, men digging graves, & others bringing the bodies to them. A little group sitting over a fire trying to cook their meat in the midst of all these scenes."

SR. MATHILDE COSKERY

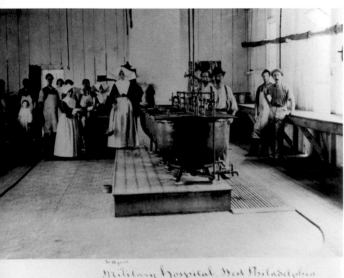

Military Hospital, West Philadelphia

ABOVE, TOP:
ILLUSTRATION OF
DAUGHTERS OF CHARITY
ON THE BATTLEFIELD.
BOTTOM:
SATTERLEE MILITARY
HOSPITAL, WEST
PHILADELPHIA.

In three days of fighting, nearly 3,000 Union soldiers were killed and 14,500 wounded. More than 5,500 Confederate soldiers were killed and 25,500 wounded.

The sisters immediately set about caring for those they could, tearing their own clothing into strips when the bandages ran out. Then they continued on into the town of Gettysburg. Churches, barns, tents, and houses were turned into makeshift hospitals. At the Catholic Church, the wounded lay on pew seats, under the pews, in the aisles, and in every available space. An operating table blocked the entry. The air was foul with the stench of gangrene, and the pitiful sounds of men in agony would not be stilled. Noted Sr. Mathilde: "Many wounds had piles of maggots in & about them which must be removed before the poor limb or wound could be soothed."

Reinforcement sisters arrived from Emmitsburg and Baltimore, along with food and supplies. The sisters distributed clothing and blankets in ambulances to the men still on the battlefield. In one of the fields near Gettysburg, the sisters served for weeks, tending the wounded until they could be moved to hospitals. Among the most

ABOVE:
SR. MARY GONZAGA GRACE
RAN SATTERLEE MILITARY
HOSPITAL DURING THE
CIVIL WAR.

valued items on the battlefield were combs, which could remove the lice and vermin from the hair of the wounded soldiers.

Thousands of wounded were taken by train to the 15-acre Satterlee Hospital complex in Philadelphia, which was run by Sr. Mary Gonzaga Grace. During the course of the war, Sr. Gonzaga and her 40 sisters cared for 50,000 Confederate and Union casualties. When patients outnumbered beds, tents were erected to handle the overflow.

SISTERS OF SAINT DOMINIC
Springfield, Illinois

In October 1874, the nation erected a monument at the gravesite of President Abraham Lincoln in Springfield, Illinois. Days before the ceremony was to occur, President Ulysses Grant asked a group of sisters in Springfield if they would unveil the monument. Because they were a cloistered order, they declined his invitation. Grant realized how much Lincoln had admired the sisters who nursed in the Civil War, and he felt their presence would be a fitting tribute to the slain leader.

The Sisters of Saint Dominic, who had distinguished themselves tending the wounded in Kentucky and Tennessee, had moved to Jacksonville, Illinois, to teach school. President Grant sought permission from the bishop to invite them and, when permission was granted, sent a special train to transport them to Springfield. On "Unveiling Day," October 15th, the bishop's telegram arrived at the motherhouse at 6 a.m. Quickly two Dominican Sisters departed for the station to board the president's special car to Springfield.

Amidst all the pomp and ceremony, Sr. Josephine and Sr. Rachel did as President Grant had asked. They pulled the cords to unveil the monument to the former president of the United States and then quietly slipped away to return to Jacksonville and their everyday lives. ❧

The nature or severity of the illness was of no consequence. Driven by faith and a desire to meet the needs, women religious rolled up their sleeves and provided care to people abandoned by others.

SISTERS OF SAINT FRANCIS
Joliet, Illinois

The Sisters of Saint Francis, a teaching order, sent five sisters to Memphis in 1871. In early summer of 1873, cholera broke out, followed a few months later by yellow fever. Mother Augustine recounted what happened.

> *"When the pestilence broke out, calls immediately came to us for help. We were not nurses; but we trusted in God and responded as best we could. Four of us, Sisters Bonaventure, Gabriel, Gertrude, and myself, volunteered to go on duty at once....*
>
> *"At first, we went to the sick only during the day; but soon we remained, taking care of them day and night. Our number could have been augmented a hundredfold, and yet there would not have been enough of us to meet the demands for help. We worked exclusively in homes.... I do not know the number of patients we nursed, as we kept no account of them; I only know the calls were so numerous, from non-Catholics as well as Catholics, and the demands upon us so great that we took no time for ourselves.*
>
> *"Sr. Gabriel, our superior,...was in a poor district of the city, nursing an aged couple, very sick with the fever, in a wretched second floor quarters of a still more wretched building, the first floor of which was used as a saloon. The click of glasses, ribald songs, and curses came up through the thin partition of the floor....*
>
> *"Sister had been there two days and the intervening night when the old man died. His wife was in a coma at the time. Lest she should wake up rational, as patients sometimes did, and find her husband dead beside her, sister spread a sheet upon the floor and summoning all her strength she removed the body from the bed to the floor and covered it with another sheet. Then she watched beside the sleeping woman until nearly morning, when the woman, without waking, passed into eternity, too.*
>
> *"Sister had a severe headache during the day, which grew worse during the night; and her last charge gone, she meant to start for home at daylight.*

Caring
When No One
Else Did

Suddenly she felt herself growing weak; she sank to the floor and was unable to rise. She had presence of mind and strength enough, however, to pull off her slipper and tap with it on the floor. She knew no more.

"The men who brought her to the convent at four o'clock that morning told this: In the saloon below they heard the tapping above. The proprietor and two other men hurried upstairs. Opening the door they saw the dead woman on her bed, the dead man on the floor, and sister lying there in a swoon, which they knew was the beginning of the fever. Tenderly they wrapped her in clean blankets and brought her home. 'I'll tell you,' one of the men said, 'the sight that met us in that room sobered us.'

"Sr. Gabriel died a few days later…. She was only 19."

THE SMALLPOX HOSPITAL
Houston, Texas

Four Sisters of Charity of the Incarnate Word—two from Galveston and two from Houston—cared for smallpox victims during an epidemic in Houston in 1891.

Smallpox victims received care at the pesthouse, and it was there that the sisters lived while the epidemic lasted. The pesthouse quickly became overcrowded as more and more victims were brought there, and tents were erected to care for the sick. The sisters often worked 20 hours a day and had only four hours for rest, which was frequently interrupted.

BELOW, LEFT:
SISTERS AT SMALLPOX
'PESTHOUSE', HOUSTON,
1890-1891.

RIGHT:
ST. JOSEPH'S INFIRMARY,
HOUSTON.

Healthcare professionals other than the sisters and physicians could not be induced to serve at the pesthouse. The dead were buried at night, and the sisters were frequently the ones who held lamps while the grave diggers worked. The sisters also carried stretchers bearing smallpox victims, because no one else would do that task.

When four smallpox victims were found at St. Joseph's Infirmary in Houston, they were banished to the pesthouse. A document from the times described their removal from the hospital:

"A large conveyance appeared at the door. It was manned by drivers and helpers so strikingly 'helmeted, booted, and spurred' as to recall to the memory the tales of romance and chivalry of the middle ages. They did not act in a chivalrous manner, however, for they refused to lend any assistance in the removal of the patients. They stood looking on, at a convenient distance from contamination, while the sisters carried these four patients on their mattresses from their beds to the wagon."

From the *Houston Daily Post*, March 29, 1891:

"God bless the dear, noble women—the Sisters of Charity. In sorrow and suffering, in pain, anguish, despair and death, the grand, sweet and lofty sympathy of these goodly women sends floods of light and warmth, love and hope to every soul that is chilled in gloom and darkness and every heart that is bathed in the shadows of death. Pure of thought, heavenly in their aspirations, worshiping God in their tender affection for suffering humanity, and making every sentiment of their life and every deed of their hand a most glorious monument to the divinely humane mission of true womanliness upon earth, they bless mankind with boundless wealth of faith, hope and self esteem, and cast a halo of sweet poetry over the cold and cheerless utilitarian philosophy of our age."

The Smallpox Hospital
Blackwell's Island, New York

*T*he smallpox epidemic of 1875 killed 1,280 New Yorkers. So intense was fear of the disease that people chose to die at home rather than go to the Smallpox Hospital on Blackwell's Island. City officials decided that the hospital had to have a new image. And they agreed that the only people who could possibly transform it were the Sisters of Charity at New York City's St. Vincent Hospital.

Eight sisters were chosen for the assignment. On their first trip to Blackwell's Island, they were accompanied by their superior, Mother Regina. "It was the most God-forsaken place…that I ever saw," she wrote.

The Sisters of Charity quickly changed the situation. The city report described what they did:

> *"The Domestic Department, including the general nursing, is conducted by Sisters of Charity…. One is in charge, and she assigns to the others their respective duties, exercising a general supervision over all. Upon one devolves the duty of housekeeper, another has charge of the laundry, and each of the others has charge of a ward, with helpers to assist under her direction….*
>
> *"No one can witness the faithfulness and self-sacrifice with which these pious women discharge their respective duties, regardless of their own comfort, and intent only on the welfare of those entrusted to their care….*
>
> *"Since the change in management has been effected, the hospital has been steadily gaining in popularity, and it is not at all unusual for us to be gratified with the sincere thanks of returned patients for the kindness and tender care which they received during the period of exclusion from their homes and from society…."*

The hospital was closed in 1880 because it was no longer needed. The building still stands near the tip of Roosevelt Island in New York City.

*O*ne of the first sights which met the eye of the unfortunate patients as the boat neared the dock was a pile of coffins at the landing place, painfully suggestive of the manner in which some of those just arriving might leave the island."

A REPORT BY THE CITY FROM 1875, DESCRIBING THE SCENE THAT AWAITED ARRIVALS TO THE SMALLPOX HOSPITAL (NEWLY RENAMED RIVERSIDE HOSPITAL).

SISTERS OF SAINT JOSEPH OF CARONDELET
St. Louis, Missouri

*I*n the fall of 1898, during the Spanish-American War, 11 Sisters of Saint Joseph of Carondelet from St. Louis nursed the wounded at Camp Hamilton near Lexington, Kentucky. The sisters took the oath of allegiance to the United States at the camp, which was a city of tents where 500 soldiers suffered from typhoid fever. Of 100 nurses at the camp, 48 were religious. Daughters of Charity, Sisters of the Holy Cross, and Sisters of Saint Joseph worked side by side.

From Camp Hamilton, the Sisters of Saint Joseph went south to Camp Gilman in Americus, Georgia. Their third assignment took them to Matanzas, Cuba, where they were the only American religious congregation to serve. They remained in Cuba until May 19, 1899.

SISTERS OF SAINT JOSEPH
Philadelphia, Pennsylvania

When the call came to nurse influenza victims in 1918, the Sisters of Saint Joseph responded, although they were primarily a teaching order. In all, 167 Sisters of Saint Joseph worked in general and emergency hospitals, while 60 sisters served in other institutions. One hundred and eighty-six sisters nursed people in their own homes.

One of the volunteers wrote to her superior:

"When called to these new duties, for which few of the sisters had any special training, there was a feeling of dread and apprehension, not of the contagion, but of fear lest inexperience and lack of training result in failure, and render our efforts ineffective.

"Entering the ward, the sisters were overwhelmed with pity and compassion at the sight of the sufferers. Many of them were so discolored as to seem black in the face.... The sisters were assigned to different phases of work: some to take temperatures; others to prepare ice caps and hot-water bags and refreshing drinks; others to prepare the diet, and others to give medicines. These definite assignments made the work more methodical and brought conditions under control. Patients were being brought in by the police and others in trucks, ambulances and wagons, and by nightfall the ward was nearly filled, and a number of extreme cases had died. There was only one orderly in the place, and the dead often lay for some time waiting to be removed."

The sisters also went from house to house, caring for victims of influenza. In one house, according to a sister, "Finding the door open, we entered. On the table was a loaf of bread and a mouse eating it. The place seemed to be headquarters for roaches and ants and creeping vermin."

On the second floor, the sisters found two sick boys, one six, the other 10, in a single bed. In the next room the mother lay next to another boy and a baby girl, all seriously ill. They had had nothing to eat since the day before. The sisters found food, changed the bed linens, and sent for a doctor and a priest.

In another instance, the sisters entered a home to find a three and a half-year-old boy trying to care for his sick parents and sibling. In still another house they found a young woman who had lain unattended for a week. After the sisters washed the woman and put her in an airy room and fed her, they urged her crippled father to get a nurse, since he could afford one. They remained until the nurse arrived.

The sisters entered each house not knowing what they would find. What they did find was people deserted by their neighbors and sometimes even by their own families. Houses were filthy and stinking; families were often starved, in addition to being ill from influenza. Some of the sisters contracted the disease or became prostrate from exhaustion.

Eight sisters died:

Sr. Irma Aloysia, age 19	*Sr. M. Rose Catherine, age 25*
Sr. Francis Xavier, age 30	*Sr. Mary Florentine*
Sr. Mary Charles Borromeo, age 26	*Sr. M. Francis Bernard, age 25*
Sr. Mary Cyprian, age 25	*Sr. Mary Catherine, age 29*
(a novice, she made her vows	*Sr. Lorenzo Donohoe*
on her death bed)	

In a letter to the Mother Superior on October 30, 1918, the bishop of Philadelphia wrote:

"I deem it my duty to send to you, and, through you, to your sisters, the expression of my profound gratitude and admiration for the heroic manner in which the members of your community risked even death in the care of the sick and dying. When the public at large were in a panic with fear and apprehension, and overwhelmed with awe and sorrow, your sisters gave an example of sublime courage and devotion which only supernatural motives could have prompted. Their fearlessness in danger, their marvelous charity, their humility, have excited the wonder of non-Catholics, and are a source of legitimate pride for those of the faith." ❧

All men and women were equal in the eyes of Catholic sisters. Resolute in the face of intimidation, women religious fought to eliminate prejudice, often at great personal risk.

SISTERS OF ST. FRANCIS
Stella Niagara, New York

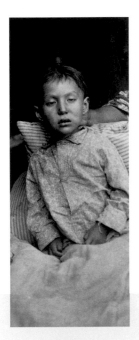

Refusing to Buckle to Prejudice

Although healthcare has never been the primary work of the Sisters of St. Francis of Penance and Christian Charity, they nursed the sick whenever the need arose.

In 1890, the sisters taught Sioux children on the Pine Ridge Reservation in South Dakota. It was a time of great unrest on the reservations and great fear among white settlers.

The following journal excerpt came from Sr. Liguori Mason, Holy Rosary Mission, Pine Ridge Reservation, South Dakota:

"In September 1890…Josephine Bee {a young student}…eluded the vigilance of the sisters and went in search of the sweets of liberty on the prairie….

"While searching for her, the sisters came upon a poor blind woman lying in a hollow…covered with filthy rags and an army of vermin. The poor creature was nearly…100 years old. She had been brought there by her children and grandchildren who supplied her with enough food to keep her alive…. She was delighted to hear that one of the 'Holy Women' had come to see her….

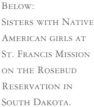

27

ABOVE:

ST. FRANCIS MISSION.

"Mother Kostka…hastened to visit her and with the help of two of the girls she carefully washed the old woman, put clean clothes on her, arranged her bed more comfortably, and gave her a soft pillow…. Clara {the name given to the woman}…was placed in the infirmary and tenderly cared for by Mother Kostka….

"New Year's Day dawned. What would 1891 bring them? News came that General Miles had arrived and would take the chief command. Alas, a report was also rife that the Indians were determined to fight and to die!…. Word was received from Fr. Stephan, director of the Indian Bureau, who was on his way to the mission…to conduct the sisters to a place of safety…. But Mother Kostka…assured Father that she would not leave the mission, and calling the sisters together, she told them that eight of them might get ready to go with Msgr. Stephan, while she and one companion would remain. But the sisters declared that, save under obedience, they would not leave, they would stay at the post of danger till the end…."

In the ensuing days, there was no fight.

ABOVE, TOP:
TWO SISTERS WITH NATIVE AMERICAN WOMEN AT ST. FRANCIS MISSION.
BOTTOM:
SISTERS WHO SERVED AT ST. FRANCIS MISSION IN SOUTH DAKOTA ON A CARRIAGE OUTING IN THE LATE 1800S.

FRANCISCAN MISSIONARIES OF OUR LADY HEALTH SYSTEM
Baton Rouge, Louisiana

Sr. Mary Reginald Slattery arrived in Monroe, Louisiana, in 1913 from Ireland. Her first assignment was as nursing supervisor of St. Francis Colored Ward, a one-story hospital for African Americans. An excellent nurse and a compassionate human being, Sr. Reginald quickly made it clear that she would not give in to bullies.

One day a lynch mob arrived at the Colored Ward seeking one of Sr. Reginald's patients. Sister was unwilling to let the mob enter the building. Behind a window facing the front entrance to the building, she stood in full view of the mob. With a cold stare, Sr. Reginald held a gun in position, ready to shoot the first person who dared to enter. Noting the pistol, the members of the mob looked at one another for a few seconds and quietly dispersed. Little did they know that Sr. Reginald had never before held a gun, that she had no idea how to shoot, and that the gun was not loaded.

Sr. Chrysostom Moynahan
Daughters of Charity
Birmingham, Alabama

BELOW:
DURING WORLD WAR I,
SR. CHRYSOSTOM LED A
BAND OF 10 DAUGHTERS
OF CHARITY AND 90
GRADUATE NURSES TO CARE
FOR THE WOUNDED IN
ITALY.

The child of Irish immigrants, Sr. Chrysostom Moynahan became a Daughter of Charity in 1891. She served as a nurse during the Spanish-American War and in 1900 founded Alabama's first school of nursing at St. Vincent's Hospital in Birmingham. In 1903, Sr. Chrysostom survived a brutal case of typhoid fever. She was administrator of St. Vincent's Hospital from 1900 to 1918. On March 10, 1916, she became the first registered nurse licensed in Alabama.

During World War I, Sr. Chrysostom led a band of 10 Daughters of Charity and 90 graduate nurses to care for the wounded in Italy. She was decorated by the Italian and United States governments for bravery and service to the military.

Sr. Chrysostom died at age 74 in 1941, and was buried with military honors in a soldier's grave in the Catholic Cemetery in Mobile, Alabama. In 1982 she was installed in the Alabama Women's Hall of Fame.

Sr. Beatrice Eyl
Sisters of Charity of Nazareth
Nazareth, Kentucky

Sr. Joseph Beatrice Eyl, known as Sr. Jo B, fought becoming a Catholic sister with every ounce of her "obstinate nature."

"I'd go out to a dance or a party until 1 or 2 am, get home, get down on my hands and knees and pray to the great good God that I wouldn't have to be a sister," she recalled in 1992.

For two years the young woman studied journalism, but something told her she was avoiding her destiny. She finally decided to become a cloistered nun. But the priest to whom she confided had other ideas. "No way!" he told her. "You have strength, you have health, and you have brains. You get yourself down to Nazareth

House." In 1928 she joined the Sisters of Charity of Nazareth.

The first job of this brainy, headstrong, healthy young woman was to dust the front stairs of the motherhouse. "I was through in 15 minutes," Sr. Jo B recalls. "I was happy as a lark because I had the rest of the day free." Little did she realize the mistress of novices was ready to put another dust cloth in her hand.

One day Sr. Jo B donned a white apron and went to work in the kitchen. She forgot to take off the apron when she went in to dinner. The sister who was administrator of the Catholic hospital was so taken by her appearance that the next morning Sr. Jo B found herself in front of the mother general. "Would you like to be a nurse?" she was asked. "Oh, no, mother," Sr. Jo B pleaded. Ten days later she was in nurses' training.

For years, Sr. Jo B taught nursing and taught in the sisters' schools. In 1969, she visited a priest who worked with migrants. He, in turn, introduced her to Catholic sisters from other religious communities who had received a federal grant to work with migrants. "I had never heard the word 'migrant' before, and they offered me the directorship of the whole program. When I got home, I looked up 'migrant' in the dictionary." Sr. Jo B refused the directorship but decided to spend the summer working with migrants.

At age 62, she arrived in Elizabeth City, North Carolina:

*W*hat I saw that summer… Those poor migrants. They were treated like beasts of burden. If they didn't do what the crew leader said, he was the devil incarnate. He carried a black snake whip and a pistol. And he used the whip on them.

SR. JOSEPH BEATRICE EYL ON THE MIGRANT WORKERS OF NORTH CAROLINA.

"This was North Carolina in July and August, and it was hot. When I first got there I saw women standing up cutting cabbage. Other women were pushing cabbage into crates just as fast as they could. I thought they were all out of their minds. I didn't realize they got one cent per crate! And if they didn't crate at least 200 crates, they didn't get any money.

"They didn't make any money anyway, because at the end of the day the crew leader would say, 'I'll pay you at the end of the week.' But at the end of the week, when the poor people thought they had $60 or $100, he would say,

One time, Sr. Jo B was stopped on her way into a migrant camp by a woman who told her she couldn't come onto the property. "I work for the government," Sr. Jo B retorted, "and I'll put my foot on anyone's property I want." The social worker who accompanied her stared open mouthed.

A pickup drove up and a man got out and ordered Sr. Jo B off the property. "I want to see the conditions in your camp," Sr. Jo B told him. The man pulled his shotgun from the back of the truck. Aiming it at her, he again ordered her off the property. The social worker prepared to hit the ground. "I work for the federal government," Sr. Jo B said. "Now put that gun back in your truck," she commanded. To the astonishment of the social worker, the man did as he was told, and Sr. Jo B walked into the migrant camp.

'Your kid broke a light and busted a window and you didn't do this or that.' And their pay would be $10 or $15.

"The food that they fed the migrants made me vomit! They'd come in from the fields after working hard all morning. There was no place to wash their hands even though they'd been rummaging around in the ground for sweet potatoes or whatever. They'd be given a tin plate with cooked pig tails hanging off the plate (they don't curl when they're cooked), half-cooked corn bread, and half-cooked beans. They'd eat sitting against a tree or on the ground in the blazing sun.

"The conditions in the camps were terrible," she continued. "And if anyone tried to run away, well, I saw a crew leader break a man's leg so he wouldn't run away from camp. The meanness, the cruelty I saw!"

The more she worked with the migrants, the angrier Sr. Jo B became. At considerable personal risk, she told her horror stories to the FBI, the State Department, the NAACP, and local and state officials. She testified about the violence of the crew leaders and the abominable conditions of the migrant camps. "I took the problems and put them in their laps," she says. "When I wasn't fighting with the government, I was fighting with doctors or the health department for my migrants."

In 1978, the executive director of the Migrant and Indian Coalition for Coordinated Child Care, Inc., Hood River, Oregon, had this to say about Sr. Jo B: "We were amazed at the ability of Sr. Joseph Beatrice to move in this environment. She removed the fears as if by magic. She is aware of realistic alternatives that are workable for the resource people and the families. She had an extreme sensitivity to our target population, giving them a feeling of worth and willingness to learn new methods."

Sr. Jo B retired at age 80 in 1987. She died on June 9, 1995.

St. Joseph's Hospital and Health Center
Paris, Texas

St. Joseph's Infirmary had already failed when the Sisters of Charity of the Incarnate Word agreed in 1911 to run it. They agreed also to assume the $14,000 debt on the property. In making the commitment, they realized that many of the people in the area were strongly anti-Catholic.

ABOVE:
THE KLU KLUX KLAN BURNED A CROSS ON THE LAWN OF THE SISTERS' INFIRMARY (CORBIS-BETTMANN).

Arriving by train in Paris, the sisters carried their luggage the mile and a half to St. Joseph's. Their first task was to clean the infirmary. They carried water for the washing from a nearby well, and by the end of the day, the sisters were too tired to eat.

The arrival of the Incarnate Word Sisters prompted the defection of the chief surgeon, who decided to build his own hospital rather than work for the sisters. He took many patients and nurses with him, leaving St. Joseph's without a chief surgeon and with few patients.

Not the least of the threats to the women religious was the Ku Klux Klan. Extremely active in Paris, the Klan burned a cross on the lawn of the infirmary. The cross burning won public sentiment for the sisters, however, and St. Joseph's began to see more patients.

To make room for the increase, two sisters volunteered to live in a tiny cottage, where the rain fell through the roof onto their beds at night. In the morning, they used water from their tin hot water bottles to wash their faces.

Sisters of St. Joseph of the Third Order of St. Francis
South Bend, Indiana

In 1945, at the request of the bishop, the Sisters of St. Joseph went to Meridian, a poor Mississippi town, to open a hospital. They went there because there was a need, not because there was strong support for the Catholic Church. Only one out of every 50 Mississippians was Catholic.

The sisters purchased an old, roach- and ant-infested shell of a building that had once been a sanatorium. After it was cleaned and painted, St. Joseph Hospital opened in June 1946. From the start, the sisters encountered difficulties. Sr. Camille Guzman remembered: "The ambulances used to pass our hospital and take patients to the other hospitals (there were three in town) even if the rule normally is, 'Take the patient to the nearest hospital.' They would bring us patients who couldn't pay or those whom no one else wanted."

The reason for this was that the sisters' policy was to accept black persons as patients on the same level as white patients. And, according to Sr. Camille: "When we first came, people thought we might make them Catholics.... However, in a relatively short time they saw we were human...."

During the Civil Rights movement in the early 1960s, St. Joseph Hospital was constantly subjected to abuse because the sisters publicly recognized the rights of blacks. In 1966, two years after passage of the Civil Rights Act, the federal government ordered Mississippi to desegregate. Sr. Mary Eleanore Wiencek, the administrator, promptly issued a news release reiterating the sisters' stand against any kind of discrimination. That same day, she sent a letter to the medical staff, admitting officers, supervisors, head nurses, and department heads, insisting that in St. Joseph Hospital, "the patient's medical and nursing needs as determined by his physician will be the sole criteria for assigning him a bed."

The role of the sisters during the Civil Rights movement further enraged the community. In St. Joseph's Hospital, the sisters fed students who had traveled to Mississippi to help rebuild black churches that had been burned down. The community boycotted the hospital and other organizations that favored civil rights. Leaflets dropped from planes read: "Attention white citizens of Meridian and Lauderdale County. Listed below are a few people and businesses

SISTERS OF MERCY
Baltimore, Maryland

Martin de Porres Hospital, Mobile, Alabama, closed in 1971 because the need for it no longer existed. During its 30-year existence, the hospital cared solely for African American patients. Established as a maternity hospital in 1941 because of the dire need for such services, Martin de Porres was taken over by the Sisters of Mercy, Baltimore, in 1942. The sisters expanded the facility several times in response to need. In 1971 they decided that Civil Rights legislation had negated the need for a hospital exclusively for African Americans and closed the facility.

who are traitors and parasites, who would sell their souls for thirty pieces of silver—integration."

Hospital occupancy dropped, and with it revenues. The sisters stood their ground and kept the hospital open. Sisters from other parts of the country raised money to help them through the difficult times. Passions eventually cooled in Meridian, as they did elsewhere in the country, and integration became an accepted practice.

SR. PROVIDENCIA
SISTERS OF PROVIDENCE
Spokane, Washington

"The story begins with my grandmother. [She] was traveling across the Plains with her sisters and others in a covered wagon in 1887. They accidentally drove into a Sioux encampment. The Sioux happened to be on the warpath at that time. They spared the lives of the white travelers because my grandmother wore a large cross. I have told many Indian tribes that I feel I have a personal obligation to Indians because they spared the life of my grandmother."

In 1948, Sr. Providencia joined the faculty of the College of Great Falls, Montana, a Catholic liberal arts college, as a lecturer in sociology. She soon was a familiar figure to Native Americans in the area.

Sr. Providencia believed in the power of the reservation to instill pride and values among Native Americans, according to Joan Bishop writing in the summer 1993 issue of *Montana, The Magazine of Western History*. She was appalled by off-reservation settlements that had sprung up in Montana. The Indians there were "people without a place," she affirmed. Residents of these settlements were not eligible for federal government funding or for county aid because they did not live on reservations.

Sr. Providencia raised money and obtained food and clothing for the Indians. Although she was successful—largely because people didn't know how to say no to her—she realized these efforts were temporary at best. What was needed was heightened awareness among legislators.

In the early 1950s, the federal government was seeking to bring to a hasty end its involvement in Indian affairs. The government also wanted to relocate Indians who lived on reservations to cities. Although they opposed both ideas, tribal leaders feared retaliation if they spoke out against these schemes.

With encouragement from Sr. Providencia and others, Native American leaders testified before Congress in 1954. Sr. Providencia became vocal with Democratic party leaders in Washington, particularly with legislators from Montana, including Mike Mansfield (who later became Speaker of the House of Representatives).

ABOVE:
SR. PROVIDENCIA WITH
NATIVE AMERICAN
WOMAN.

With her students, Sr. Providencia published several studies to support her advocacy efforts. Among her findings: Native Americans who moved away from reservations experienced "a slight rise in economic opportunities," but "a loss in group status and individual attainment."

In September 1955, the House Subcommittee on Indian Affairs came to Great Falls from Washington, D.C., for hearings chaired by Sr. Providencia.

In December of 1955, the National Congress of American Indians gave Sr. Providencia their annual merit award "for her inspiring leadership of Indians and whole communities." The ensuing publicity frustrated Sr. Providencia. She believed the attention detracted from the plight of Native Americans. And she was coming under attack for her efforts. Among her critics were sisters from her order who felt she was spending too much time

on the Indians. Ire was aroused because Sr. Providencia ignored the
accepted custom of traveling with other sisters and frequently visited
Capitol Hill with college students. Nevertheless, her congregation
continued to support her. And Sr. Providencia continued to fight for
the rights of Native Americans. She demanded federal attention
to the problems of subsistence, health, education, and welfare.
At the same time, Native American advocacy efforts grew stronger
as tribal representatives became increasingly outspoken.

In 1959, Sr. Providencia and others greeted Lyndon Johnson in
Great Falls, where, at a reception in his honor, he acknowledged that
the case of the landless Indians was primarily a federal responsibility.

Gradually, legislation paved the way for better education,
housing, and job opportunities. In 1966, Sr. Providencia wrote,
"I warn the dinosaurs who still think the Indians are 'things' to get
pushed around—to move out of the way."

When she died in 1989 at age 80, Sr. Providencia was remembered as someone who could "make the sparks fly and help us hear
the thunder roar in the land of the shining mountains."

Sisters of Saint Joseph of Wheeling
Wheeling, West Virginia

"Twenty-five staff nurses at St. Francis Hospital have agreed to leave the institution unless three Negro nurses employed there are dismissed immediately," reported the *Charleston Daily Mail* on May 12, 1951. When the hospital administrator, Sr. Helen Clare Bauerback, refused to meet their demands, 20 white nurses quit.

Reported the *Daily Mail*: "It appeared that the attitude of the Sisters was to continue their present practice regardless of its effect on the good name of St. Francis in this community, and in expressed opposition to the majority of the staff physicians of the hospital...."

To keep the hospital from closing, the sisters airlifted Sisters of Saint Joseph from other West Virginia hospitals.

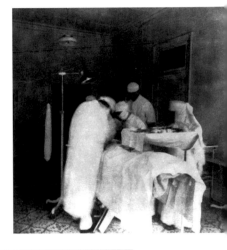

If the local community took issue with the sisters' stance, other parts of the country viewed their refusal to accede to the nurses' demands as an act of tremendous courage. Father John LaFarge, SJ, chaplain of the Catholic Interracial Council of New York, called the move "a historic turning point in the history of interracial relations in this country."

The sisters received letters from hundreds of individuals and organizations. Among them was this from U.S. district court judge John F.X. McGohey of New York City: "Your magnificent Christianity in refusing to dismiss the Negro nurses from your hospital has been a great inspiration. I hope you realize that, apart from the spiritual value of your action, you made a great contribution to true democracy and Americanism...."

> Sr. Helen Clare was confronted with the challenge and met it bravely.... The Sisters announced: 'As a Catholic institution it will continue to uphold Christian principles of charity and justice as well as the spirit of the United States Constitution.' We believe the brave stand taken at St. Francis Hospital is an event of national significance....
>
> *THE INTERRACIAL REVIEW*, JUNE 1951.

Some physicians left Saint Francis in sympathy and the patient census went down, but Saint Francis weathered the controversy. The strike lasted about three months.

Maryknoll Sisters
Maryknoll, New York

> *Kansas City, Missouri, June 10, 1955—"There has been a Baptist Ministers Conference here in Kansas City this week. A minister from Texas attending the conference was stricken with a heart attack. Hospitalization was necessary, and the man, being colored, had a hard time gaining admission to the hospitals in the city. He was finally brought to our hospital."*
>
> FROM THE DIARY OF A MARYKNOLL SISTER

Queen of the World Hospital opened in April 1955. Run by the Maryknoll Sisters, who are known for their missionary work, the hospital ignored color, a radical concept at the time. Graduate sociology students from the University of Chicago commented that, "no other hospital in the United States is attempting integration as is the Queen of the World Hospital." Approximately 30 of the hospital's 140 physicians were African American, and white and black nurses worked side by side tending to patients from both races. At the time, no other accredited hospital in Kansas City would accept black physicians. The Maryknoll Sisters worked in administration at the hospital and served as nurses. They also opened a nursing school in 1956 that accepted applicants of all colors.

Queen of the World Hospital remained open until December 31, 1965.

Sr. Antona Ebo
Franciscan Sisters of Mary
St. Louis, Missouri

It was a Sunday afternoon in March 1962 that linked Sr. Antona Ebo with a town in Alabama she'd never heard of: Selma.

Sr. Antona, a Franciscan Sister of Mary since 1947, was watching television when the program was interrupted. She sat stunned as she watched footage of troopers beating a group of citizens who were marching for the right of Negroes to register to vote. She said to herself, "If I wasn't a nun, I'd be there."

RIGHT:
SR. ANTONA EBO
IN SELMA.

UPO31010-3/10/65-SELMA,Ala.:Nuns who were in forefront of 3/10 attempted march on the Dallas County courthouse delivers statement to city officials who halted the march less than a block from its starting point.Marchers were turned around on orders of Selma Mayor Joe Smitherman. UPI TELEPHOTO -iwl

St. Louis' Cardinal Ritter sanctioned Catholic participation in an interfaith group that would go to Selma to march. The group consisted of 48 priests, rabbis, Protestant clergy, and six Catholic women religious. Sr. Antona was asked to be one of the six—the only African American woman religious. "One side of me said, 'I don't want to be a martyr.' But the other side said, 'Put up or shut up.'" She agreed to go to Selma.

The night before she left, the TV news showed a young white minister being beaten to death on the streets of Selma. "I didn't sleep too well," she recalled.

The group boarded a chartered flight from St. Louis to Selma on March 10. Volunteers greeted the marchers at the airport and drove them into town. To get to the church where they were to gather, they had to walk past a housing project.

"A little black girl was playing outside," smiled Sr. Antona. "She took one look at me and ran to me with her arms outstretched. She'd never seen a black nun before. I embraced her, and it was the kind of affirmation you can't get anywhere else in the world."

*S*r. Antona Ebo remembers: "There were Confederate flags everywhere and squad cars, policemen in helmets, police dogs, and bullies with clubs in their hands."

Finally, they were face to face with the mayor. "I have never seen such hatred in anyone's eyes," Sr. Antona said. "If I get arrested," she thought, "I won't be in the same jail as the other sisters." The jails were segregated.

RIGHT:
SISTERS OF CHARITY
MARCHING IN NEW YORK
IN SOLIDARITY WITH THE
CIVIL RIGHTS MARCHERS
IN SELMA.

The church was overflowing with people. As they walked in, the crowd began to stir. "They brought the nuns, they brought the nuns!" people murmured.

Sr. Antona, originally a Baptist who converted to Catholicism, was singing songs she hadn't sung since her early days. "I was having myself a good ol' relaxing time," she grinned, "until someone asked me what my name was." Organizers wanted her to speak. "I was so scared," she admitted. "In St. Louis, everyone had told me not to say anything. I thought, 'This is the South! I can't do this.'"

But the Reverend Anderson was speaking. "For the first time in my life," he declared to a hushed church, "I am seeing a Negro nun. To see her tells me you don't have to be white to be holy."

Sr. Antona stepped up to the microphone as the people stood and applauded her. As she surveyed the crowd, she noticed people with bandages, casts, and missing teeth, survivors of the violence that had already erupted. Somehow she introduced herself and explained how she had wanted to be in Selma to walk with the people, that she believed in the right of Negroes to vote. What she did not say was how afraid she was, how she'd bargained with God and told him if it hadn't been for her habit she'd have gone to Selma, and how he'd called her bluff.

When the group began to march, someone asked her to take her glasses off.

In the midst of it all, the microphone was once again thrust at Sr. Antona. She faced the mayor, the helmeted policemen, and the bullies. Into a sea of Confederate flags, she said, "I am here because I am a Negro, a nun, a Catholic, and because I want to bear witness." Her presence and her words were broadcast around the world. The violence she had so feared never came to pass that day.

In 1967, Sr. Antona became the first black woman religious to head a hospital. She was named administrator of St. Clare Hospital in Baraboo, Wisconsin. Today she is a pastoral associate at St. Nicholas Church in St. Louis. ◔

ABOVE, LEFT:
A FELICIAN SISTER OUT-
SIDE A PRIMITIVE HOUSE
IN THE 1900S.

ABOVE, RIGHT:
THE FELICIAN SISTERS
WITH ORPHANS IN
POLAND, 1878.

*Catholic women religious defy stereotype. Some worked quietly
to meet the needs, while others were vocal in advocating justice.*

THE FELICIAN SISTERS
Livonia, Michigan

*I*n their earliest days as a religious order, the Felician Sisters traveled from village to village in Poland, establishing dispensaries,
or *ochrony,* for peasants. In addition to treating people's ills, the sis-
ter-infirmarians would teach hygiene to replace health practices
guided by superstition. Also in Poland, the sisters established an
orphanage, a home for the elderly, and a 40-bed hospital.

Invited to teach Polish immigrants in rural Wisconsin, five
Felician Sisters came to the United States from Poland in 1874.
Although teaching was their primary mission, they responded eager-
ly to other community needs. The sisters opened 10 orphanages over
the next 50 years. In 1888, they took over a small hospital in
Manitowoc, Wisconsin, until a larger one could be built by the
Franciscan Sisters.

For 29 years, the young congregation was guided by Father
Joseph Dabrowski, who had sought help from the Polish Felicians. A
quiet man of good deeds, he told the sisters, "Only small and narrow

souls hunt for recognition and applause from the crowds. A great and noble soul passes through life so quietly and unobtrusively that she draws no one's attention. Even when she must exert herself heroically, she never considers that she is doing anything above the call of duty."

SR. STANISLAUS MALONE
DAUGHTERS OF CHARITY
New Orleans

The Daughters of Charity had served at Charity Hospital in New Orleans for half a century when Sr. Stanislaus Malone arrived there as a young sister in 1884.

When Sr. Stanislaus arrived, there were no electric lights. Sisters made their night rounds by lantern light. The beds were so high, the sisters had to climb on a stool to reach their patients.

A physician described Sr. Stanislaus in her early years at Charity as "a petite, vivacious and agile figure flitting through the hospital as a white-winged messenger.... But she had a mind of her own right from the start. And could she put a young intern in his place and teach him a lesson?"

The doctors quickly recognized Sr. Stanislaus' abilities, and she was sent to school to study operating room techniques. In 1895, she received her diploma in nursing.

On December 26, 1913, Sr. Stanislaus wrote to another sister about her work as assistant administrator of Charity Hospital:

"There will always be enough of this kind of work, and this is all a Sister of Charity desires. Do you know that we are a sort of mystery to these new doctors? They cannot understand our lives. The untiring devotedness and sincere interest manifested by our sisters in their various duties puzzles them.

"I have been reported a few times to the superintendent, but in each case I was able to secure my pardon without fine or imprisonment. It is a standing joke among our regular doctors—'Sister Stanislaus was reported.'—I have been offered so many positions. All eyes are on the one I am holding. Two doctors got into a conversation about it... 'I wonder how much salary Sister receives

CATHOLIC CHAPLAINS
ARMY AND NAVY

VICARIATE
PROVINCE OF NEW ORLEANS
2452 NAPOLEON AVENUE
NEW ORLEANS

ORDINARIATE
142 EAST 29TH STREET
NEW YORK

INCLUDING THE STATES OF
ALABAMA
ARKANSAS
LOUISIANA
MISSISSIPPI
TEXAS
OKLAHOMA
NEW MEXICO

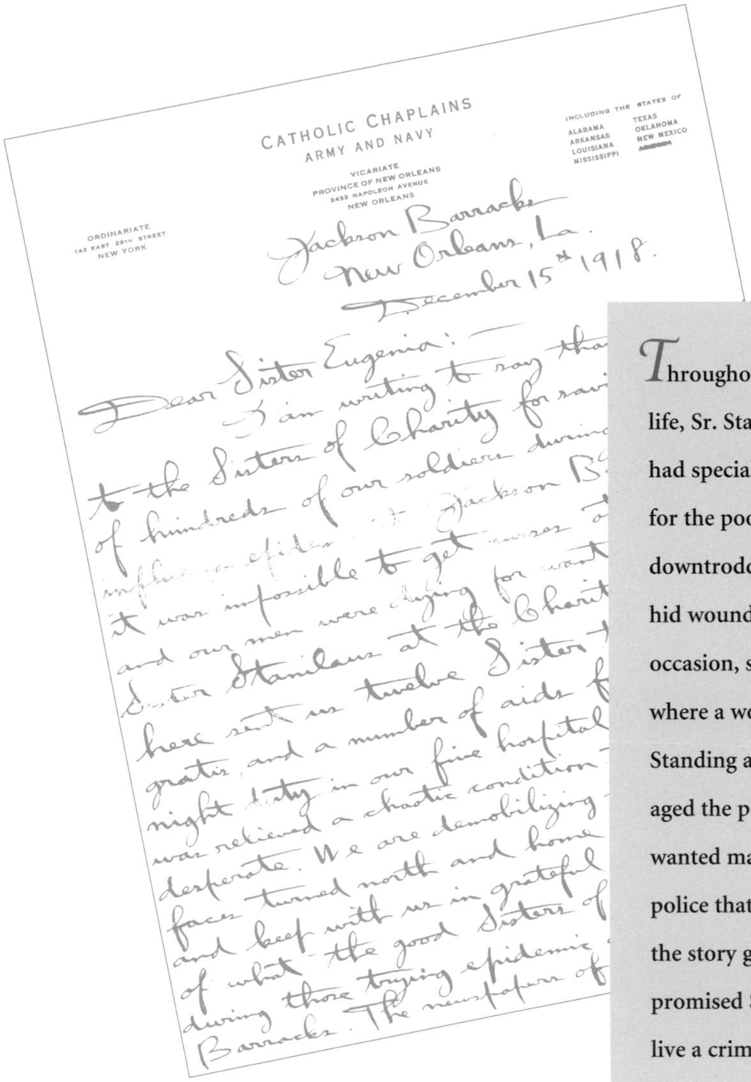

Jackson Barracks
New Orleans, La.
December 15th 1918.

Dear Sister Eugenia:—
I am writing to say tha
to the Sisters of Charity for savi
of hundreds of our soldiers durin
influenza epidemic at Jackson B
it was impossible to get nurses
and our men were dying for want
Sister Stanislaus at the Charit
here sent us twelve Sisters
greater, and a number of aids f
night duty in our five hospital
was relieved a chaotic condition
desperate. We are demobilizing
faces turned north and home
and keep with us in grateful
of what the good Sisters of
during those trying epidemic
Barracks. The newspapers of

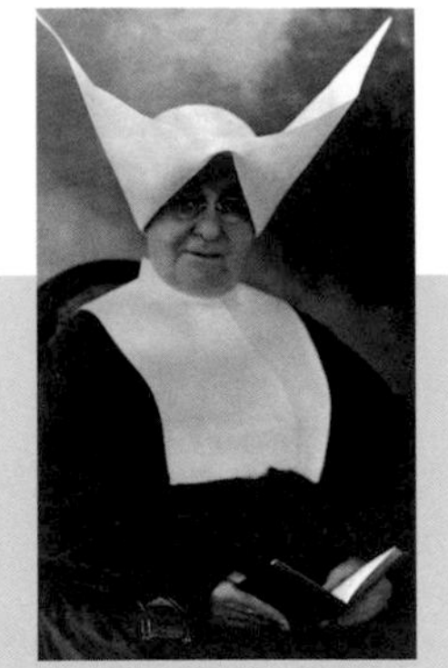

Throughout her life, Sr. Stanislaus had special feelings for the poor and the downtrodden. Stories abound about how she hid wounded outlaws from the police. On one occasion, she took the police into the ward where a wounded bandit was lying in bed. Standing at the foot of his bed, she encouraged the police to search carefully for the wanted man. Her presence so distracted the police that they left without their man. And, the story goes, weeks later the bandit humbly promised Sr. Stanislaus he would no longer live a criminal life.

Left:
Letter from John J. Donovan, a Chaplain, thanking the Sisters of Charity and Sr. Stanislaus (shown in inset) for their efforts during the influenza epidemic of 1918.

for her work,' said one. 'She must get a goodly sum for running that place.' His companion said: 'I never heard, but it must bring her something quite worthwhile.'

"In the course of the day wishing to gratify his curiosity he said to me: 'Sister. I hear you get some good money for your work around here.' 'Yes,' I said. 'I am getting such a large salary that I do not tell anyone. Too many are looking for my position.'

"Sometime afterwards, he went to the superintendent to make inquiries. The next time that superintendent met me, he said, 'Sister Stanislaus, how could you let Doctor So-and-so think you are getting a big salary?'

"'Well,' I said, 'I am getting a big salary. The biggest in the world. I am working for the honor and glory of God.'"

In 1914, Sr. Stanislaus was promoted to superioress of Charity Hospital. The doctors and board were delighted. A newspaper report at the time quoted two physicians: "She is a great woman. Splendid, alert, magnanimous." "And she can wield a scalpel as well as any man."

During the influenza epidemic of 1918, the Army asked Sr. Stanislaus for sisters to nurse the soldiers at Jackson Barracks. She promptly assigned 19 teaching sisters to Charity Hospital and sent 12 nursing sisters to care for the soldiers.

In the 1930s, during a trip to New Orleans, President Franklin D. Roosevelt requested that his motorcade route be changed so he could visit Charity Hospital and meet Sr. Stanislaus.

A surgeon who worked with her said: "Sr. Stanislaus was the most remarkable woman I've ever known—remarkable because of her great understanding of human nature, her genial Irish mirth, her ever-ready smile, her enthusiastic optimism, and her boundless energy and tact, which enabled her to accomplish much with little effort."

When the new, $12 million hospital building was completed in 1937, Sr. Stanislaus gave it her highest praise. "This," she said proudly, "is a hospital fit for the poor."

In April 1944, at the age of 81, the "angel of charity" resigned from her demanding position. Sr. Stanislaus Malone died June 8, 1949.

ST. FRANCIS HOSPITAL
Colorado Springs, Colorado

*A*s a surgeon on the battlefields of the Civil War, Dr. Anderson could not help but be impressed by the sisters who cared for the wounded. So when the Midland Railroad Company asked him to

open a hospital for men injured on the job, he invited the Sisters of St. Francis Seraph of Perpetual Adoration from Lafayette, Indiana, to join him.

On September 1, 1887, the first patient arrived at the hospital in Colorado Springs. Fortunately, it was also the day the sisters arrived. The sisters laid down their baggage, rolled up their sleeves, and went to work to make a place for their first patient. They arose at midnight to do the washing, scrubbing, and cleaning in time to care for the patients in the morning.

Only a few days after their arrival, a Midland construction train wreck killed several men and injured 60. The tiny hospital was inadequate to care for so many injured, so the sisters set about begging so they could build a larger facility. The new Saint Francis Hospital opened in the spring of 1888.

St. Joseph Hospital and Medical Center
Paterson, New Jersey

*I*n 1906, Sr. Mary Clare Reilly, the administrator of St. Joseph's Hospital and a Sister of Charity of Saint Joseph, demanded the resignation of the entire medical staff.

Her decision was triggered by the death of a St. Joseph's surgeon. When Sr. Mary Clare selected his successor and new physicians assistants, the disgruntled physicians ignored her choices. Instead, they made their own slate, which they forwarded to her.

Several days later she asked them all to tender their resignations. A flurry of newspaper articles ensued. At issue, said one, was:

"Shall supervision and control of the medical staff rest with the sister directress, or shall the power to make appointments and fill vacancies be exercised by the physicians serving upon the staff?

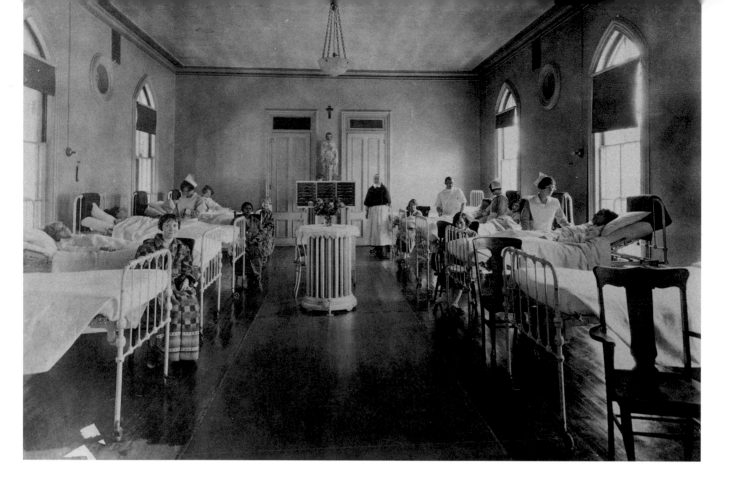

"St. Joseph's Hospital has been of great good in the community. It is no easy matter to successfully manage such a large institution, and Sr. Mary Clare's executive ability has received wide recognition. This is the first time that open friction has occurred, although this question of control of the staff appointments has been a burning one for several years."

Although Sr. Mary Clare offered the physicians an opportunity to reapply for their positions, none did at the time. Several returned to the hospital later.

Sr. Mary Clare remained administrator of St. Joseph's Hospital for 44 years. She died in 1919.

The priest who delivered her eulogy said of her: "The life of a woman like this Sr. Mary Clare—this superioress of that big hospital—is a story of tenderness towards humanity, of self-sacrifice in accord with high belief, and of loyal service to the general community." ❧

The life of a Catholic sister required an adventurous spirit and a disposition strong enough to confront the danger in the next valley or behind the mask of a notorious outlaw.

SISTERS OF CHARITY OF LEAVENWORTH
Leavenworth, Kansas

Five sisters and a laywoman left Leavenworth, Kansas, on September 29, 1869, and headed to Montana. The last leg of their journey—from Utah to Helena, Montana—was by stagecoach.

When the harrowing journey finally ended on October 10, no one met them in Helena, nor was anyone expecting them. They were the first sisters to arrive in the Montana Territory to serve white settlers.

By 1870, the sisters had opened a school and a hospital. In 1875, two sisters were sent to Laramie, Wyoming, to open a hospital. Sr. Martha wrote to the motherhouse on January 2, 1876:

> *"Dear Sisters at Home:*
>
> *"(When I wrote the word 'home', a tear dropped on the page before me. I hear you exclaiming, 'Sister Martha homesick! Impossible; she is too brave. Nothing of the kind, my dear young sisters; I am not at all brave; a greater coward seldom traveled toward the setting sun; but I am courageous enough to conceal my sentiments from Sister Joanna, who, I think, is slightly affected in the same manner...)"*

Sr. Martha went on to describe the sisters' daily life:

> *"We have our breakfast, then to work. 'Man's work is from rise to set of sun, but woman's work is never done'—and it might be added that a hospital sister's work is not infrequently from the rising of one sun to the rising of another."*

Back in Montana, life was not easy. Among the health problems the sisters had to deal with were gunshot wounds, frozen feet and

---

Dear Mother,

Words cannot describe the first night in the [stage] coach, nor the second, nor the third, nor the fourth, and I fancy if there had been a fifth night, I should have had a strong temptation to remain over at one of the relay stations, and to sleep for a day or two to make up for lost time.

FROM A LETTER WRITTEN BY SR. MARTHA TO THE MOTHERHOUSE IN 1869.

Facing the Unknown

hands, alcoholism, typhus, snakebites, and wounds from brawls. Early records indicate other diagnoses: "kicked by horse," "run over by wagon," and "morphine fiend."

SISTERS OF ST. JOSEPH OF CARONDELET
Tucson, Arizona

On April 20, 1870, seven Sisters of St. Joseph of Carondelet said good-bye to sisters they never expected to see again and began a perilous journey from St. Louis to Tucson, Arizona. They'd been called to Tucson by the bishop to open a school. One of the seven, Sr. Monica Courigan, kept a journal.

From St. Louis, the sisters traveled by rail to Kansas City, Omaha, and across the Rockies, "a frightful and desolate region." From Salt Lake City they journeyed to San Francisco, where they boarded a boat to San Diego. From there, they traveled by wagon to Tucson.

On May 7, the seven sisters began the most difficult part of their journey. The wagon was too small for all of them to ride in, and one of the sisters volunteered to ride outside with the driver.

"It is beyond description what she suffered in riding 200 miles…without protection from the rays of a tropical sun," wrote Sr. Monica.

BELOW:
FROM ST. LOUIS, THE SISTERS OF ST. JOSEPH OF CARONDELET TRAVELED BY RAIL TO KANSAS CITY, OMAHA, AND ACROSS THE ROCKIES. FROM SALT LAKE CITY THEY JOURNEYED TO SAN FRANCISCO, WHERE THEY BOARDED A BOAT TO SAN DIEGO. FROM THERE, THEY TRAVELED BY WAGON TO TUCSON. THE MAP TRACES THE LAST PART OF THEIR JOURNEY.

Journal of The Sisters of St. Joseph
en route to Arizona — 1870
Rev. Mother & Dear Sisters :

*Before leaving Carondelet I
promised to write a "Journal" of our
trip to Arizona...
the fulfillment...
almost out of da...
scarcely time t...
our habits before...
I was obliged to de...
of our trip until...
not have courag...
it, were it not th...
is reminding me continually...
have time now it is true...
capacity for such a task. Va...
less I shall do the best I ca...
on the kind indulgence of ou...
Sisters.*

April 20 — 1870 -
*"After bidding adieu to our go...
Sisters in Carondelet we started on our
long and perilous journey to Arizona*

These burial places looked so sadly neglected. The desolate, lonely places in which these poor creatures were laid to rest, and still more, their melancholy and frightful death, cast a damper over our spirits, as we had no certainty of not meeting the same fate. And yet, why should we be sad? Did we not risk our lives for the love of Jesus?

FROM THE DIARY KEPT BY SR. MONICA COURIGAN, COMMENTING ON THE GRAVES OF PEOPLE KILLED BY NATIVE AMERICANS.

LEFT:
THE SEVEN SISTERS OF
ST. JOSEPH OF CARONDELET
WHO JOURNEYED FROM
ST. LOUIS TO TUCSON IN
1870 AND A PAGE FROM
THE DIARY OF SR. MONICA
DOCUMENTING THEIR
JOURNEY.

On the first night, they camped at the foot of a mountain. Three sisters slept outside, two stretched out inside the wagon, while the other two sat up.

"Sr. Euphrasia and I sat in a corner and tried to sleep," wrote Sr. Monica. "We had scarcely closed our eyes when the wolves began to howl about us…. During the night, Sr. Euphrasia was startled from her sleep by one of the horses licking her face. She screamed fearfully, and we concluded she was a prey of the wolves."

At a ranch where the sisters rested the following day, they found many men, but few women. Some of the ranchers "proposed marriage to us, saying we would do better by accepting the offer than by going to Tucson, for we would all be massacred by Indians."

By May 9, after climbing up and down the mountains, they had reached the desert. As they descended the last mountain on foot, Sr. Monica observed, "The sides of the road were covered with teams of horses, oxen, and cattle that had dropped dead trying to ascend. At one place we counted 14 oxen, which had apparently died at the same time. When Mother beheld so many dead animals, she wept, fearing we might share their fate."

When the sisters reached the ranch where they were to spend the night, "there were upward to 20 men there, some of whom were intoxicated. They annoyed us very much," Sr. Monica wrote, "some offering to shake hands with us, others trying to keep them off, and all swearing. We shall never be able to tell our dear sisters all the mortifications and humiliations we had to endure there." Four of the sisters slept in a shanty, with "the men coming in and going out all night."

At 5 a.m. on May 10, the sisters began their trek across the desert. The sisters passed 1,000 head of cattle, all dead, and later the remains of 1,500 sheep smothered in a sandstorm. The temperature reached 125 degrees in the shade.

"We could get water only in one place and when we did get it, it was not only hot, but so full of minerals that we suffered more after taking it than before," Sr. Monica noted in her journal.

They walked until late at night and rested during the heat of the day. When they were finally able to bathe, on May 11th, one sister found that her stockings were stuck to her feet by congealed blood. She discovered 22 bleeding sores from cactus sticks.

On May 13, the sisters narrowly escaped drowning when their wagon fell over as they crossed the Colorado River on a raft.

During the portion of the journey when the sisters most feared an Indian massacre, they stopped at noon, but "there was no room for us in the inn." With "not even a tree to shelter us from the burning rays," the sisters lay down in the shade of some nearby ruins. A troop of nude Indians appeared and "had the consideration to be quiet" and let them sleep. One "noble warrior...stole softly up and sat down beside [Sr. Martha] as her Guardian Angel."

When they were 65 miles from Tucson, a cavalcade of soldiers arrived to escort the sisters through the dangerous territory. The sisters finally reached Tucson on May 26 and were awed by the spectacle awaiting them. The crowds numbered 3,000, "some discharging firearms, others bearing lighted torches..." wrote Sr. Monica.

Their new home in Tucson was a one-story adobe building. The sisters taught school, but with the arrival of the Southern Pacific Railroad in the late 1870s, the need for a hospital became acute. Ten years after their arrival in Tucson, the sisters opened St. Mary's Hospital.

Sr. Blandina Segale
Sisters of Charity of Cincinnati
Mount St. Joseph, Ohio

Sr. Blandina Segale went out west from Cincinnati in 1872 to teach school. When the railroad tracks ended, she continued by stagecoach to her destination of Trinidad, Colorado.

She had received numerous warnings from her friends about the wild cowboys who inhabited the West. To her horror, one night the stage picked one up. When he demanded to know who she was, she replied that she was a Sister of Charity, a person who gives her life for others. She soon got over her fear of the man, and by journey's end had made him promise to write to his mother, with whom he had not corresponded for years.

In 1876, Sr. Blandina learned that an outlaw had been wounded in a gunfight and was dying in a hut outside of Trinidad. Local physicians had refused to care for him, but Sr. Blandina bathed and bandaged his wounds and nursed him back to health.

The grateful outlaw introduced her to his boss, Billy the Kid (not *the* Billy the Kid, but a Billy the Kid and nonetheless an outlaw). Not only did Sr. Blandina offer her greetings to Billy, she talked him out of killing the four doctors who had refused to treat the wounded outlaw.

The following year, Sr. Blandina was traveling by stagecoach with the husband of a friend, when the travelers learned that Billy the Kid was likely to attack.

Sure enough, as they were traversing the northern plains of New Mexico, they spotted a man on horseback galloping toward the stagecoach. Sr. Blandina's friend reached for his revolver. "Put your gun away," the sister demanded. She leaned out of the coach and caught the outlaw's eye. When he realized who it was, Billy raised his hat in salute, bowed, waved, and rode away leaving the cowering travelers unassailed.

ABOVE:
TWO ILLUSTRATIONS FROM *THE CATHOLIC LITERARY FOUNDATION*, SEPTEMBER 1948, DEPICT THE ADVENTURES OF SR. BLANDINA SEGALE.

During her stay in Colorado, the five-foot, three-inch Sr. Blandina built an adobe school and opened an orphanage and a hospital for workers building the Santa Fe Railroad.

After her stint in the West ended in 1894, Sr. Blandina returned to Cincinnati, where she worked to improve conditions for Italian immigrants. She also fought for laws to end child labor and was a lifelong proponent for the rights of Native Americans. She died on February 12, 1941, a month after her 91st birthday.

SISTERS OF MERCY
Council Bluffs, Iowa

Srs. Mary Xavier Clinton and Mary Clare Clifford journeyed to Ireland in 1928, where they recruited the "Irish Fifteen." Fifteen young women, most of them in their mid or late teens, set sail on the *Metagama* for the week-long journey to the United States.

Sr. Martina Woulfe, 15 at the time, was one of the group. Many years later, in an interview, she recalled the ocean crossing:

> *"We reported to County Cork, and our parents were with us.... We were all crying, carrying on, you know, feeling sad. And the gangplank was slanted, and we walked up there, got up on deck, waved, tears streaming. It was very cold too. It was a wet day...."*

The tears soon gave way to seasickness. But, "when we got over the sickness," remembered Sr. Martina, "we used to dance the Charleston. We used to do so many steps. Sr. Clare decided...no it was Sr. Xavier...she would start a novena. We had to be present for these prayers every night. Many of us didn't show up because we were either dancing or playing cards. Having a good time. There was a British businessman who saw that we got to the captain's table, so we got first class treatment all the way...."

They arrived in Des Moines on December 5, 1928.

Sr. Martina's career in healthcare has spanned more than 60 years and included numerous jobs. Her life has been like the lives of many sisters, in that she often had to leave for a new assignment at a moment's notice.

In an interview years later, she remembered: "One Sunday Sr. Alberta [the superior] came to me and said: 'Sister, I want you to go up and take charge of the operating room on Monday.' I started to argue.... I was there for two years under a head nurse. Then on a Thursday she came to me and said: 'You are to go to a school in Chicago. Be ready to leave by train on Sunday. And you're going to take operating room management and methods of teaching in the school of nursing.' So I went to Chicago."

At age 82, she is patient care coordinator at the Bishop Drumm Retirement Center in Johnston, Iowa.

LEFT:
IN 1928, CATHOLICS IN COUNCIL BLUFFS, IOWA, MADE A CONCERTED EFFORT TO RECRUIT YOUNG WOMEN FROM IRELAND. A LETTER FROM THE BISHOP TO THE SISTERS OF MERCY SAID: "WE NEED MANY MORE NUNS TO CARRY ON THE SCHOOLS AND THE HOSPITALS, AND TO OPEN NEW ONES ALREADY DEMANDED. THE FIELD IS RIPE FOR HARVESTING. GOD SEND THE WORKERS...." SHOWN IN THE PHOTO ARE THE IRISH RECRUITS ABOARD THE *METAGAMA*.

The Work Continues…

Sr. Mary Rose McGeady

DAUGHTERS OF CHARITY
Covenant House
New York, New York

Advocating for Children

"Did you know that one million American kids run away from home each year?" asks Sr. Mary Rose McGeady. "Every night there are 300,000 kids on the streets of the United States. It's an indictment of our country that we have so many unhappy kids."

When Speaker of the House Newt Gingrich made his infamous comment in 1994 about taking children away from their families and putting them in orphanages, Sr. Mary Rose called him up. "We need to talk," she told him over the phone. When they met in Washington, Sr. Mary Rose told him about her experiences with homeless kids—and about just how effective she thought orphanages would be in solving the problem. (Not at all!) And then she gave him a book to convince him that he had erred in making his statement. A few weeks after their meeting, she got a letter from Gingrich. He apologized for the orphanage comment, calling it a poor choice of words, and promised not to go down that road again.

"A lot of people in power just don't get it," she declares. "So many good programs for kids are being cut right and left."

Homeless children could not have a more effective advocate than Sr. Mary Rose. At 66, this Daughter of Charity is tireless in her efforts to raise awareness about the plight of our nation's children.

RIGHT:
A STREET KID IN
TIMES SQUARE.

As head of the international organization Covenant House, Sr. Mary Rose spends a lot of her time traveling and speaking out on behalf of homeless children. Wherever she goes, she takes time to meet and talk to the children—in shelters, on the streets, and at seminars.

Life on the streets is hard for anyone, let alone a 13-year-old. "Prostitution rings look for boys and girls age 13," explains Sr. Mary Rose, noting that young children are less likely than older prostitutes to be infected with HIV. "There is an enormous market for homeless and runaway teenagers. You offer these kids $60 a trick or $40 with a condom, and it's a way for them to survive. It's amazing what kids will do for a few dollars."

By the time a kid comes to Covenant House, he or she is desperate, with nowhere else to go, Sr. Mary Rose explains. Many times their families have broken apart. "These kids come in off the street so empty. They are grieving the loss of any attachment they've had."

*S*ometimes kids sleep in cardboard boxes. It's freezing in the winter. We can't eat when we want to. Some nights we get no sleep at all. I see kids with no shoes on, freezing. One kid's foot was all puffy and green. He said the doctors told him they'd have to cut it off, but he said he'd rather die.

KEITH, A STREET KID IN NEW YORK CITY.

BELOW: A HOMELESS ADOLESCENT COUPLE AT PORT AUTHORITY BUS TERMINAL, NEW YORK CITY.

Located in cities throughout the United States, Central America, and Canada, Covenant House offers shelter, medical and psychiatric care, education, drug counseling, and even job training and placement. After their immediate needs are met, the children look at options for the future. Some can be reconnected with their families, but such an option is not always possible. For some kids, "getting into the world of work is the ultimate answer. We don't want to breed dependency," says Sr. Mary Rose. Kids stay at Covenant House anywhere from one night to two years. There is no set limit.

She is responsible for the annual budget of $71 million, 90% of which comes from donations from individuals. The remainder comes from organizations. Covenant House receives no federal funding.

"The issue," says Sr. Mary Rose, "is that kids have lost a sense of belonging, which is one of the most basic human needs. Our kids tell a million versions of family failure. They get shipped off during a crisis and the family never gets back together. The kids blame themselves."

ALL PHOTOS FOR THIS
SECTION, ROMAN SAPECKI.

Family failure, she is quick to point out, occurs among all socioeconomic levels, although it's often convenient to think it happens primarily among the poor. "It gets America off the hook to blame someone else," she says. "But let's not point to any one group as a scapegoat. National policy has to address the reality that a large percentage of our youth will be lost to us without the proper intervention."

Sr. Mary Rose's life reflects her dedication to people in need. She lives in Brooklyn's tough Bedford-Stuyvesant neighborhood. It is said that she can tell from the sound what type of gun has been fired.

"I have learned so much by living there," she says. "At the grocery store, I see mothers put food back because they can't afford it.

"I never have any trouble getting up in the morning because it's so exciting. There's nothing like this kind of work to convince you you're spending your life the right way." ❧

There's nothing so wonderful as seeing a kid dirty and depressed come in off the street and then 9, 12, or 15 months later that same kid working, having gotten his or her act together, feeling good. You can turn a kid around. We find that if you love a kid, there are very few you can't reach.

SR. MARY ROSE
MCGEADY ON HER LIFE
AT COVENANT HOUSE.

BELOW:
A PARTICIPANT IN THE
SUBSTANCE ABUSE PROGRAM
FOR ADOLESCENTS.

ABOVE:
MARISOL, A YOUNG WOMAN
AIDED BY COVENANT
HOUSE, WITH HER
DAUGHTER.

LEFT:
TWO HOMELESS BOYS AT
PORT AUTHORITY.

Vision

The future of the world will be
what women make it.

MOTHER CLARE CUSACK, A SISTER OF ST. JOSEPH
OF PEACE, ENGLEWOOD CLIFFS, NEW JERSEY

*F*or some it was a dream. For others it was a determination
to do the things they believed in. In every case, these
women religious were driven by a vision of a better way and
powered by the strength of their convictions.

MOTHER JOSEPH

SISTERS OF PROVIDENCE
Seattle, Washington

*Architect
of the Pacific
Northwest*

In Statuary Hall in the Capitol, Washington, D.C., is a statue of Mother Joseph. Not only is she one of only a few women represented in the Capitol, she is the only Catholic woman religious. The inscription on the base of the statue summarizes her life: "She made monumental contributions to healthcare, education, and social services throughout the Northwest."

Mother Joseph was born Esther Pariseau on April 16, 1823, in St. Elzear, a village near Montreal, Canada. Esther was the daughter of a coachmaker and his wife, and she learned carpentry at an early age. On December 26, 1843, Esther became the thirteenth woman to join the newly formed Sisters of Providence in Montreal. When presenting her to the mother superior, her father said: "Madame, I bring you my daughter Esther, who wishes to dedicate herself to religious life. She can read and write and figure accurately. She can cook and sew and spin and do all manner of housework well."

LEFT:
SISTERS OF PROVIDENCE
JOHN OF GOD, LEFT, AND
JEANNE DE CHANTAL WITH
CHIEF CHARLO AND HIS
COMPANIONS ON THE
FLATHEAD INDIAN
RESERVATION IN
MONTANA DURING THE
LATE 1800S.

In her early days as a sister, she cared for victims of typhus. In 1851, Mother Gamelin, the young foundress of the religious community, died of cholera, and the following year the archbishop asked the community to come to the northwest United States. The journey from Montreal to Ft. Vancouver, Washington Territory, was 6,000 miles across treacherous waters: first to New York, then on to Jamaica, Panama, Acapulco, and, finally, San Francisco. Five sisters departed, but the people they expected to serve had left for the California gold rush. They decided to return to Montreal, but were forced by illness and the weather to stop in Chile, where they took over an orphanage.

Four years later, in 1856, community leaders selected a second group to make the journey. This time, Mother Joseph was the leader.

Mother Joseph and the other sisters suffered from intense seasickness during the journey. In San Francisco, they stayed with the Sisters of Mercy at Saint Mary's Hospital before making the difficult journey up the Columbia River to Ft. Vancouver. When they reached their destination, the five women settled into a tiny room in the bishop's attic. The bishop who had sent for them

How much more agreeable for me to remain at home. But with the large debt we still carry and the needs of the poor, the sick, and the orphans pressing, it is with all my heart I leave my solitude for the toilsome task of begging.

MOTHER JOSEPH, 1876, BEFORE EMBARKING ON A BEGGING TOUR.

was in Europe when they arrived, and the vicar-general wanted them to move to Olympia.

Under the leadership of Mother Joseph, the sisters soon settled in their first convent, an old fur-storage building in Ft. Vancouver abandoned by the Hudson Bay Company. Mother Joseph herself designed the chapel and built the altar.

The sisters made home visits to the sick and cared for Native Americans displaced by warring. They took in orphans and started teaching, establishing Providence Academy, Vancouver, Washington, the first permanent school in the Northwest. In 1858, they opened the four-bed St. Joseph Hospital (the first permanent hospital in the Northwest) in a tiny building intended for a laundry and bakery. Also that year, Mother Joseph incorporated the Sisters of Providence — one of the earliest organizations in the state to become incorporated — enabling the religious community to legally acquire property.

Not only did Mother Joseph open schools, orphanages, and hospitals, she designed and built them. In his book *Cornerstone,* Ellis Lucia described her: "There was Mother Joseph striding across the ground near Fort Vancouver, Washington, hammer dangling from her belt like the sheriffs of the Old West carried their six-guns, and wielding a saw in her hand.

"There was no stranger sight around Ft. Vancouver than Mother Joseph in her black habit bouncing on a high cross beam to test its strength or wriggling out from beneath the ground level where she had been inspecting a foundation."

During the next 50 years, Mother Joseph opened, designed, and built hospitals, orphanages, and schools throughout the Northwest. To raise money for the buildings, she begged in the mining camps. The begging tours often lasted for months and exposed Mother Joseph to harsh weather and primitive living conditions (including wolves, snakes, and bandits). But each series of trips to the mining camps could yield up to $5,000.

ABOVE, TOP TO BOTTOM: MOTHER JOSEPH AND ANOTHER SISTER ON HORSEBACK WITH GUIDES. FIVE SISTERS OF PROVIDENCE, INCLUDING MOTHER JOSEPH. OPERATING ROOM OF ST. VINCENT HOSPITAL, PORTLAND, OREGON.

There was Mother Joseph striding across the ground near Ft. Vancouver, Washington, hammer dangling from her belt like the sheriffs of the Old West carried their six-guns, and wielding a saw in her hand.

There was no stranger sight around Ft. Vancouver than Mother Joseph in her black habit bouncing on a high cross beam to test its strength or wriggling out from beneath the ground level where she had been inspecting a foundation.

FROM THE BOOK *CORNERSTONE,* BY ELLIS LUCIA.

ABOVE, TOP:
PROVIDENCE HOSPITAL,
SEATTLE, 1885.
BOTTOM:
ST. PETER'S HOSPITAL,
OLYMPIA, WASHINGTON,
1887. MOTHER JOSEPH
DESIGNED AND BUILT BOTH
HOSPITALS.

On a trip to Denver, it is said, masked men seized the stagecoach and thrust guns through the windows. They demanded that the travelers hand over all their baggage and belongings. When the baggage was piled up, the passengers were ordered back into the coach. Mother Joseph lagged behind.

"My boy," she said to one of the bandits over fierce protests to be quiet from the other passengers. "My boy, please give me that black bag." "Which one?" the surprised bandit asked. She indicated her bag.

He lifted an ample carpetbag. Mother Joseph nodded and ordered him to give it to her. Astounded by her audacity, the bandit carried the bag to her. "Thank you. God bless you, my boy," Mother Joseph said. The looting of the other bags continued, but the $200 Mother Joseph had collected remained safe.

Another time, a farmer who had been impressed by her on a begging trip wanted to send her a cow that she could auction for money. He attached a tag to its horn reading "For Mother Joseph" and sent it along to her as freight. The cow arrived and yielded $250 at auction.

Even as she grew older, Mother Joseph remained in command. On one construction job, she pointed out to workers that the chimney they had just built needed to be rebricked. They ignored her. The next morning they found the chimney rebricked the way she wanted it.

Mother Joseph was a woman of multiple and contrasting abilities. She was not only skilled at building design and construction, but was an able needle worker, wax worker, and wood carver. She was honored by the American Institute of Architects and the West Coast Lumbermen's Association.

"Oh, if I were young!" Mother Joseph wrote in 1897. "We would do much good on a mission where there would be misery, and where it would be necessary to make sacrifices. Nowadays, we look for too much comfort in this land which offers so much."

Before she died on January 19, 1902, of a brain tumor, Mother Joseph told the sisters: "Whatever concerns the poor is always our affair." Mother Marie Antoinette, superior general, eulogized her: "She had the characteristics of genius: incessant works, immense sacrifices, great undertakings; and she never counted the cost to self...." ᴏ

When hospitals and nursing homes needed to be constructed from the ground up, these sisters took matters into their own firm and capable hands.

St. Joseph Hospital
New Bedford, Pennsylvania

*A*fter immigrating to the United States from France in 1864, the Sisters of the Humility of Mary settled in New Bedford, Pennsylvania. During the smallpox epidemic that fall, the sisters were nurses in the homes of people stricken with the disease.

Sr. Mary of the Angels Maujean, a woman in her 30s, fell victim to smallpox while nursing and wrote the following note in French on scrap paper. Frightened, ill, and unsure of what to do, she asked for her mother superior, who would be able to assess the situation.

> *"I am scribbling these few words to tell you my situation. I can hardly see. More plainly, I fear to lose my sight if I lack care. I have some pimples in a fine way indeed. The patient has just told me that her son will do whatever ought to be done for the cold. But I'm afraid of being unable to do the rest. Have the kindness, please, to send our superior. If she sees that it's all right, I will remain. She will come in our carriage. She will bring to me my cloak and my hood. It is necessary that she see this so as to be able to explain to the patient, who will be very upset."*

Sr. Mary of the Angels did indeed lose her sight. But she recovered it eventually and went on to found the Congregation of Humility of Mary in Davenport, Iowa.

• • •

In the late 1870s, when the railroad crews came to New Bedford, Pennsylvania, the need for a hospital increased. But the Sisters of the Humility of Mary, who had earlier in the decade agreed to care for local railroad workers, had no money to open a hospital. Thinking creatively, the French-born Mother Anna Tabourat, the community's first major superior in America, hit

upon a solution. She worked out an agreement whereby railroad officials agreed to buy as many railroad ties as she could produce.

Quickly setting up a sawmill in the woods, Mother Anna hired vagrants who had lost their jobs on the railroad. But first she made them pledge, "I'll never touch a drop of the old stuff as long as you boss us."

By 1879, Mother Anna's sawmill had supplied enough railroad ties to pay for a hospital...with lots of lumber left over for the building itself. A two-story facility housed an emergency/operating room on the first floor and patient rooms on the second floor. The sisters slept in the attic. They washed everything in two large black iron kettles in the washhouse yard. In winter and summer, patients' linens and clothes were laundered in the open and hung out to dry.

When construction on the transcontinental railroad moved west, the need for a hospital declined in New Bedford. In 1911, the sisters closed the hospital, moving the last remaining elderly patients to St. Elizabeth Hospital in Youngstown, Ohio.

Mother Valencia
Saint Francis Hospital and Medical Center
Hartford, Connecticut

With $9.65 in her pocket, Mother Valencia came to America from France in 1897 with orders to start a hospital. From her first days in Connecticut until her death, Mother Valencia was Saint Francis Hospital.

Newly arrived from France, Mother Valencia spoke little English but was an experienced nurse, trained at Hotel Dieu Hospital in Lyons by the Sisters of Charity. Accompanying her were three sisters who spoke English but knew little about nursing. They had been sent to America to answer the call of the bishop of Hartford.

Mother Valencia was vigilant about all aspects of running Saint Francis. In her early years as superintendent, she relied on construction crews when expansion of the hospital was necessary. But in one instance, after months of work on a new wing, the building inspectors condemned the addition. After thinking the matter through, Mother Valencia asked some friends to teach her about construction. From then on, in addition to her myriad responsibilities, she supervised all remodeling and construction on the hospital.

Mother Valencia insisted that all patients, regardless of financial status, receive compassionate care. The book *So Falls The Elm Tree* by John Louis Bonn, SJ, a history of her life, tells of a young boy suffering from gunshot wounds who was brought to the hospital one night by the police.

A bell in Mother Valencia's bedroom announced all late-night emergency room arrivals. That evening she dressed quickly and rushed to the emergency room, where she convinced the policemen, who were bent on questioning the ailing boy, to leave him in her

> *M*other Valencia was Saint Francis Hospital's heart, its head, its hands. Its walls are saturated with her spirit. Its efficiency is borrowed from her person. Its very bricks and stones echo with her voice, for to it she dedicated her life-blood and her life.
>
> From the writings of Msgr. Anthony Murphy, 11 years after the death of Mother Valencia.

charge. The physician did not arrive so quickly. Half an hour later he appeared and curtly nodded to Mother Valencia as if to dismiss her. He roughly probed the boy's wounds as the lad clenched his fists in pain. "How did this happen?" he demanded.

Mother Valencia motioned the doctor into the hall. Why had it had taken him so long to appear in the emergency room, she asked. The doctor was unabashed.

"On the day you came here did you not hear the regulations of the hospital?" she demanded. "And these, *monsieur le docteur*, serve the high purposes of the institution. Are they not the result of experience; also of much long thought? Yet you assume the privilege of disregarding them. So first, I warn you. With a shrug of the shoulder, with a laugh, you throw off my comments. Perhaps it is that you think I am a woman? You resent that, no? Then you say I wear the habit of the religious. Consequently, I do not know the world? Is it perhaps that?"

The doctor said nothing, and Mother Valencia continued. "Because I know human nature, I know more about the world than you do. Go now," she bade him.

On another occasion, Mother Valencia fired a renowned surgeon who refused to come to Saint Francis in the middle of the night to perform an appendectomy on a poor elderly woman. When the surgeon showed up in Mother Valencia's office the next morning, he refused to believe he had been fired. "We have no stars here," she told him. Outraged, he promised to open a hospital and take all of Saint Francis' patients.

He did open a competing hospital, but years after their confrontation, he sold it and wrote the following:

"Dear Mother Valencia,
Enclosed is what I realized on the sale of my hospital. It never was, really, my hospital. My hospital was always yours…."

He ultimately returned to Saint Francis Hospital.

Mother Valencia died on November 29, 1936 at age 82. ☙

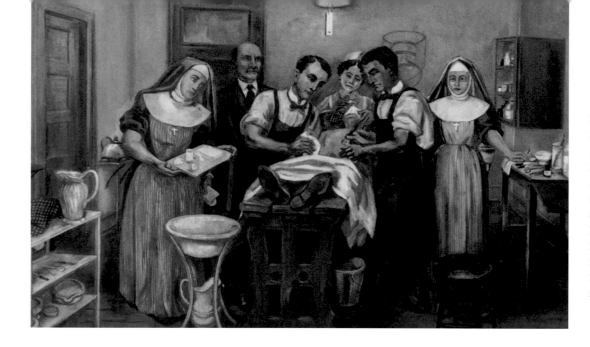

Standing Firm in the Face of Authority

Adjectives such as stubborn, maverick, impulsive and strong-minded described these sisters, who bucked convention in pursuit of their vision.

MOTHER ALFRED MOES
SAINT MARY'S HOSPITAL
Rochester, Minnesota

Mother Alfred Moes was born to govern. So said members of her congregation at the time of her death. She was strong minded, impulsive, and made enemies of priests.

Some of her character traits were not what Church officials liked in a woman religious in the nineteenth century. Bishops put Mother Alfred out of office in two religious communities — including one that she founded — before she founded still another in Rochester, Minnesota, near the end of her life.

Mother Alfred seemed to have a propensity for standing up to Church officials. In an 1861 letter, the bishop demanded that she be replaced as the head of a school in LaPorte, Indiana. In part, the letter says:

"As long as sisters & brothers keep their place, they are most useful & beneficial to religion, but when they begin to oppose the pastor (whose assistants they are) & seek to boss and rule him, it is turning things upside down, they loose {sic}

God's grace & blessing & become a nuisance.... You will therefore do me the favor to recall her as soon as possible & without noise."

Maria Catherine Moes entered the School Sisters of Notre Dame in 1852 at the age of 24, but left before taking her final vows, possibly because teaching was not in her immediate future there. She entered the Marianite Sisters of Holy Cross in Notre Dame and made her final vows in 1858.

After leaving Holy Cross because of questions about which male Church official was in charge, Sr. Alfred and her companions established a new congregation, the Third Order of St. Francis of Joliet, Illinois, in 1865. She had the full approval of the Chicago bishop for the endeavor. As a founder of this teaching community, Mother Alfred became its first general superior. And her headstrong behavior continued. In one instance, when the pastor indicated his displeasure over Mother Alfred's selection of a school principal, she withdrew all the sisters from the school.

In 1877, the bishop expelled her from the Joliet congregation. Twenty-three sisters went with her to Rochester, Minnesota, where Mother Alfred had already opened a school. The sisters established a branch of the Joliet congregation there.

Eventually, the two communities split, and in 1878, the bishop of Rochester, after initial misgivings, approved a new congregation, the Sisters of St. Francis of Our Lady of Lourdes. At age 49, Mother Alfred was again a founder.

For most of her life, Mother Alfred was a teacher. But in 1883, when a tornado devastated Rochester, she began to think along different lines. The sisters cared for many of the injured at a makeshift hospital, under the guidance of the town physician, Dr. W.W. Mayo.

Years later, an area newspaper offered an account from the then-aged Dr. Mayo describing Mother Alfred's actions in the aftermath of the tornado. The headline was, "A Nun's Dream Built the Mayo Hospital."

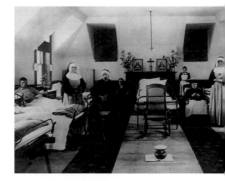

ABOVE, TOP:
SAINT MARY'S 10-BED WARD IN 1889 CONTAINED ROCKING CHAIRS AND A SPITTOON FOR PATIENTS. IT WAS FURNISHED WITH WOODEN DRESSERS, A CRUCIFIX, AND A PAINTING OF JESUS AND THE BLESSED VIRGIN. PICTURED WITH PATIENTS ARE SR. JOSEPH DEMPSEY AND SR. CONSTANTINE POUTAL.
BOTTOM:
MOTHER ALFRED MOES, LEFT, AND SR. STANISLAUS KOSTKA.

Another account was related by Dr. Mayo in 1894:

"The mother superior came down to my office and in the course of her visit she asked, 'Doctor, do you not think a hospital in this city would be an excellent thing?' I answered, 'Mother Superior, this city is too small to support a hospital.'

"'With our faith and hope and energy it will succeed,' she responded. I asked her how much money the sisters would be willing to put into it, and her reply was, 'How much do you want?' 'Would you be willing to risk forty thousand dollars?' I said. 'Yes,' she replied, 'and more if you want it. Draw up your plans, Dr. Mayo, it will be built at once.'"

Saint Mary's Hospital opened on September 30, 1889, staffed by the Mayo physicians. Within four years, patients had come from Iowa, Illinois, Kansas, Minnesota, Montana, Nebraska, North Dakota, New York, Ohio, South Dakota, Michigan, and Wisconsin. To this day, Mother Alfred's collaborative vision lives on. Physicians from the Mayo Clinic have staffed Saint Mary's for 107 years.

Mother Alfred died on December 18, 1899.

BELOW:
DR. WILLIAM WORRALL MAYO, HIS WIFE LOUISE, AND THEIR DAUGHTERS, SARAH, PHOEBE, AND GERTRUDE.

MOTHER DOLORES
SAINT MARY'S HOSPITAL
Reno, Nevada

"It was the maverick Mother Dolores who established the Dominican Sisters in Reno. She came one jump ahead of the archbishop, and with her arrival began the chain of events that created Saint Mary's Hospital." So begins a history of Saint Mary's in Reno.

Mother Dolores was among the first of her St. Catharine's, Kentucky, Dominican order to volunteer to nurse the sick and wounded soldiers in the Civil War. She served in field hospitals and at least once was caught in a hail of bullets, one of which passed through her hair.

In 1876, Mother Dolores sought permission to go west and settle in San Francisco with four teaching sisters and two novices. The archbishop there granted her permission if she would join an already existing convent. That was not what Mother Dolores had in mind. When she arrived in San Francisco, the archbishop refused to let her establish her own community.

On the morning of July 14, 1877, as the other sisters slept, Mother Dolores left a note, slipped out of the convent, went to the train station, and caught the train to Sacramento. When the sisters discovered her note, they raced to the depot, boarded a train, and reencountered Mother Dolores on a platform at the Sacramento train station ready to board the train to Kentucky. They boarded the train together. The sisters' journey did not last long. As the train lurched over the Sierra Nevada, one of the sisters became violently ill. The seven women left the train to seek help at the next stop after Sacramento: Reno. The Lightning Express proceeded to Kentucky without the Dominican Sisters. When the local priest learned of the sisters' arrival, he asked them to establish a school for the daughters of prosperous Catholics. Mother Dolores agreed to stay.

But for that to happen, the Reno priest had to seek permission from his bishop, who, in turn, had to appeal to the archbishop of

BELOW:
MOTHER DOLORES WAS
AMONG THE FIRST OF HER
ORDER TO VOLUNTEER TO
NURSE THE SICK AND
WOUNDED SOLDIERS IN THE
CIVIL WAR.

San Francisco—the one with whom Mother Dolores had battled. The archbishop sent back a note: "I shall give her to you as a present."

Things were never easy for the feisty Mother Dolores. According to a manuscript in the Dominican archives, she was "continually in trouble with the priests and the bishop." Nevertheless, she opened Mount Saint Mary's Academy in 1877 and within two years had raised enough additional funds to construct a new three-story $30,000 school. But as the mining boom began to fail in Reno in the late 1880s, enrollment declined. Mother Dolores borrowed heavily to finance the school, but fell behind in her financial commitments. She also began to bully the sisters. A fundraising trip to Kentucky in 1892 failed to raise funds, and when Mother Dolores returned to Reno, she found Mount Saint Mary's padlocked. Friends found her prowling around the empty building. Not long after, she departed Reno. She died in 1915.

However, that fateful train stop to Reno eventually led to the founding of Saint Mary's Hospital. The sisters stayed on in Reno after Mother Dolores left, and in 1907, a doctor asked one of the sisters to open a Catholic hospital. When a second sister returned from a recruiting trip to Ireland with five young girls who expected to teach, she found a hospital where the convent had been. Today, Saint Mary's Regional Medical Center remains in Reno, sponsored by the Dominican Sisters, Congregation of the Most Holy Name.

MOTHER FRANCIS CLARE CUSACK
SISTERS OF ST. JOSEPH OF PEACE
Englewood Cliffs, New Jersey

Mother Francis Clare Cusack was reinstated as the founder of the Sisters of St. Joseph of Peace in 1970, 82 years after she was forced to resign as head of the religious congregation she founded.

Born in Ireland to an aristocratic family, Margaret Anna Cusack converted to Catholicism and joined the cloistered Irish

Poor Clare Nuns in Newry, Ireland. The well-educated woman religious wrote prolifically, publishing about 50 books in her lifetime. The proceeds from her works went to the poor, and Sr. Francis Clare became known as the Nun of Kenmare, the Irish County where she lived. Keenly aware of social justice and women's issues, she published in 1874 a work titled *Woman's Work in Modern Society*. "I appeal to women," she wrote. "I beg them to lay aside for a little the sensational romance and to look stern facts in the face; for so sure as there is a sun in the heavens this day…the future of the world will be what women make it." She outlined the problems facing women of her day: lack of meaningful education, financial dependency, and frivolous role models. In the aftermath of the article, Sr. Francis Clare's life was threatened. The document angered Protestant landowners and conservative Catholics. She became a nationally known figure, and songwriters wrote ballads about her.

Sr. Francis Clare wanted to help alleviate the suffering of the Irish and decided to open an industrial school. But she felt that a new religious congregation was needed to focus on the education and training of women. She left Kenmare to found the Sisters of St. Joseph of Peace.

Despite a cold reception from the Church hierarchy, she managed to set up a convent and open a kindergarten and industrial school in Knock, Ireland. But in 1883, the archbishop demanded that she turn over the convent to him and cut all links with the Sisters of St. Joseph of Peace. In 1884, Sr. Clare traveled to Rome, where Pope Leo XIII gave his approval to her plan to set up homes for Irish immigrant girls in the United States.

She arrived in the United States in November 1884, where she intended to open residences for Irish immigrant girls and to raise money. Her plan was to settle in New York City, but the archbishop, having heard about her reputation, refused to see her. So, the fledgling community moved across the Hudson River to

ABOVE:
BORN IN IRELAND TO AN ARISTOCRATIC FAMILY, MARGARET ANNA CUSACK CONVERTED TO CATHOLICISM AND JOINED THE IRISH POOR CLARE NUNS.

New Jersey, where the sisters opened a home and employment bureau for immigrant girls in Jersey City on March 10, 1885. Taking the name of the archdiocese in which they found themselves, the congregation became known as the Sisters of St. Joseph of Newark. Quickly realizing the breadth of the needs of the girls, the sisters offered daycare, home nursing, and food. The sisters also began caring for blind adults and children.

In 1888, Mother Francis Clare published a pamphlet that was seen by the Church as "an unwarranted, unjust and scandalous attack on Archbishop Corrigan [the New York archbishop] and his council." In retaliation, the bishop refused to allow novices to take their vows with the sisters and would not let the sisters admit any women to their congregation. In July of that year, ground down and seeing no alternative, Mother Clare left the order she had founded. Bitter about the treatment she had received at the hands of the Catholic Church, she found solace with Anglican friends. Eventually she left the Catholic Church altogether. She continued her writing—as it was her sole means of financial support—but went on to criticize the Church as the institution of mean and small-minded men. In her final days, she returned to England, where she died in 1899.

St. Joseph's School for the Blind was founded in 1891 by Mother Clare's Sisters of St. Joseph (who took back their original name in 1970). In the early 1960s, St. Joseph's began offering a curriculum for multiply disabled children.

Mother Cusak is not well known in Catholic Church history. The book *Nuns in Nineteenth-Century Ireland* by Caitriona Clear speculates: "No doubt her persistence in trying to justify herself and her position, her refusal to take lessons in 'humility' and self-abnegation from males in the Church, and her reputation as an articulate, able woman, added the deadly sin of pride, and worse, the female sin of 'immodesty' to her original sin of independent initiative." ❧

*Whether it is a Meals on Wheels program in the inner city
or a home for disabled youths, these sisters recognized
a specialized need and found a way to meet it…sometimes with
miraculous results.*

MOTHER CABRINI
MISSIONARY SISTERS OF THE
SACRED HEART
New York, New York

Maria Francesca Cabrini was born in Santangelo, Italy, on July 15, 1850, the thirteenth child of Agostino and Stella Cabrini. Frail and sickly, Frances dreamed of traveling to China as a missionary. Twice she sought to enter religious communities, but was rejected each time because of her poor health. At age 18, she obtained her teaching certificate.

After teaching in public school, Frances took a position as director of a school for orphans, where her kindness and religious conviction were widely recognized. One day in 1880, she was summoned by her bishop. He knew of her desire to become a missionary, but told her that to do so she would have to found her own religious community. Frances moved into an abandoned monastery with several other women and on November 14, 1880, at age 30, founded the Institute of the Missionary Sisters of the Sacred Heart.

Within years, this frail and determined woman had established houses in other parts of Italy and had opened orphanages and schools. But she still longed to go to China. A meeting with Pope Leo XIII in 1889 convinced Mother Cabrini to travel to the United States. "Not to the east, but to the west," he told her. "Your China is in the United States.

On March 23, 1889, two weeks after her conversation with the Pope, Mother Cabrini began her first journey across the Atlantic. On a rainy evening eight days later, she and six other Missionary Sisters of the Sacred Heart landed in America. They spoke not a word of English. No one was there to meet them. And their first night in New York City was spent in two run-down, roach-infested hotel rooms. But Mother Cabrini was determined to begin her work: the education of orphaned Italian girls.

Before long her work gained recognition in New York. A daily paper commented:

> *"In the past few weeks we have been seeing some dark-skinned women in our midst. They are little, slender, delicate women. They speak a few words of English. They climb narrow staircases, descend into filthy basements, and enter some places where a policeman would be afraid to go alone… These five or six sisters, newly arrived in our city, are breaking ground for the work of their sisterhood in the United States."*

*B*etween 1880 and World War I, three million Italians arrived in the United States and nearly half a million settled in New York. The death rate from measles, diphtheria, scarlet fever, tuberculosis, and pneumonia was higher among Italian immigrants than any other nationality. In 1888, the average mortality rate in lower Manhattan among Italian children under age five was 24 percent.

In 1891, Mother Cabrini was asked to take over a hospital. She hesitated, since hers had been founded as a teaching order, but eventually agreed. She recruited 10 sisters from Italy to take over a financially unstable hospital from the Scalabrinian Fathers, but they were unable to make the effort a success. The bank foreclosed in the summer of 1892.

The effort had convinced Mother Cabrini of the need for a hospital for Italians, and she obtained permission from the archbishop to open a hospital of her own. Using $250 she had received in donations, Mother Cabrini rented two adjacent apartment

BELOW:
MOTHER CABRINI, THE WOMAN WHO WAS TOO FRAIL TO GAIN ACCEPTANCE TO OTHER RELIGIOUS COMMUNITIES, FOUNDED 67 HOSPITALS, SCHOOLS, AND ORPHANAGES THROUGHOUT THE UNITED STATES, CENTRAL AMERICA, SOUTH AMERICA, AND EUROPE.

buildings on East 12th Street and bought 10 inexpensive metal bed frames. The sisters sewed the bed linens and made the mattresses. They slept on blankets on the floor.

The hospital opened on September 17, 1892. The sisters named it Christopher Columbus so Italian immigrants would know it was their hospital. During the first week there was no running water or gas. The sisters purchased meals at a nearby restaurant and brought them to the patients. The hospital's reputation spread rapidly and by 1903, it had grown to nearly 200 beds.

The woman who was too frail to gain acceptance to other religious communities founded 67 hospitals, schools, and orphanages throughout the United States, Central America, South America, and Europe. She crossed the Atlantic Ocean many times, traversed the Isthmus of Panama, and sailed the Gulf of Mexico on a banana boat and the Pacific Ocean on a steamer. At age 45, still frail and sickly, Mother Cabrini trekked across the Andes on a mule in the snow and ice. She wrote: "We rode above ravines that were several kilometers deep, and I didn't want my mule to ride so close to the brink. He just went straight on his way, paying no attention when I tugged on the reins. And when he leaned out so far that his head and neck projected beyond the cliff, then I would shout at him in as much Spanish as I knew. It didn't do any good."

Even as her health declined, Mother Cabrini continued to visit the organizations she had founded. On December 20, 1917, during a visit to her hospital in Chicago, Mother Cabrini learned that the 500 orphans in her Italian parochial school would not have their usual Christmas candy because of war shortages. The next day she insisted that the children get their goodies. She rose early and helped pack 500 boxes for the children.

Before noon on December 22, Mother Cabrini met with the supervisor of Columbus Hospital. She died a short time later in the room where she resided during her visits there. Mother Cabrini was canonized in 1946, less than 30 years after her death.

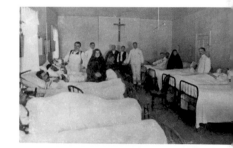

THE NEW YORK FOUNDLING HOSPITAL
New York City

RIGHT:
ORPHANS FROM THE NEW
YORK FOUNDLING
HOSPITAL IN THE 1920S.

With $5 and a vision, four Sisters of Charity moved into a flat on East 12th Street in New York City on October 11, 1869. They were planning to receive babies in January, but the first infant arrived that very night. From then on, the sisters placed a bassinet outside the door to receive abandoned babies and children.

Today, the New York Foundling Hospital is celebrating 127 years in New York City. It offers a spectrum of services aimed at meeting the needs of children.

SISTERS OF ST. JOSEPH
Ann Arbor, Michigan

St. Anthony's School for the Feeble Minded was opened by the Sisters of St. Joseph in 1899 in Kalamazoo, Michigan. It was among the first such institutions in the country specifically for children. St. Anthony's offered a home-like setting with private rooms for each child. Among the activities: croquet, swings, and play houses.

An early brochure emphasizes: "This is not an Insane Asylum. It is a school for feeble minded children who will be given the attention and care such as only Sisters can give.

BELOW:
"DOVES, BELGIAN HARES AND VARIOUS KINDS OF POULTRY ARE READY TO RECEIVE THE ATTENTION OF THOSE WHO FEEL INCLINED," EXPLAINED A BROCHURE ADVERTISING ST. ANTHONY'S SCHOOL FOR THE FEEBLE MINDED.

"The worst forms of feeble mindedness are improved by a course of training such as is given at this school," notes the document. Parents "will be relieved when they are assured that such germs of faith as are naturally in the hearts of their children will be nourished under the kind and sympathetic treatment of the Sisters in charge, who will do everything in their power for the spiritual and bodily welfare of the children committed to their care."

MOTHER M. ANGELINE TERESA
CARMELITE SISTERS FOR THE AGED AND INFIRM
Germantown, New York

*A*s a Little Sister of the Poor, Mother M. Angeline Teresa loved working with the elderly. But she saw needs that were not being met by the sisters. She wanted nursing homes to offer a homelike atmosphere where people could keep the freedom they'd had for their first 70 or 80 years. Although they offered homes for the destitute poor, the Little Sisters of the Poor had no such facilities for the middle class — and could not offer them because of the rules governing the congregation.

It became obvious that Mother Angeline Teresa could not make the changes she sought within her religious congregation. After years of prayer and pondering, Mother and the Little Sisters decided that the dilemma was God's way of bringing into existence a new congregation in the United States to care for all classes of the aged.

In 1929, seven sisters requested dispensations from Rome to leave the Little Sisters of the Poor and to continue to work as religious caring for the aged in a new way. With the approval of the archbishop of New York, the new order would care for the elderly regardless of their financial status, national origin, or religious belief. The environment would be homelike.

Leaving the Little Sisters — the congregation to which they had dedicated their lives — was painful. They had enjoyed many happy years there, loved the sisters, loved their work with the aging, had positions of responsibility, and had a secure future spiritually, physically, and financially. Such a risk! Leaving meant an uncertain future. Finances were nonexistent, and failure was a distinct possibility. Not only were they opening a nursing home, Mother Angeline was beginning a new congregation.

Mother Angeline was the youngest of that pioneer group of seven who walked out the door of their convent on August 11, 1929.

There was no going back. The worst
Depression this country has ever known
would happen in less than three months.

    The sisters spent three weeks with
another congregation, praying and preparing for the next step.
On September 3, they moved to the old rectory of an abandoned
church on Broadway and 187th Street in New York City. It had
seven beds. With no financial resources of their own, the seven
women religious relied on the kindness of friends to meet their
simple needs.

    Not long after they moved to St. Elizabeth's Rectory, the
sisters opened it to a small number of needy older persons. From
the very beginning, the sisters encouraged each elderly resident to
use his or her talents in the home. The first resident, Mr. Thomas,
took charge of the furnace room. Miss Savage was an experienced
cook. And so it went. During their first summer, the sisters did
something unheard of for a nursing home: they took the residents
to the Catskills for the summer.

    On July 16, 1931, Mother Angeline realized her greatest
dream when she received a cablegram from Rome granting her

ABOVE, RIGHT:
THE FIRST RESIDENTS
TAKEN IN BY THE NEW
CONGREGATION.
LEFT:
THE COTTAGE IN THE
CATSKILLS WHERE MOTHER
ANGELINE TOOK HER FIRST
SEVEN ELDERLY RESIDENTS
ON VACATION.

permission to form the Carmelite Sisters for the Aged and Infirm, a new congregation. That settled, Mother Angeline found a larger facility to use as a home for the aging, a motherhouse, and a novitiate. The little group moved into St. Patrick's Home in the Bronx on September 29, 1931, and began accepting postulants.

One of the delightful stories about the early years of the nursing home describes Mother Angeline's sensitivity to the fact that the residents liked a cocktail before dinner or a glass of wine with a meal. So it was with pleasure that she accepted a gift of confiscated liquor from the director of Catholic Charities.

In 50 years, Mother Angeline opened 59 facilities, plus daycare, senior centers, and outreach programs. Twenty-three organizations remain open today, and the congregation numbers just under 300. For her work—and for the love with which the sisters cared for the elderly—Mother Angeline received numerous honors, including the

BELOW:
THE ORIGINAL
ST. PATRICK'S HOME.

You are one of those rare and wonderful people who started to do something about a problem years before most of us even acknowledged that a problem existed.

SENATOR THOMAS DODD ON MOTHER ANGELINE.

86

1969 National Award of Honor from the American Association of Homes for the Aging. The late Senator Thomas Dodd wrote of her: "You are one of those rare and wonderful people who started to do something about a problem years before most of us even acknowledged that a problem existed."

When Mother Angeline celebrated 50 years of religious profession in 1965, the journalist Jim Bishop wrote:

"One could say that Mother Angeline is a leader, a born leader. But the word is malleable and weak and it tells little. It might be proper to say that she is a builder, but this is the puny accolade of the ambitious. It might be closer to say that, deep down, there is a streak of stubbornness which could never comprehend the word defeat, but that is a characteristic common to all good generals. It is more fitting, I think, to point out that Mother Angeline was born to wash the feet of the aged, the infirm, and to do it on her knees with love."

DAUGHTERS OF CHARITY OF ST. VINCENT DEPAUL
Evansville, Indiana

Sister Loyola Ritchie was among the first women religious to settle in Michigan. She and three other Daughters of Charity arrived in Detroit at the request of the bishop in May 1844 to open two schools, one for girls and one for boys. Eventually officials decided that the school for boys should be discontinued, and Sr. Loyola proposed the opening of a small hospital. A history recounts how "providence furnished an occasion which tended to convince the bishop of the utility of such a good work."

One of the schoolgirls found a man covered with sores lying in an abandoned shed. She told Sr. Loyola, who immediately went to him. She inquired if he would be willing to be moved to a more comfortable place where he could be cared for. The man gratefully agreed. When the sisters told the bishop, he consented to use the boys school as a hospital. It was the beginning of Providence Hospital, Southfield.

The Work Continues…

SR. JANET GILDEA

SISTERS OF CHARITY OF CINCINNATI
El Paso, Texas

Horizon City, Texas," reads the billboard.
"Life in the not so fast lane."

It's brown in the desert, brown and
flat for almost as far as you can see. And just when you think the
desert will go on forever, you see the mountains. El Norte, the path
to the north, winds through the mountains; for some Mexicans the
path leads to what they hope will be a better life. A rooster crows
relentlessly and dogs bark. It's another morning in the colonias.

The colonias are at the edge of the desert. Dusty and flat,
dotted with sagebrush, they are tiny communities of trailers,
shacks, and crude houses. Some colonias have electricity, some
don't. Some have water and sewers, others don't. The residents
are poor. Some are undocumented persons who have nowhere else
to go; others live there because they love the way the stars look,
so vivid against the pitch-black sky.

The Clinica Guadalupana is a tiny building that sits all by
itself in the middle of the desert. Outside the clinic several women
sit with their children absorbing the morning sun. "We used to
look out our windows and see only the desert," says Gloria
Morales, a resident of the colonias. "Then one day the clinic was
here. It was like a mirage. I thank God that we have the sisters,"

*W*e used to look out our windows and see only the desert. Then one day the clinic was here. It was like a mirage. I thank God that we have the sisters. And to think they don't care about money! They are wonderful people. And they have programs for the children. It's not like a health place. It's like a fun place.

GLORIA MORALES,
A RESIDENT OF THE
COLONIAS.

says Morales. "And to think they don't care about money! They are wonderful people. And they have programs for the children. It's not like a health place. It's like a fun place."

Sr. Janet Gildea is a physician. But she's always been more interested in the service dimension of medicine than in the science. What didn't interest Sr. Janet was becoming a sister. In fact, when the idea entered her mind in high school, she told herself, "Not on your life." But at some point during college, she read about a sister in Kentucky who was also a medical resident. And she began to entertain the idea of a dual vocation. After she finished medical school in 1982, she joined the Sisters of Charity of Cincinnati, which she describes as a progressive religious congregation. "We are committed to social justice," she observes. "We don't wear a habit, we discern our own ministries, and we choose who we live with."

Being a sister, she explains, "frees me to be the kind of physician I want to be. I can serve the poor and be in community with other sisters."

RIGHT:
THE COLONIAS ARE AT THE
EDGE OF THE DESERT—
TINY COMMUNITIES
OF TRAILERS, SHACKS, AND
CRUDE HOUSES.

FAR RIGHT:
THE CLINICA
GUADALUPANA.

Sr. Janet never expected to work in El Paso. "I always thought I'd work in Appalachia," she smiles. One thing she's always known for sure is that she wanted to serve on the front lines—where the needs were greatest. In 1991, she was part of a small group of Sisters of Charity who decided to live more fully the words of the congregation's new vision statement. The women committed themselves to working with Hispanics and the materially poor.

As they looked throughout the Southwest for a place to relocate, Sr. Janet learned that another religious community was looking for a medical director for a clinic in El Paso. She took the job, but the other sisters went to El Paso without jobs. Explains Sr. Janet, "We knew that, as a border city, El Paso would always have needs. Someone has written that religious life will be rewoven at the periphery," Sr. Janet explains. "Well, El Paso is a peripheral place and the colonias are on the periphery of El Paso."

After working at the medical clinic for two and one-half years, Sr. Janet wanted to deliver care in the colonias. Clinic Guadalupana is as far out on the colonias as you can go and still have running water. Sr. Janet and Sr. Peggy Denewith chose the site based on the recommendation of their "sugar daddy."

"When we were talking about what we wanted to do, we kept telling ourselves the only way we could do it was if we found a sugar daddy," laughs Sr. Peggy, who became a registered nurse in 1993. "That's what the sisters did in the early days," she reminds.

In the brief time we've been here I think we have made a difference. The people think the Church cares about them because the sisters have chosen to come here. It's what we want to be doing: healthcare on the front lines.

Sr. Janet Gildea, Sisters of Charity of Cincinnati, on working at the clinic Guadalupana in Texas.

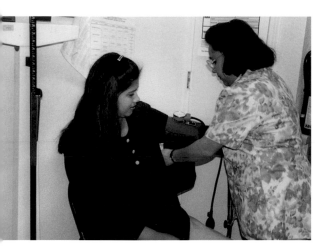

ABOVE:
LUZ PATINO TAKES A
BLOOD PRESSURE READING.

LEFT:
CHILDREN AT THE CLINIC
LIBRARY.

ABOVE:
ENRIQUETA JIMINEZ AND
HER DAUGHTER AT THE
CLINIC.

Adds Sr. Janet, "I thought the stories about our early sisters were just stories of the past. But since I've been here I realize that all you have to do is ask for what you need. People want to help and they trust the sisters."

Sr. Janet and Sr. Peggy met their "sugar daddy" after mass one Sunday. It turned out that he owned a construction company and helped them purchase land for $500, an amazingly low price. With his assistance, financial help from their congregation, and the donated services of many, the sisters built the Clinic Guadalupana for less than $15,000. It opened on January 16, 1995.

The clinic is a public-private partnership. On the day Sr. Janet approached the health department to propose a clinic, the department had lost funding for another clinic. "They jumped at the chance," laughs Sr. Janet.

The department of health pays the sisters' salaries for 20 hours a week, as well as for various screenings and exams. The Sisters of Charity of Cincinnati pay for an additional 20 hours of the sisters' salaries. About one fourth of the patients are on Medicaid, and patients without insurance pay on a sliding scale, with most asked to pay $10 per visit. "It's a small clinic doing primary and preventive care in a very simple way," says Sr. Janet.

In addition to providing healthcare, the sisters offer TEAM (Together Everyone Achieves Miracles), a program aimed at building self-esteem among young girls. On Saturdays at the clinic, the girls dance, do arts and crafts, read, and sing. They also have a library of children's books at the clinic, and youngsters are encouraged to borrow the books.

Many people who live in the colonias have no legal status in the United States, and the Border Patrol is a frequent sight in the

tiny communities. Immigration vans drive down the dirt roads and the illegals run for their lives, says Luz Patino, a nurses aide at the clinic. The people don't realize that if they just stayed in their places, they'd probably be safe, she adds. When they run, the van just picks them up and deports them. Sr. Janet describes such action as harassment. At the clinic people only have to produce evidence that they reside in a colonia to receive care. Clinic Guadalupana serves people from 11 colonias.

Before the clinic was built, people had to travel 20 miles or more to get healthcare. When a child got sick, the woman would get everyone up at 5:30 in the morning and the entire family would travel by car with the husband who was on his way to work. She would wait at the clinic or outside or at a McDonald's the entire day with the sick child and her other children until her husband picked them up after work.

"I pray that the sisters stay a long time," says Gloria Morales.

"It's beyond my wildest dreams," says Sr. Janet. "I never thought I'd be in the middle of the desert."

"In the brief time we've been here I think we have made a difference," she says. "The people think the Church cares about them because the sisters have chosen to come here. It's what we want to be doing: healthcare on the front lines.

> *L*ike the early sisters, we came to a community where we didn't speak the language, and we had to learn it. We also had no money—just like the early sisters. Collaborating with the laity—as we're doing—was natural in the early days because there were fewer sisters then.
> SR. JANET GILDEA

"With our commitment as sisters, we've foregone family and financial rewards. What we're doing demands faith and a willingness to take the first steps into the dark. But we feel the call to serve and the freedom to respond. Women of faith will always take risks." ❧

Sr. Sam

DAUGHTERS OF CHARITY OF ST. VINCENT DEPAUL
ST. VINCENT MEDICAL CENTER
Los Angeles, California

*S*r. Alice Marie Quinn, "Sr. Sam" to most people, did not mince words. "I want to raise the money to build a kitchen big enough to prepare 3,000 meals a day," she declared one day in 1991. Sr. Sam is the founding director of St. Vincent Meals on Wheels in Los Angeles.

Then, say those in the know, a miracle happened. The St. Vincent Medical Center board gave permission for her to expand her current kitchen, which fed 100 persons.

An architect drew up the plans, and a fund-raising campaign raised $1.6 million. Today, Sr. Sam, a Daughter of Charity for 41 years and a registered dietitian, has a state-of-the-art kitchen with the capacity to prepare 3,000 meals a day.

Her Meals on Wheels program began informally in 1977 when she prepared a few meals for seniors attending a program in a church not far from St. Vincent's. Her goal was to provide nutritional meals daily to the poor, the homebound, and the elderly. Word spread quickly and the program grew. Today, Sr. Sam oversees the daily preparation of approximately 2,000 meals. Each day 1,400 hot lunches and 625 cold suppers are delivered to individuals in the community. Through Sr. Sam's efforts, 200 breakfasts and 300 frozen meals go to people in need each week. In 1995, Sr. Sam delivered 744,000 meals. ❧

Sacrifice

We offer you no salary; no recompense;
no holidays; no pensions, but much hard
work; a poor dwelling; few consolations;
many disappointments; frequent
sickness; a violent or lonely death.

ADVERTISEMENT FOR RELIGIOUS LIFE BY
MOTHER M. JOHN HUGHES, FIRST SUPERIOR, ABERDEEN
PRESENTATION SISTERS, 1831-1897

*O*n accepting their call, these women religious willingly
accepted hardships. In leading lives of sacrifice,
they experienced spiritual growth and personal fulfillment.

MOTHER MARIANNE OF MOLOKAI

SISTERS OF ST. FRANCIS
Syracuse, New York

"*I am hungry for the work… I am not afraid of any disease, hence it would be my greatest delight even to minister to the abandoned 'lepers'.*"

In June 1883, during the second year of her second term as provincial superior, Mother Marianne Cope, a Sister of St. Francis of Syracuse, New York, received a letter from a priest in Hawaii begging for help. He had sent a similar letter to more than 50 religious communities in the United States, but Mother Marianne's was the only response that offered him hope. On October 22, 1883, Mother Marianne and six other sisters left Syracuse bound for Hawaii. She expected to be gone for only a few weeks. Little did she know that she would never return.

The Branch Hospital at Kakaako, Honolulu, had been established in 1881 as a "receiving station" for people suspected of having leprosy. Built to accommodate 100, Kakaako housed more than 200 people when Mother Marianne arrived in November 1883. The book

FAR LEFT:
LEPER GIRLS FROM THE BISHOP HOME WITH MUSICAL INSTRUMENTS.

LEFT:
A GROUP OUTSIDE ON A PICNIC WITH SISTERS ON MOLOKAI.

ABOVE, RIGHT:
PORTRAIT OF MOTHER MARIANNE AS A YOUNG WOMAN.

A Song of Pilgrimage and Exile by Sr. Mary Laurence Hanley, OSF, and O.A. Bushnell, describes Mother Marianne's first view of the facility. "She looked full into the face of horror that day, and she did not turn away."

A diary kept by one of the Franciscans, Sr. Leopoldina, described the patient wards: "Fat bedbugs nested in the cracks [of walls]. Brown stains upon walls, floors, and bedding showed where their blood-filled bodies had been crushed by desperate patients. Straw mattresses, each more or less covered by a dirty blanket, lay upon the unswept floor… Blankets, mattresses, clothing, and patients all supported an ineradicable population of lice. No attempt had been made to separate patients according to age, sex, or stage of illness…."

"Above all," continues *A Song of Pilgrimage and Exile,* "permeating everything—air, clothes, straw pallets, greasy blankets, even the wood of the walls and the dirt on the floors—hung the stink of lepers: the revolting stench rising from sores unwashed and uncovered, the miasma of dead and rotting flesh, in which voracious microorganisms by the billions eagerly devoured the debris from the tissues that they, and the implacable causers of leprosy, had killed in the bodies of their hapless hosts."

In January, the sisters began their work at Kakaako. Mother Marianne required stringent handwashing and other sanitary procedures and promised that no Franciscan Sister would ever contract leprosy. None ever has.

The first thing the sisters did when they went to work at the Branch Hospital is what sisters always do when they come face to face with chaos: they rolled up their sleeves and began to clean. Of all their tasks, the most difficult was dressing the lepers' sores. Notes *A Song of Pilgrimage and Exile:* "Each sister-nurse learned to wash away the scabs, the pus, the maggots, the rot from those fetid ulcers, to cut away the dead putrescent flesh at the margins of the sores, to apply soothing ointments to the raw wounds, and to bind them about with clean cloths."

Lawlessness prevailed at Kakaako. With a diagnosis of leprosy came the abandonment of hope. Rape and other types of violence were a way of life. Men, women, and children lived together, and the children ran in packs. Mother Marianne quickly realized that the corrupt power structure at the hospital perpetuated the lawlessness, and she tactfully stipulated the conditions under which the sisters would continue to help the lepers. Chief among her demands was the firing of the corrupt administrator. On April 2, 1884, the sisters were given full charge of the hospital.

Mother Marianne believed that the healthy children of leprous parents were at high risk of contracting leprosy. But the children had nowhere else to live, and when their parents died, they ran wild. In November 1885, she opened a home for healthy girls with leper parents. The Kapiolani Home was begun with a group of 10 girls from Molokai.

In the summer of 1886, the sisters took care of Father Damien when he visited Honolulu. The priest had first noticed signs of leprosy in 1882. In her journal, Sr. Leopoldina noted, "It was very sad to see the young priest so disfigured, his hands, neck, and face a deep purplish red, his ears so red and enlarged that they were hanging nearly to his shoulder and his nose twice its natural size and great leper lumps on his lips and face, his eyes were heavy and red but he was cheerful and happy...." Father Damien explained to Mother Marianne that he wanted the sisters to take over for him on Molokai when he died. At the time, he had been there 13 years.

Mother Marianne wanted to visit the Leper Settlement on Molokai before she made a final commitment. On September 20,

*A*s Father Damien and Mother Marianne had learned very soon, lepers judge the quality of a clean person's character by testing his willingness to shake their hands.

A SONG OF PILGRIMAGE AND EXILE, BY SR. MARY LAURENCE HANLEY AND O.A. BUSHNELL.

Reverend Sister Maryanne
        Matron of the Bishop Home
                Kalapapa.

To see the infinite pity of this place,
The mangled limb, the devastated face,
The innocent sufferers smiling at the rod,
A fool were tempted to deny his God.

He sees, and shrinks; But if he look again,
Lo, beauty springing from the breast of pain! —
He marks the sisters on the painful shores,
And even a fool is silent and adores.

                        Robert Louis Stevenson

Kalawao. May 22ᵈ 1889.

THE SAME BOAT THAT
BROUGHT THE SISTERS TO
MOLOKAI BROUGHT THE
POET ROBERT LOUIS
STEVENSON, ABOVE, WHO
STAYED FOR A WEEK. HE
LATER SENT MOTHER
MARIANNE THE POEM AT
LEFT.

1888, she visited the island. "She went," says *A Song of Pilgrimage and Exile,* "to see if she should send any of her sister-companions into that hell hole, into that land of the living dead." She decided she should.

Mother Marianne and two other Franciscan Sisters set sail for Molokai on November 13. Forty or so lepers, about half women and children, traveled on the boat with the sisters. The lepers were forced into cattle pens for the journey. At Kalaupapa on Molokai, 1,000 lepers awaited the sisters' arrival. It was a sad, isolated, dreary place. The lepers had neither the energy nor the inclination to improve their pathetic living conditions. Most lived in hovels.

Upon their arrival on Molokai, the sisters took charge of the new Bishop Home for Unprotected Leper Girls and Women. Among the first things Mother Marianne did to improve the bleak environment was to grow fruit, vegetables, and landscape plants.

The male lepers were constant threats to females in the Bishop Home. Sex was among the few pleasures left to the lepers, and they were not willing to give it up without a struggle. Mother Marianne and the sisters were constantly on their guard, often wielding clubs to keep the men from raping the girls. They also attempted to create a moral conscience among some of the willing girls. Sr. Leopoldina's diary references a plot to murder Mother Marianne.

On April 15, 1889, the sisters learned that Father Damien had died. Mother Marianne and Sr. Leopoldina went by wagon to his tiny house. Recounted Sr. Leopoldina: "When we reached the home there was a dead silence everywhere[.] The poor boys were in little groups…like sheep without their shepherd." Mother Marianne prepared Father Damien for burial.

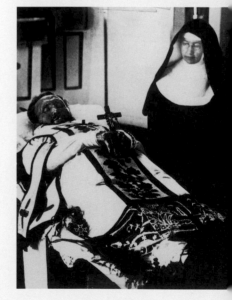

*I*t was very sad to see the young priest so disfigured, his hands, neck, and face a deep purplish red, his ears so red and enlarged that they were hanging nearly to his shoulder and his nose twice its natural size and great leper lumps on his lips and face, his eyes were heavy and red but he was cheerful and happy…

FROM THE DIARY OF SR. LEOPOLDINA, SISTERS OF ST. FRANCIS.

Fulfilling her promise, Mother Marianne took over the boys home the leprous priest had run. She brought two new sisters to

Molokai to be in charge. The same boat that brought the sisters brought the poet Robert Louis Stevenson, who stayed for a week. According to *A Song of Pilgrimage and Exile,* Stevenson visited with Mother Marianne and the sisters and taught the leper girls how to play croquet.

During his stay, Stevenson wrote a poem:

To see the infinite pity of this place,
The mangled limb, the devastated face,
The innocent sufferers smiling at the rod,
A fool were tempted to deny his God.

He sees, and shrinks; but if he look again,
Lo, beauty springing from the breast of pain!—
He marks the sisters on the painful shores,
And even a fool is silent and adores.

A week after Robert Louis Stevenson left Molokai, a piano was delivered to the Bishop Home for Girls, a gift from the famous poet. After that, "there was always music," wrote Sr. Leopoldina.

The annual census at the leprosarium hovered between 1,000 and 1,100 between 1889 and 1900. After that, the number of cases fell below 1,000 and continued to decline slowly but steadily.

The Franciscan Sisters couldn't offer a cure for leprosy—that would come later in the century at another home for lepers in Louisiana where the Daughters of Charity served. What they could offer the lepers was some semblance of dignity and as pleasant a life as possible. When the mother superior from Syracuse visited

BELOW, TOP:
THE LIVING QUARTERS FOR
WOMEN AND CHILDREN AT
THE BISHOP HOME.
BOTTOM:
MOTHER MARIANNE MADE
SURE THE GIRLS WORE FINE
DRESSES.

RIGHT, TOP:
MOTHER MARIANNE
CONSENTED TO HAVE HER
PICTURE TAKEN OUTSIDE
IN HER WHEELCHAIR; THE
SISTERS STOOD BEHIND
HER, AUGUST 1, 1918.
BOTTOM:
GROUP OF WOMEN AND
GIRLS FROM THE BISHOP
HOME.

Molokai in 1900, Sr. Leopoldina remarked in her journal: "She was very much surprised to see them enjoying life, being so sadly afflicted."

In 1908, the U.S. government began building the United States Leprosy Investigation Station on Molokai. Included were hospital wards, research laboratories, and housing for healthcare professionals and their families. When the facility opened in 1909, the people of Molokai saw electricity for the first time. Unfortunately, neither the lepers nor the sisters were allowed to pass through the barbed wire barricades to enter the facility. In its first two years, only nine of the 700 lepers participated in the research program. The magnificent investigation station closed in 1913.

In her later years, Mother Marianne suffered from pulmonary hemorrhages and endured a chronic racking cough. In 1916, in her seventy-eighth year, she wrote to Syracuse asking to be relieved of her managerial responsibilities in Hawaii. Although her request was denied, the superior appointed another sister as Mother Marianne's representative.

On January 23, 1918, the sisters celebrated Mother Marianne's eightieth birthday. By then, the once beautiful woman was completely broken. Confined to a wheelchair, she was disfigured and bloated from physical ailments.

On August 1, Mother Marianne consented to have her picture taken. She was carried outside in her wheelchair and the sisters stood behind her. In the photograph, she is bent, broken, and disfigured. Wrote one of the sisters: "I would look at her feeble body and bent shoulders thinking, 'What a pity that you wore out your frail body doing work befitting the strongest man.' But her heart and thoughts were all for Molokai."

Mother Marianne Cope died on August 9, 1918. ◈

The specter of death was always near as the sisters tended to the sick and impoverished. In trying to ease the pain of others, they stepped in the path of danger, and many sisters died well before their time.

St. Vincent's Hospital
New York City

The pear tree planted by Peter Stuyvesant in 1647 was 202 years old when the Sisters of Charity arrived on East Thirteenth Street on November 1, 1849, to start St. Vincent's Hospital. The hospital opened on November 12. Staffed by five physicians and four Sisters of Charity, the hospital was quickly crowded with patients. According to a history:

> *"The sisters slept on mattresses brought out at night and laid on the floor of the small room which they reserved for their living quarters. For the first four years, the mortuary was located on a porch opening off this room. This was the least of the inconveniences, for the hospital had no running water, no bathing facilities of any kind except for water carried from a nearby well, no light but oil lamps, no heat but that provided by a small stove in the cellar. Under these conditions, nursing was grueling physical labor. And in the entire United States, there was not a single thermometer to gauge a soaring temperature, much less a hypodermic syringe to relieve pain."*

Of all the cases in St. Vincent's history, undoubtedly the most famous emergency call came in April 1912. The "unsinkable" cruise ship *Titanic* had sunk in the icy waters of the North Atlantic with 1500 passengers and crew. The 700 survivors who escaped in lifeboats were picked up by the *Carpathia* and brought into New York harbor.

On April 16, the day after the tragedy, Sr. Maria Isidore, administrator of St. Vincent's, sent word to the White Star office that the hospital would receive without charge up to 150 of the *Titanic's* passengers.

At 8 p.m. on April 18, a contingent from St. Vincent's met the ship at the pier. Of the 174 survivors who were cared for in seven

ABOVE:
FRONT PAGE OF *NEW YORK TIMES*, APRIL 16TH, 1912.
HEADLINE: TITANIC SINKS....
(CORBIS-BETTMANN).

institutions, 117 went to St. Vincent's. They represented 14 nationalities and the majority could not understand English.

In recent times, St. Vincent's has provided care to the survivors of notorious crimes, including the Bernhard Goetz subway shooting victims, the Hasidic students shot crossing the Brooklyn Bridge, and the model whose face was slashed with a razor by thugs hired by a former friend. St. Vincent's paramedics were first on the scene of the World Trade Center bombing in 1993.

The hospital was among the first to support persons infected with HIV and, through its Department of Community Medicine, provides healthcare to homeless persons and the homebound elderly.

St. Mary's Hospital
Galveston, Texas

*I*n 1866, diphtheria, yellow fever, and typhoid were rampant in Texas. In May, the second bishop of Galveston—a diocese that encompassed the entire state—set out for his native France to seek help. In Lyons, he asked the Sisters of the Incarnate Word and Blessed Sacrament to help him found a new congregation to respond to the health needs of the people in Texas.

On October 24, Srs. M. Blandine, Joseph, and Ange arrived in Galveston. They were the first three women religious in a new congregation, the Sisters of Charity of the Incarnate Word. A small building served as both hospital and convent.

ABOVE:
SR. VINCENT COTTIER WAS ONE OF THE 10 SISTERS WHO DIED AT THE ORPHANAGE DURING THE 1900 STORM.

BELOW:
ST. MARY'S HOSPITAL BEFORE THE 1900 STORM.

ST. MARY'S INFIRMARY.

Charity Hospital opened on April 1. Its mission: to care for the sick and for orphans. A mere three months later, Galveston experienced the worst yellow fever epidemic in its history. Two of the sisters fell ill. Mother Blandine died, and Sr. Ange eventually recovered. The period after the yellow fever epidemic was difficult for the two remaining sisters. With few patients to care for and no regular source of income, they opened a private school on one floor of the hospital.

Six more sisters arrived in 1868 from France, and Charity Hospital changed its name to St. Mary's Infirmary. To ensure an income, the sisters entered into a contract for the care of U.S. Marine patients at $1 per patient per day. In addition, they began offering private insurance for $1 a month paid in advance.

In the days before antibiotics, many of the people admitted to a hospital died there. It was not uncommon for both parents in a family to be stricken by a deadly disease, leaving their children orphaned. It was to meet the needs of these times that the sisters housed orphans on a floor of the hospital. After an outbreak of smallpox in 1872, they purchased a building on another site and moved 28 children to the new orphanage.

Begging was a daily activity. The sister in charge of the kitchen often had to wait for the other sisters to return from begging at the market before preparing dinner. When sisters went to beg in distant parts of the state, they often brought back so many new orphans that the money they had collected was immediately used up.

By 1900, 93 orphans were living with the sisters. On September 8, 1900, the "storm of the century" struck Galveston. To this day, it remains the worst natural disaster in U.S. history, having killed 6,000 people.

The orphanage sat on the shores of the Gulf of Mexico. That September day, as the waters rose, the sisters moved all the children into the newer and stronger girls dormitory. Still the water rose, and the sisters moved the children from the first to the second floor.

Each of the 10 sisters in that building tied 10 orphans to her body with clothesline. To calm the children, they sang "Queen of the Waves."

At 7 p.m., a tidal wave lifted the entire girls dormitory up for a few moments, and then the roof crashed down, trapping the sisters and their young charges inside. All but three boys perished. William Murney, then 13, remembers holding the hand of his seven-year-old-brother as they watched the water rise. When the roof collapsed, Murney lost his grip on his brother and never saw him again. The three survivors clung to the branches of a tree and were rescued after a day in the water. The bodies of the sisters were identified by the laundry numbers on their clothing. Many still had the children tied to them. They were buried where they were found, still tied together.

A Jesuit priest wrote:

"Ah, far removed from human aid, bravely did these Sisters of the Incarnate Word battle with the tide and hurricane to save their little charges... These brave, good, and holy nuns died as they had lived—caring for others."

Every year on September 8, Sisters of Charity of the Incarnate Word around the world remember the 10 sisters and 90 orphans who died in the storm. And every year, the sisters sing the hymn "Queen of the Waves" in their memory.

On September 8, 1994, a plaque commemorating the sisters' heroism was placed by the State of Texas at the site of the orphanage.

WHEATON FRANCISCAN SISTERS
Wheaton, Illinois

In 1872, Mother Clara Pfaender, founder of the German order Franciscan Daughters of the Sacred Heart of Jesus and the Immaculate Heart of Mary, sent three sisters to the United States to nurse the sick. Over the next several years, additional sisters joined them.

By 1875, Mother Clara had decided the fledgling community, based in St. Louis, could best be governed locally. She chose Henrica Fassbender, a 28-year-old sister, to head the U.S. province, now known as the Wheaton [Illinois] Franciscan Sisters. On December 2, 1875, Mother Clara said good-bye to Sr. Henrica and the four sisters who were to accompany her to St. Louis. The oldest was 32 years old.

When Mother Clara returned to her room after bidding good-bye to the women, she found a poem written by Sr. Henrica (see opposite page).

Four days after they left the convent, the five sisters perished at sea. The *Deutschland,* the ship on which they had sailed from Germany, hit a sandbar off the coast of England. The sisters gave their seats on the lifeboat to children and their parents.

Sr. Henrica was not the only one to write a poem that December. Gerard Manley Hopkins, a young Jesuit at the time, was so moved by accounts of the tragedy that he wrote the famous poem *The Wreck of the Deutschland* "to the happy memory of five Franciscan Nuns…drowned between midnight and morning of Dec. 7th, 1875."

The five sisters who died were Sr. Barbara Hueltenschmidt, Sr. Henrica Fassbender, Sr. Norberta Reinkober, Sr. Aurea Badziura, and Sr. Brigitta Damhorst. The bodies of four of the sisters lay in state in England. The body of Sr. Henrica was never found.

Lebe wohl...!

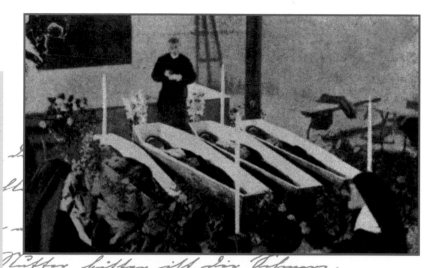

Now the solemn hour of departure is at hand,
And my heart, deeply touched, throbs with fear;
'Tis bleeding as though pierced by many a spear,
For in bitter pain we leave you and our land
   so dear.

I leave—yes, depart gladly and in peace—
In obedience to your wishes, O' Mother most dear;
Though distant, I know that your prayers will
   ne'er cease,
For your love will follow—hov'ring ever near.

But oh! as once again before you I kneel,
Allow these tears of departure free reign—
Thus consoled, I shall depart; for I shall feel
Your precious blessing coming to us o'er the main.

Oh pray that this office upon me now laid
Shall not too heavy for my weak shoulders prove;
May I learn to bear all with soul unafraid
While for God's highest honor, I labor with love.

Farewell! also to you, my sisters fond—
Ever preserve in your hearts your love for me!
Thus, uniting more firmly the consecrate bond
That binds our hearts for all eternity.

DEDICATED TO OUR DEARLY BELOVED MOTHER AT
OUR DEPARTURE FOR AMERICA BY YOUR LOVING
DAUGHTER, GRATEFUL UNTIL DEATH, SR. M. HENRICA,
DECEMBER 2, 1875.

ABOVE:

INSURANCE TICKET SOLD
BY BORGESS HOSPITAL.

SISTERS OF ST. JOSEPH HEALTH SYSTEM

Ann Arbor, Michigan

At the Michigan State Fair in 1885, a young boy was found stumbling along the sidewalk and was jailed for drunkenness. Amid the garbage and drunken curses of the inmates, he died just after a priest, Father Frank O'Brien, gave him the last rites.

The boy's death in such grim circumstances prompted Father O'Brien to seek to open a hospital. A few days before Christmas in 1888, he received a note from a bishop friend, Caspar Borgess, along with a check for $5,000:

> *"I am sending you $5,000, which is the last payment on my mother's property which was disposed of in Cincinnati… I was touched with your description of the death of the young man in jail, who, on account of lack of place where he might be taken, dealt such a crushing blow to his parents. If you feel you want to use this sum for that purpose, do so but…let me advise that you will be sorely tried with opposition. It will be worth the effort, but don't get discouraged with the many obstacles which will be placed in your way."*

In July 1889, 11 Sisters of St. Joseph of Nazareth arrived in Kalamazoo to run Borgess Hospital. It opened on December 8, 1889. Sr. Leonard Sage, a nurse at Borgess, described the times:

> *"The sisters did most of the work—cleaning walls, windows, and floors—and there were no mop wringers. They painted and varnished, did the kitchen work and laundry and sat up nights with patients following every major operation —at no charge to the patient…*

> *As if the sisters did not have enough worries…they also tilled a produce garden and maintained cows and chickens to supplement the hospital food supply."*
>
> SR. LEONARD SAGE, A NURSE AT BORGESS HOSPITAL IN THE LATE 1800s.

Father O'Brien's younger sister was a physician. After completing her studies, she joined the Sisters of St. Joseph of Nazareth and became Sr. M. Raphael O'Brien. Sr. Raphael, M.D., was an attending physician at Borgess Hospital, with privileges in medicine and surgery. She also practiced dentistry.

During the influenza epidemic of 1918, the hospital was placed at the disposal of health officials. Every available sister in Kalamazoo reported for duty at Borgess, caring for hundreds of the suffering day and night. Wards were packed with influenza victims and hallways were jammed with cots containing moaning patients. The sisters gave up their own beds, snatching a few hours of sleep in storerooms, closets, or wherever else they could find a vacant space. The death toll remained low in Kalamazoo. Across the state, however, thousands died and 13 nursing sisters lost their lives.

SISTERS OF MERCY OF THE AMERICAS
Cincinnati, Ohio

When asked to care for stricken Kentucky miners during the influenza epidemic of 1918, 16 Sisters of Mercy from Cincinnati volunteered. Traveling in mule carts, the sisters went wherever their services were needed, visiting as many as 40 families in a single day. Often they visited families devastated by the disease, as neighbors fled in fear.

BELOW:
SR. RAPHAEL O'CONNOR
DIED WHILE HELPING
INFLUENZA VICTIMS
DAYS BEFORE HER 58TH
BIRTHDAY.

Sr. Raphael O'Connor died while helping influenza victims days before her fifty-eighth birthday. An official of the American Red Cross wrote to the congregation's mother superior, praising the work of the sisters:

"I am so distressed to hear that one of your number paid 'the supreme sacrifice' after her heroic work in helping others. She no less gave her life for her country than did our brave boys; for this flu epidemic threatened our country most seriously, and nowhere was the suffering more than in our mountain section. I know that you did everything to save her, but that her life went as she wanted it to be in doing for others."

Combating disease and poverty was complicated by the sisters' lack of funds. When they had nothing at all, their faith kept them going.

MARIANITES OF HOLY CROSS
Princeton, New Jersey

The Marianites of Holy Cross came from France in 1847 to work with the Holy Cross Brothers at St. Mary's Orphan Boys' Asylumin New Orleans.

Conditions were deplorable for those three earliest sisters. The 40 boys lacked beds and mattresses and slept on the floor. The bed coverings were so filthy they had to be burned.

The sisters' only means of feeding the boys was begging. Their trips yielded sacks of bread, meat, vegetables and fruit, with the occasional cigar stub, peelings, knives, forks, and dish towels. The sisters would pick through the leavings, wash and clean the food, and prepare it for the orphans. On many days, these collections were the only food in the house. In the early years, the poverty was so intense that it was only the charity of the Ursuline nuns that kept the sisters from dying.

When the brothers withdrew, the sisters began accepting boys from families who could pay for their care. By 1851, 200 boys were being cared for. The sisters lived in the orphanage attic where, in the sweltering New Orleans summers, the heat was unbearable. Yellow fever was a constant threat. To upgrade the building, the sisters again turned to begging. After two months they had enough money to purchase a small house for themselves, which served as the first Marianite Novitiate in Louisiana.

The Marianite women became aware of another need in the city: the growing number of orphaned girls ages 12 to 15. Too old for the girls' orphanage and too young to remain without guidance, these girls were abandoned to the streets. The sisters offered them shelter, food, and an opportunity to learn to sew.

Bedrock of Faith

Things proceeded smoothly with the two ventures until 1862, when the Union forces made their way into New Orleans. Food and clothing became scarce and Confederate money was worthless. The sisters begged daily, often to little avail. An entire day's begging could yield as little as two small bags of flour—to feed 200 boys and the young women of the industrial school—not to mention the sisters.

The story goes that one day a sister met a well-to-do man on her begging tour. "You are having difficulty procuring food, are you not?" he asked. She nodded. The man entered a nearby shop, purchased a snuffbox for 25 cents and presented his gold one to the sister, who sold it for $80.

When gunshots announced the takeover of New Orleans by federal troops, Sr. Mary of Calvary was on the streets. At home the cupboard was bare. As she left the French Market carrying a shoulder of salt pork, she caught the last streetcar home. The city was in flames, but Sr. Mary of Calvary made it home with the meat.

Through a series of epidemics in the 1800s and the influenza outbreak of 1918, the Marianites cared for their young charges. St. Mary's Orphanage continued until 1932, when the boys were moved to a new facility opened by Catholic Charities. The sisters gracefully stepped out of a ministry they'd known for nearly 100 years.

FRANCISCAN SISTERS OF THE HOLY FAMILY
Dubuque, Iowa

On November 3, 1869, Mother Xavier Termehr and 15 other German women vowed to "live in obedience, without property, and in chastity…in the service of the sick and poor children."

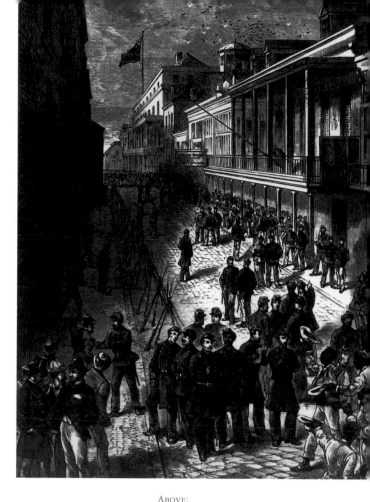

ABOVE:
THE OCCUPATION OF NEW ORLEANS BY FEDERAL TROOPS, UNDATED WOODCUT (CORBIS-BETTMANN).

BELOW:
MOTHER XAVIER TERMEHR CAME TO THE UNITED STATES WITH 28 OTHER SISTERS IN 1875.

In taking those vows, they became Sisters of Mercy of St. Francis. In 1875, fearing oppression in Germany, Mother Xavier and 28 other sisters went to the United States, where they settled in Iowa City. Such was their poverty that during their earliest days there, the entire food bill for each sister came to less than three cents a day.

In Iowa City, they opened the state's first orphanage. They also changed their name to the Sisters of St. Francis of the Holy Family. Later, Mother Xavier moved them to Dubuque, where they opened an orphanage and a hospital and taught school.

When a poor man told Mother Xavier he longed to send his children to the sisters' school but was too poor to buy the necessary books, she said, "Just send your children to school. We shall supply them with whatever they need." Overcome with gratitude, he departed. Mother Xavier turned to the sisters and said, "Our mission in this world is surely not to become rich."

MERCY HOSPITAL
Iowa City, Iowa

When the University of Iowa opened a medical school in Iowa City in 1870, patients who underwent surgery in the lecture room were sent to a rooming house to recover. Physicians were uncomfortable with this arrangement because they believed clinical medicine could not be learned properly without hospital experience.

On September 6, 1873, four Sisters of Mercy alighted from the Chicago train at the dusty prairie depot in Iowa City. They were hungry, tired, covered with dust, and laden with furnishings and medical supplies. The four women had agreed to open Mercy Hospital for the Medical School of the University of Iowa.

Three weeks later, on September 27, the hospital opened.

The Sisters of Mercy who served in Iowa City had received no formal training as nurses. They learned through experience and from other Sisters of Mercy in Davenport, Iowa.

The sisters lived in extreme poverty. When the hospital had more patients than beds, they slept on the floor. When they finished their daily nursing responsibilities, they spent part of each night washing sheets and other linens by hand in the basement. Reports from the time fail to recognize the sisters for the services they provided. Nor is there any indication that the sisters were compensated financially for their work.

St. Francis Regional Medical Center
Wichita, Kansas

> *"Wichita, November 1964—The community of sisters here who received word from the motherhouse in Rome to sell a debt-ridden hospital and return to Europe 65 years ago will mark 75 years of service to Wichita and Kansas next Wednesday."* From the *Wichita Catholic Advance*.

The sisters' decision to defy orders from Rome was not an easy one. Hunger, hard labor, and hardships were routine for them in 1899. Because people dreaded hospitals in those days, the newspaper account explains, "the number of admissions was dreadfully low. As few as 32 patients were admitted in one year. Eighty percent… were charity patients. And the sisters, handicapped by being unfamiliar with the English language and American ways, found it increasingly difficult to continue…"

The bishop managed to dissuade the sisters from leaving, and the advent of surgery helped financially, as more and more people began using the hospital. A century later, the Sisters of the Sorrowful Mother operate hospitals throughout the United States.

To provide food for the hospital and themselves, they had to beg from house to house. Next they went to work as nurses in private homes—for 50 cents for a day's work.

In 1893, in the midst of all their want, the sisters purchased the building they had been renting—with borrowed money.

This debt, joined with all their other difficulties proved to be one huge nightmare, so that in 1899 word came from the motherhouse to pull out of Wichita.

Newspaper account of the history of the Sisters of the Sorrowful Mother and St. Francis Regional Medical Center, Wichita, Kansas, from the *Wichita Catholic Advance*, 1964.

St. Vincent's Hospital
Jacksonville, Florida

ABOVE:
RESEARCH AT
ST. VINCENT'S HOSPITAL
EARLIER IN THE CENTURY.

The Daughters of Charity cared for yellow fever victims in Jacksonville, Florida, during the 1898 epidemic. They also tended the wounded from the Spanish-American War at Camp Cuba Libre in Springfield, Florida. With their reputation firmly established in the minds of the citizens of Jacksonville, the city asked them to take over a sanatorium. They agreed and renamed it St. Vincent's Hospital in 1916.

A segment of a letter written in 1916 by the first administrator, Sr. Mary Rose, to the mother superior in far-off Emmitsburg, Maryland, describes some of the hardships endured by the pioneer women.

> *"Sr. Louise has the operating room, drug room, and maternity hall, and as she says herself, she does not know a thing about any of these duties. She is under a strain all the time, suffers severe headaches with nausea and looks badly; she does try to be generous and has a good spirit. I must admit we all feel the heat very much, and though it seems to agree with Sr. Andrea, as she seems to be soaking wet all the time, she has gained about 10 lbs.*
>
> *"May I be on the lookout for a graduate nurse to look after the maternity and teach some things to the nurses that the srs. are not supposed to teach?"*

ABOVE:
A DAUGHTER OF CHARITY
IN JACKSONVILLE, FLORIDA.

Sisters of St. Joseph
Parkersburg, West Virginia

The September 18, 1920, issue of the Parkersburg newspaper offered the following comment:

> *"The Sisters of St. Joseph living among us for 20 years have earned our gratitude in every crisis when their help was required. During the influenza scourge, crowded beyond capacity, they imperilled their lives doing heroic work among the afflicted... When floods caused devastation in the low lands of*

Parkersburg, victims found comfort and a domicile with these charitable nuns…

"According to their vows, these good women have abandoned earthly affections and pleasures to cheerfully accept the substitute in sacrifice which is ever-present with the sick of every creed and class. They receive no compensation. They work and save and struggle in order to enlarge their sphere of usefulness… The Sisters of St. Joseph labor quietly, cheerfully and efficiently."

St. Joseph's Hospital was begun by the Sisters of St. Joseph in 1900.

ST. FRANCIS HOSPITAL
Blue Island, Illinois

When Blue Island, Illinois, became a city in 1901, the closest hospitals were 16 miles away in Chicago. After unsuccessful attempts to convince Chicago hospitals to open a branch in Blue Island, one of the local physicians approached a priest for help. The priest wrote to another priest and on September 18, 1904, five Sisters of St. Mary of the Third Order of St. Francis left St. Louis with $50 in cash bound for Blue Island.

Their motherhouse had paid $10,000 down on a $30,000 house that would become a Catholic hospital. When one of the sisters expressed misgivings about going so deep in debt, the priest advised, "Trust in God and be kind to the poor and all will be well."

For the first three months after their arrival, the sisters' diet consisted chiefly of bread, potatoes, pumpkins, and pancakes. Soup made from hot water, bacon grease, and chunks of bread varied the menu a bit.

One Sunday, when the doctor stopped in to see how renovations were progressing, he asked the sisters what they were having for Sunday dinner. They had given no thought to the matter, as they were helping the carpenter remove nails from boards, so the boards could be reused. The doctor returned with two ducks for their meal.

St. Francis Hospital opened on March 25, 1905. Because it had

BELOW:
AN EARLY PHOTO OF
ST. FRANCIS HOSPITAL.

no elevator, heavy patients were kept on the first floor, light ones on the second floor. A few weeks after the opening, an operating room was added, but since the sisters could not afford sufficient equipment, the kitchen table had to be carried upstairs for every operation.

Among the sisters who served at St. Francis in its earliest years was Sr. Mary Honoria Peckskamp, who arrived in 1910 and spent the next 50 years of her life as a cook in the hospital.

It was nothing, says a history, for sister to lift a half slab of beef onto the meat block or to wash walls and scrub floors after a long day at the stove.

Her sense of humor was well known. On one occasion, she called the butcher (who was a friend of the sisters) and inquired, "Do you have any brains?" When he answered "no," sister responded, "Well, then, please send someone to the phone who has brains."

The year after Sr. Honoria's arrival, money was scarce. She recalled, "With 27 patients on the census we had nothing in the house to cook, so we went out collecting. There are eight of us sisters, and we take turns begging at the market for a little cheap meat or whatever else they will give us."

HOSPITAL OF SAINT RAPHAEL
New Haven, Connecticut

In May 1906, a group of Catholic physicians in New Haven formed a Catholic Health Association with the intent of opening a Catholic institution of healing. They appealed to the Sisters of Charity of St. Elizabeth from Convent Station, New Jersey, to help them run the facility. Four sisters arrived in New Haven in February 1907, and ground was broken for the Hospital of Saint Raphael in April.

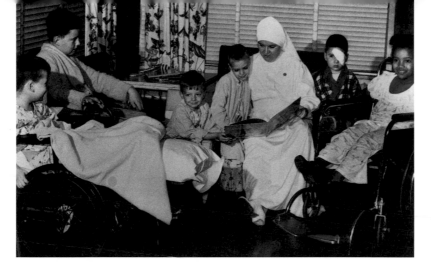

Newspaper reports of the day described the new building as "the best in New England," with such modern features as "an electric elevator." Another feature garnered national attention: "All walls and ceilings will have rounded corners to make them perfectly sanitary in every respect."

In the hospital's earliest days, the four sisters slept in the attic. In the evenings after surgery, they washed all the linens by hand for the next day's surgery. At night, to get the orderlies to do a better job scrubbing the floors, the sisters would tell them, "Okay, I'll do half and you do half."

DOMINICAN SISTERS OF SPOKANE
Spokane, Washington

The Dominican Sisters came from Speyer, Germany, in 1925 to take charge of a college in Helena, Montana. In 1929 they expanded their ministry to include hospitals, and by World War II they operated four hospitals and a mission for Native Americans.

A history of the congregation explains that "the sisters knew poverty that far exceeded the promise of their vows." During World War II, there were times when they did not have even three cents to mail a letter.

Despite their extreme poverty, at the end of the war the sisters sent packages of supplies to friends and family in Europe. Remembered one sister: "Many of us did not eat candy or cookies in those years. We saved all sweets to add them to our parcels of love." ❧

SISTERS OF ST. FRANCIS
Williamsville, New York
December 25, 1907. Owing to extreme poverty, Christmas presents were very few. However, each sister received one pair of shoe strings.

FROM THE ARCHIVES ON THE BEGINNINGS OF MT. ST. MARY'S HOSPITAL, SISTERS OF ST. FRANCIS.

**Prayers
Answered**

*Prayer was the sisters' source of strength. Sometimes that
strength was bolstered by the arrival of a much-needed miracle.*

SISTERS OF MERCY
St. Louis, Missouri

The Sisters of Mercy arrived in St. Louis in 1856 to teach young
girls. They also began visiting the sick, opened a home for
young working girls, taught black adults and children, and prepared
for religious services each Sunday at the city jail.

The winter of 1857 was a difficult one for the sisters. They had
little warm clothing and often went hungry because they gave their
only food to others more hungry than they. They took in laundry to
help support their efforts.

So intense was their poverty that Mother M. de Pazzi Bentley
considered returning to New York. One day, when she was reflecting
on what to do, one of the sisters told her there was not a loaf of
bread in the house and they had only $1. Mother M. de Pazzi went
to the chapel to pray. While she was in there, a man rang the door-
bell and left an envelope. In it was $100.

In 1871 the Sisters of Mercy opened the Infirmary for Women
and Children, a hospital for indigent women. So meager was the
revenue from this new venture that the sisters gave up their own
beds and slept on the floor to accommodate extra patients. Within
two years, pressure from physicians had convinced the sisters to open
the hospital to men, as well as paying patients.

SAINT JOSEPH HOSPITAL
Denver, Colorado

*A*t the persistent requests of the bishop of Denver, four Sisters of Charity of Leavenworth, Kansas, journeyed to Denver in 1873 to open St. Vincent's Hospital.

The tiny hospital could not keep up with patient demand and was moved to a larger building in the town's red-light district. When someone commented on the "questionable" nature of the neighborhood, one of the sisters is said to have replied, "We'll take the question out of the neighborhood."

The bishop wanted an even larger facility and enthusiastically planned for a 50-bed hospital. In the meantime, the sisters did the day-to-day work in the old building. In addition to nursing the patients day and night, they washed the laundry (often over an open fire outdoors), cooked, cleaned, and traveled across Colorado collecting funds. Because most patients had no money, the physicians scolded the sisters for taking in "dead-beats." Not infrequently, the hospital was full, but the sisters had no money at all.

One morning a woman arrived at the hospital, pleading for 30 cents to buy medicine for her sick husband. In arguing against giving the woman the money, a young sister said to her elder: "We have only 30 cents in the whole house." The older woman religious replied, "Sister, give her that and God will restore a hundred-fold."

*I*n 1900, Sr. Felicitas McCarthy was named superintendent of St. Joseph Hospital. A former teacher, Sr. Felicitas was a short woman. Upon her arrival, the chief of the medical staff said to his colleagues, "Boys, we'll have a good time. She won't know much about a hospital."

The next morning, Sr. Felicitas met him as he entered the building and gave him a report on each of his patients. At noon, when the medical staff met, the doctor said to them, "Boys, I made a mistake. Button your coats and get to work. There'll be no good time as long as she's around."

Sure enough, that afternoon the sisters were visiting a sick man, who presented $10 to each of them. On their way home, another man approached them and begged them to accept a donation of $10.

St. Vincent's was renamed Saint Joseph's Hospital in 1876. ❧

Sisters devoted their lives to treating broken bodies and wilted spirits. While they could not always ensure a remedy, their commitment to people in need was deep and unselfish.

St. Vincent's Hospital
Erie, Pennsylvania

LEFT:
DETAIL OF OIL PAINTING
OF MOTHER AGNES
SPENCER, FOUNDER
OF SAINT VINCENT
HOSPITAL.

In 1865, four Sisters of St. Joseph of Northwestern Pennsylvania opened a home for orphans in Erie, Pennsylvania. One day in 1874, an elderly man fell outside the orphanage and broke his leg. The sisters took him in and cared for his injury. Several months later, the bishop of Erie convened a committee to look into opening a hospital. The outcome: the Sisters of St. Joseph were commissioned to canvass the city for money. They were successful, and the three-story, 12-bed, $6,000 St. Vincent's Hospital opened in September 1875. The sisters served as nurses.

On December 27, 1879, the *Lake Shore Visitor* reported:

"The hospital is besieged every day by tramps.

"The institution has four new patients, three of whom are charity. With these there are 15 inmates in the hospital besides the eight sisters. A few of the patients pay for their keeping, but it is only one in about every five....

"The only resources the hospital has is what it gets from the patients and the earnings of the two sisters who teach the German school at St. Joseph's parish, and which is about $300 a year. How in the world Mother Agnes and her assistants, the sisters, manage to live, keep the institution in repair, in fuel, and give four or five patients all the nursing, nourishment, and care on this slender income, is a query none but a self-sacrificing band of sisters can solve.... There is no reason why the general public should not take an interest in this institution for it is the only place in the city where a stranger who happens to sicken in our midst can go for care."

A report from the July 1, 1882, *Erie Morning Dispatch* commented:

> *"There are nine sisters in all at St. Vincent's who do all the household work and furnish the medical attendance. The hospital is made self-supporting by the industry of these nine devoted women. Three of the sisters teach school at a neighboring Catholic educational establishment and their salaries, instead of being expended upon themselves, are applied to the funds of the hospital. So that the poor fellow upstairs groaning in agony from the effects of a misspent life, can, if he knows it, lay and ponder upon the novelty, not to say nobility, of those devoted women out working to support him. This is vacation time, and the three teachers are 'home for the holidays'. To them it does not mean a couple of weeks' pleasure, but is merely a change of employment."*

And:

> *"Their somber dresses with the peculiar collar of spotless white strike the eye at first as being melancholy, but the dark-hued habiliments are relieved by pleasant smiling faces and the visitor soon finds that the sisters do not minister to their sick with long faces and solemn words.... Were it so the hospital would register fewer cures."*

ST. MICHAEL'S HOSPITAL
Stevens Point, Wisconsin

When the citizens of Stevens Point decided to build a hospital, they wanted sisters to run it to ensure its success. In the November 1, 1912, issue of the *Stevens Point Daily Journal*, the City Hospital Association and the Woman's Club explained why sisters were crucial:

> *"Under no other management could a hospital meet with success in a city as small as ours. The reasons are plain. Every detail of hospital work, from the janitor service and scrub women to cooks, nurses and finances, will be scrupulously accomplished by those who have renounced the world and are devoting their lives to the care of the sick and afflicted, without money and without prize. It requires but a glance to see how impossible {it would be} to meet the financial requirements should it become the duty of the hospital association to pay in big round dollars for all the details of running a successful hospital."*

The Sisters of the Sorrowful Mother came to Stevens Point in 1912 to run the hospital and continue there to this day.

SISTERS OF SAINT JOSEPH
Concordia, Kansas

On June 28, 1914, Saint John's Hospital was dedicated in Salina, Kansas, with the Sisters of Saint Joseph in charge. In his dedication address, Jesuit Father A.J. Kuhlman offered the following comments:

> "Today is a great day for Salina. Something is being done here that calls out the citizens of all classes to this event... It is not for one; not for a few; not for one body only but for all. It is something permanent....
>
> "This represents something that is a benefit; something that is good. It is true it has been built and is being dedicated by one form of religion alone. But its charity is for all. All will find equal welcome here. Wide indeed it is opened for all. All that are human can find an entrance here. This is a work in which we all have an interest....

> "And then the sisters behind the walls are back to their work. It is the beginning of a great labor for them. These women whose services could not be bought are giving themselves. They are giving to Salina generation after generation of sisters. They are to live and die here and others will be called to take their place....
>
> "We need the example such as women of this kind can give. The sisters do not want money for themselves when they ask for money in the building of a hospital.

> "A sister comes here and stays 50 years and when she leaves it, she leaves as she came—without a cent. The nation needs a lesson in the use of money. These sisters have given up all. Home ties are broken for those who enter here. There can be no cry of mother love, no love as a wife, but only a spiritual love."

SAINT MARY'S REGIONAL MEDICAL CENTER
Reno, Nevada

Sr. Mary Seraphine Murray entered the convent in 1917 at age 26 after six years in the business office of a California vintner. Although she expressed an interest in nursing, she was told to work in the business office of a Catholic college.

ABOVE:
THE SISTERS OF THE SORROWFUL MOTHER ON THEIR
ARRIVAL IN TULSA IN 1914.

At age 39, Sr. Seraphine was recovering
from ulcers when she was sent to Reno to be
the administrator of Saint Mary's Hospital.
She arrived in July 1931, terrified that she
was unqualified for the responsibilities that
awaited her.

Years later, she recalled:

*"When I came I had to do everything. I kept the
books, and I relieved the switchboard operator
for lunch. If she didn't come to work, I would
fill in there and do my work between telephone
calls. I took care of purchasing,...personnel,...
practically everything: the assigning of rooms to
patients... It was terrific, keeping things covered, but we lived through it.*

*"Afterward we would all go to bed in the con-
vent at night. A bell would ring and we would
all go to bed, into our rooms anyway....*

*"I would come over to the hospital again at about 7:30 and stay until 10
or 11 and then go home again.*

*"We were up at five o'clock in the morning. But it was just life and
it was interesting, every minute of it, and very hard, and I was frightened
to death...."*

ST. JOHN'S MEDICAL CENTER
Tulsa, Oklahoma

*P*ersons who work within such close confines
all day require a change of scenery or
atmosphere to keep in good physical, mental,
and spiritual health. That is the reason why
the superiors are concerned when a sister
cannot take time out for her meals, sleep,
recreation, and prayers. If an ordinary
machine needs occasional periods of rest to
be cleaned and replenished with fuel, then the
sister must also have time to take care of her
physical and spiritual needs. Anyone who
has been privileged to join the sisters at
recreation, or who has observed them from
a window, knows how little it takes to make
them happy. The most innocent joke gives rise
to a peal of laughter.

The happiness of their charges is also their
concern. Methods of improving hospital care,
of serving meals, or preparing more tasty dishes, of really surprising the patients, etc., form
a frequent topic of conversation. Joys that are
shared double in value, while sorrows that are
shared ease the pain for the afflicted spirit.

FROM THE SISTERS OF THE SORROWFUL MOTHER
HISTORY OF ST. JOHN'S MEDICAL CENTER, TULSA,
OKLAHOMA.

*T*here were criticisms that came up, you know. And I would feel it, I was sensitive, oh I was sensitive. It would hurt me, but I would get over it...

"I knew nothing about a hospital, and I said to Mother Raymond, 'If I only had my nursing.' And she answered, 'Well, you take care of that office, Sister dear, and don't let the bills accumulate.' So little by little we worked things out, but it was very hard."

Sr. Mary Seraphine Murray on working as the administrator of Saint Mary's Hospital in Reno, Nevada.

The winter of 1931-1932 was especially difficult. Victims of the Dust Bowl passed through Reno on their way to what they hoped would be a better life in California. Saint Mary's admitted all who sought admission. Most could not pay for their treatment, but Sr. Seraphine would turn away no one.

She successfully fought to have the hospital declared tax exempt. In 1932 when the tax assessor visited Sr. Seraphine, he demanded she call off her fight. Her reply was emphatic: "Definitely not, sir!"

When the assessor told her he was only trying to save her trouble and promised to "knock off a couple thousand dollars," Sr. Seraphine, who was less than five feet tall, faced the man in fury. "You won't take a cent off your evaluation," she told him. "The hospital has paid unfair taxes for years... You don't make any changes on our evaluation, and we'll see how the county commissioners view your figures." In 1933, the Nevada legislature passed a bill making charitable institutions such as Saint Mary's Hospital exempt from property tax.

Sr. Seraphine struggled with her responsibilities at the hospital and feelings of unworthiness. In 1932, she wrote to her superior, "I would love to be released...if you can see your way clear. I really don't feel qualified for the work or the responsibility...." Her request was denied.

Ulcers continued to plague Sr. Seraphine. For 34 years, she ran Saint Mary's. In 1971 she received the Brotherhood Award from the National Conference of Christians and Jews, one of many honors throughout her lifetime. She retired in 1981.

In 1982, during a conversation with a Saint Mary's patient who was dying, Sr. Seraphine began to talk of God. The man's wife invited her into the hall and said, "My husband does not believe in God." Sr. Seraphine smiled: "Isn't he going to be surprised," she responded.

Sr. Seraphine had the first of several strokes in 1984. She died in 1987 at age 95.

Dominican Santa Cruz Hospital
Santa Cruz, California

A group of five Adrian Dominican Sisters arrived in Santa Cruz, California, at the request of the bishop in 1941. Their charge was to reopen a 28-bed hospital. They found the building filthy. Work days ran 16 to 18 hours long. Sr. Georganne Duggan, the only registered nurse among the five, remembers:

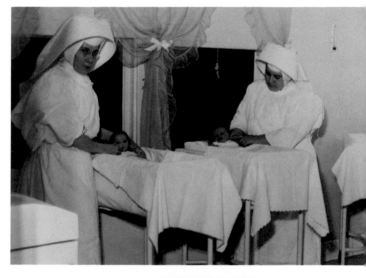

"When we went inside, I was convinced that I had made the mistake of a lifetime.

"Everywhere I looked increased my panic. Having come from one of Chicago's most modern and beautiful hospitals made it difficult to even imagine how this cottage-like building would ever become functional as a hospital.

"It was an impossible situation to begin with. Utterly impossible.

"To make a long story short, we opened about eight weeks later. We had to start from scratch. I don't know how we ever did it.

"Whatever sister was on night duty started breakfast. The days kind of ran together sometimes."

"We've come a long way since then," says Sr. Georganne. She retired in 1992. ❧

BELOW:
SR. GEORGANNE WITH A BABY BORN AT DOMINICAN SANTA CRUZ HOSPITAL.

ABOVE, TOP:
SR. GEORGANNE DUGGAN, RIGHT, AND SR. ANNE HERRINGER IN THE NURSERY, CIRCA 1946.
BOTTOM:
SR. GEORGANNE IN 1991, MANAGER OF STERILE PROCESSING AT DOMINICAN SANTA CRUZ HOSPITAL.

Creativity

*H*ard work and faith in God were powerful forces for the Catholic sisters, but they were not sufficient remedy for every problem. In many instances, the sisters' best resources were their creative imagination and a determination to sculpt obstacles into opportunities.

BELOW:
SR. IGNATIA, SECOND ROW, SECOND FROM RIGHT, WITH OTHER SISTERS OF CHARITY OF ST. AUGUSTINE.

Sr. Ignatia

Sisters of Charity of St. Augustine
Cleveland, Ohio

*A Co-Founder
of Alcoholics
Anonymous*

When Sr. Mary Ignatia Gavin died on
April 1, 1966, Cleveland, Ohio, was
besieged by mourners. At her funeral,
the church overflowed with people, while TV crews jockeyed to
cover the event.

Sr. Ignatia was a tiny, frail woman who suffered from physical
and emotional problems during her early years. For 21 years she
taught music for the Sisters of Charity of St. Augustine.

At age 39, when she was recovering from a nervous breakdown,
Sr. Ignatia received an assignment that meant leaving her life of
music. In 1928 she went to work as the registration clerk
in the admissions office of the sisters' new hospital, St. Thomas,
in Akron, Ohio. Her assignment there would change the world.

At St. Thomas, she met Dr. Bob Smith, a physician trying
to reestablish his reputation after a long history of drinking.
Sr. Ignatia and Dr. Bob established an immediate rapport, since both

were recovering from devastating problems: hers emotional, his alcohol related.

In 1939, Dr. Bob and Bill Wilson, a recovering alcoholic from New York, published a book, *Alcoholics Anonymous,* which outlined their philosophy on recovering from alcoholism and the importance of spiritual healing to the alcoholic. On a legal pad, Bill Wilson crafted The Twelve Steps based on their conversations around the kitchen table in Bob and Anne Smith's home.

By the end of 1939, according to the book *Sister Ignatia: Angel of Alcoholics Anonymous* by Mary Darrah, "AA emerged with a name, an identity, a new independence, and an effective program for sobriety. Still needed, however, was a sympathetic hospital that would tend to the alcoholics' medical needs while allowing the spiritual medicine of Alcoholics Anonymous to take hold."

In August 1939, Dr. Bob asked Sr. Ignatia to help him. He wanted to hospitalize alcoholics so they could begin a recovery program. Dr. Bob wanted to use St. Thomas as a place where the alcoholic could detox and then learn a new way to live—without alcohol. The idea was that the alcoholic would receive visits and encouragement from other recovering alcoholics. However, the St. Thomas administration had made it clear to him that they did not want alcoholics in their hospital.

Even before Dr. Bob's request, Sr. Ignatia had been quietly hiding alcoholics in the hospital. She admitted the men during shift changes, so nursing supervisors could not protest.

But Sr. Ignatia's surreptitious actions had come back to haunt her. One day she had placed a drunk in the hospital's tiny Flower Room, where sisters watered patients' flowers. She described what happened when she returned to the hospital: "When I came over early the next morning, the night supervisor…was standing in the doorway. She said, 'The next time you take a DT in this place, please stay up all night and run around after him as we have.'… I decided then that's enough. I often felt sorry to see them turned away, but

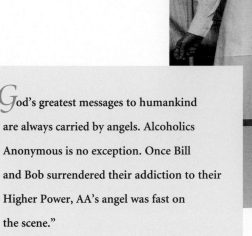

> *G*od's greatest messages to humankind are always carried by angels. Alcoholics Anonymous is no exception. Once Bill and Bob surrendered their addiction to their Higher Power, AA's angel was fast on the scene."
>
> FROM THE BOOK *SR. IGNATIA: ANGEL OF ALCOHOLICS ANONYMOUS* BY MARY DARRAH.

I was not the last word in the hospital."

"So," Sr. Ignatia recalled, referring to Dr. Bob's request, "you can imagine my misgivings." But because she trusted Dr. Bob, she agreed to take in a patient.

When Dr. Bob sought admission for another alcoholic, Sr. Ignatia decided to put the two men together. It soon became obvious that a policy change was needed, and Sr. Ignatia was determined to include alcoholics in the St. Thomas admitting policy. Sr. Ignatia, Dr. Bob, and several AA members met with Sr. Clementine, the hospital administrator, and asked her permission to officially care for alcoholics. Sr. Clementine boldly agreed, and the board and diocesan authorities followed suit. St. Thomas Hospital, noted Darrah, "became the first religious institution in history to officially adopt a permanent policy that recognized the rights of alcoholics to receive hospital treatment."

Things went smoothly for awhile, but Sr. Ignatia never paid much attention to finances, a cause for concern among hospital administrators. The alcoholics admitted to St. Thomas were at a low point in their lives. Many had lost their jobs and were unable to pay for their care. The Sisters of Charity of St. Augustine absorbed the debts from the alcoholic ward at first, but eventually asked Sr. Ignatia to be more fiscally responsible. Fortunately, she had made lasting friendships with the alcoholics she had helped through recovery, and they often raised the necessary funds for patients new to the alcoholism ward.

The minimum length of stay for alcoholic patients was five days. Alcoholics were the only patients not admitted to the hospital by physicians. Some of the doctors and nurses criticized St. Thomas for admitting "undesirable" patients. In her book, Darrah explained, "Akron's magic blend — the scientific with the spiritual — succeeded where previous attempts to treat addiction had miserably failed." Between 1939 and 1950, more than 5,000 alcoholics recovered through the Akron program.

Sr. Ignatia was much loved by the alcoholics to whom she ministered. Any attempts by hospital administrators to curb her advocacy for alcoholics met with staunch protests from the people she had helped. But as her power increased, so did resentment toward her from members of her religious community. Dr. Bob died in 1950, and in 1952 Sr. Ignatia was transferred to Cleveland's St. Vincent Charity Hospital.

*W*e're just like people in the Army, you know. We go where we are sent... I was there [in Akron] for 24 years...and finally the obedience came that I was to go to Charity and work with AA there."

SR. MARY IGNATIA GAVIN ON BEING TRANSFERRED TO
ST. VINCENT CHARITY HOSPITAL, 1952.

On August 7, 1952, at age 63, the "angel of Alcoholics Anonymous" arrived in Cleveland for her new assignment. Planning began for an alcoholism wing at the hospital. Darrah recounted the following story:

> *"As part of the ward's setup, {Sr. Ignatia} requested a coffee bar for the patients, similar to the one in Akron. However, a board member who reviewed the plan questioned the need for it. He returned the plan to Sr. Ignatia and said, 'A table will have to do.' But...Ignatia would not compromise. She knew what she wanted for the AAs, and she put the future of the ward on the line with her reply: 'Let's forget about it if you're not going to give us the proper setup.' The coffee bar remained in the drawings."*

With the help and contributions of the many people Sr. Ignatia had helped, Rosary Hall Solarium (its initials in memory of Dr. Bob, Robert Holbrook Smith) accepted its first patient on December 15. Darrah wrote: "It was a kind of recovery mecca where physical medicine, spiritual nourishment, and brotherly love regularly produced miracles of recovery.... Sr. Ignatia was Rosary Hall's breath and spirit."

Through the years, the program successfully treated thousands of alcoholics. Sr. Ignatia was among the first to acknowledge alcoholism among priests and nuns. She was also instrumental in implementing the first Al-Anon program, for families of alcoholics.

To each person who completed the five-day program, Sr. Ignatia presented a Sacred Heart Badge. Those who accepted it promised to return the badge to Sr. Ignatia before taking another drink of alcohol. The custom is carried out to this day with tokens awarded for sobriety.

Even as her health declined, Sr. Ignatia continued to care for alcoholics at Rosary Hall. Thousands of alcoholics knew first-hand Sr. Ignatia's honesty and nonjudgmental love. In 1961, she was recognized for her work by President Kennedy.

Sr. Ignatia retired in May 1965. She died less than a year later on April 1, 1966. ❧

ABOVE:
THOUSANDS OF ALCOHOLICS KNEW FIRST-HAND SR. IGNATIA'S HONESTY AND NON-JUDGMENTAL LOVE. IN 1961, SHE WAS RECOGNIZED FOR HER WORK BY PRESIDENT KENNEDY.

Ingenuity

One sister wrote the first book on nursing. Others developed a much-needed health insurance plan for miners. Whatever the problem, Catholic sisters have used their imaginations to find unique solutions to formidable challenges.

MOUNT CARMEL HOSPITAL
Pittsburg, Kansas

*I*n 1877, the first coal-mining shaft was sunk in Crawford County, Kansas, prompting an influx of immigrants looking for work as miners. By 1882, mine shafts and nearby coal camps had spread throughout the county.

Miners and their families lived in wooden shacks. Their camps had no sewers, no running water, no electricity, and no paved streets or sidewalks. When someone got sick or when the miner was carried out of the pit broken and bloody, the only sickroom was his own hot, overcrowded, fly-infested shack.

By the turn of the century, Pittsburg had a hospital, but it was located far from the mines. So the bishop called on Mother Mary Bernard Sheridan, founder of the Sisters of St. Joseph of Wichita and the only area nun with any hospital experience. The Sisters of St. Joseph worked out an agreement with the Santa Fe Operating Companies to take care of the firm's employees for $80 and 15 tons of coal each month, perhaps the state's first example of managed care.

An early-day sister wrote of the sisters' work at Mt. Carmel Hospital: "Year after year brought more sick and wounded to our door. Lest the increasing struggle to meet expenses should grow monotonous, the dear lord sent variety.

"There were biting Kansas blizzards and parching over-hot winds. There were epidemics and droughts and floods and shut downs and strikes. There were wars that stripped the hospital of its best doctors, nurses, and sisters just when they were needed the most. And, to climax the litany of catastrophes, the very ground caved in," she wrote, referring to the loss of the hospital's garden when a mine shaft caved in.

Mount Carmel Hospital opened on April 14, 1903. The city had promised electricity, but backed out at the last minute, so the hospital was lighted by oil lamps. When one prominent businessman attended the dedication ceremony, he remarked that he didn't see how Mother Bernard was going to pay for everything. Years later, she admitted she had had little more than $45 in her pocket when the hospital opened.

For 25 cents a month, each miner and his family was assured of hospital care for as long as it was needed. But, according to hospital history, the sisters had to go after that 25 cents before the saloon got it.

Local lore has it that Sr. Anthony Mahoney would travel by horse and buggy from mine to mine, where she would hail each grimy miner, weary from a day's work, to collect his payment. It was the first prepaid hospital insurance plan in Kansas, and it remained in effect until 1923.

ABOVE, LEFT:
POSTCARD FEATURING
MOUNT CARMEL HOSPITAL,
WHICH OPENED ON APRIL
14, 1903.
RIGHT:
A POSTCARD AND
A PORTRAIT OF MOTHER
MARY BERNARD SHERIDAN,
FOUNDER OF THE SISTERS
OF ST. JOSEPH OF
WICHITA.

Sr. Mathilde Coskery
Daughters of Charity
of St. Vincent de Paul
Emmitsburg, Maryland

The first comprehensive document on nursing was written by a Catholic sister who based the information on her own first-hand experience. Born in 1799, Sr. Mathilde Coskery wrote *Advices on Care of the Sick* in the mid-1800s. It is a no-nonsense, practical guide for nurses, with heavy emphasis on cleanliness. Included is information on caring for alcoholics and the insane.

"The office of 'nurse'," wrote Sr. Mathilde, "is one of awful responsibility if its duties be properly considered; for on the faithful discharge of them will the life of a fellow being, in very many instances, almost exclusively depend."

Among Sr. Mathilde's recommendations: do not shake the bed linens because such action will spread germs; if the patient can't tolerate liquids, have him suck on a chicken bone boiled in salt water to inspire thirst; rub whiskey on the patient's body as a disinfectant.

She suggests: "do not laugh at" alcoholics "or suffer others to treat them with contempt, though this should be the hundredth time he has been brought to your care."

Some excerpts:

"In fever, the face, hands, arms & feet should be often wiped with whiskey, bay rum or weak spirits of camphor. If he is in his senses & strong enough to use a mouth-wash, let it be by his bed, to rinse his mouth often with, & his tongue may be scraped with a thin whale-bone to prevent it from becoming coated....

"If the illness has been long, it helps them to move to another room once or twice...but should they become house-sick for the room they had left, let them

return to it, this indulgence will help them.... Every reasonable gratification is an important means of recovery.... Do not let them wait for their remedies, nourishment, drink or other comforts, for by this delay, besides the harm you may do the body, you irritate & discourage them."

Sr. Mathilde cared for soldiers at Antietam, Gettysburg, and at other Civil War battle sites.

SR. LUMBERJACK
AND THE BENEDICTINE SISTERS
Duluth, Minnesota

In 1887, Mother Scholastica Kerst, superior of the Benedictine Sisters of St. Joseph, Minnesota, sent seven sisters to Duluth to open a hospital.

By 1893, St. Mary's Hospital had two sources of income: patient fees and payment from the county for charity patients. The sisters decided to implement a creative idea as a source of additional income: insurance. Health insurance had proved popular with the cowboys at the sisters' hospital in Bismarck, North Dakota. Tickets entitled the cowboys to free hospital care if they got hurt or sick.

Northern Minnesota in 1893 was experiencing a logging boom. Logging camps opened weekly, and the huge logs were sent to sawmills in Duluth. Because thousands of men in the timber industry had no access to quality medical care, the Benedictine sisters decided to offer a "lumberjack ticket." Purchasers of the lumberjack ticket were entitled to free medical care at St. Mary's Hospital and any other Benedictine hospital in northern Minnesota. The ticket cost from $1 to $5.

The chief saleswoman for the program was Sr. Amata Mackett, who stood six feet tall and weighed more than 200 pounds. By train, handcart, ox, or snowshoe, Sr. Amata traveled to the lumber camps

ABOVE, TOP:
THE BENEDICTINE SISTERS
TOOK A BREAK WHILE THEY
WAITED FOR ONE OF THEIR
HOSPITALS TO BE BUILT.
BOTTOM:
NORTHERN MINNESOTA IN
1893 WAS EXPERIENCING A
LOGGING BOOM.

of Minnesota's north woods to sell the men on the value of a lumberjack ticket.

While in the camps, Sr. Amata darned their socks, listened to their problems, and baked them pies. Eventually she became known as Sr. Lumberjack.

> *W*hile in the camps, Sr. Amata darned their socks, listened to their problems, and baked them pies. Eventually she became known as Sr. Lumberjack.
>
> One time Sr. Amata arrived at a camp to find a logger with a mangled leg surrounded by wide-eyed and helpless men. She deftly took the situation in hand, cleaned and bandaged the wound, and demanded a horse and cart to transport the injured man to the nearest hospital.

But even as she took care of the lumberjacks, she did not let them take advantage of her. When the money they owed her for lumberjack tickets was slow coming in, she would chase men out of their bunkhouses with a poker to collect.

On her way back to Duluth late one evening after a collection trip, Sr. Amata was attacked by a man who tried to steal her money. She wielded her umbrella on the hapless thief, who quickly turned tail and ran—leaving the money with her.

The lumberjack ticket was abandoned in 1913 when legislation in Minnesota mandated workers' compensation.

PRESENTATION HEALTH SYSTEM
Sioux Falls, South Dakota

The Presentation Sisters who arrived in Aberdeen, South Dakota, in the late 1800s were Irish immigrants who taught the children of pioneers. But when a diphtheria epidemic raged through the town, Mother Joseph Butler, the superior, asked some sisters to attend to the sick. Soon, doctors and businessmen persuaded the sisters to build St. Luke's Hospital. It opened in 1901.

The sisters' competence as nurses led to invitations from other communities. Within a decade, they owned and staffed four hospitals in South Dakota and Montana. They also taught in 10 diocesan schools.

Hard times hit the northern plains when food prices and land values dropped sharply after World War I. Farmers couldn't repay their loans, and by 1925, 175 South Dakota banks had failed. After the stock market crash, a devastating drought shriveled crops and nurtured dust storms and grasshoppers. By 1934 almost 40 percent of the state's population was receiving public assistance.

The sisters worked long hours for no pay and practiced prudent household economies. They refinanced buildings, begged for lower interest rates, and considered selling Holy Rosary, their hospital in Montana. After receiving encouragement—but no cash—from the bishop of Great Falls, they decided to hang on, although they were unable to make payments on the mortgage until 1939.

The sisters' struggles during the Great Depression ended with a dramatic act in 1940. St. Luke's was overcrowded, but Mother Raphael McCarthy, exasperated by financial worries, refused to add new construction to the community's debts. For a bargain price, she bought an empty four-story building 10 blocks from St. Luke's. She hired a moving company, and from September through April, the 5,000-ton building plodded through the icy streets of Aberdeen, pushed and pulled by tractors and, at times, by horses. Incredibly, the building sustained little damage and remains open and vibrant to this day.

ST. JOSEPH'S HOSPITAL
Lowell, Massachusetts

Lowell Corporation Hospital was founded in 1839 to provide healthcare to employees in textile mills.

Hard times hit the New England textile industry in the 1920s. On November 1, 1930, Lowell Corporation Hospital became St. Joseph's Hospital when the Oblate Fathers of St. Joseph's Parish

agreed to take charge. They promptly turned the management of the facility over to the Grey Nuns of the Cross of Ottawa (now called the Sisters of Charity of Ottawa) because of their reputation in hospital management.

The first superior, Sr. St. Alphonse Rodriguez, arrived to a cold reception by both the superintendent of nurses and the medical superintendent. She quickly assured employees that their positions were safe. That done, the sisters set about the arduous task of cleaning, painting, and revitalizing the neglected facility.

One of the physicians, Dr. Marshal Alling, told a story about Sr. St. Alphonse:

"One particular event showed true executive genius. It became known to Sr. St. Alphonse that one of the mills in the Merrimack Mill yard was being torn down. This served a golden opportunity to build a laundry…. She called the office…and was referred to the agent.

"To him the bricks were a nuisance, so he told her to take all she wanted — 70,000 or 80,000. She contacted several trucking firms, but all wanted $4 per thousand to transfer them to the hospital yard. Her perseverance paid off, however, for the last one promised to deliver them at no cost, if she was in no hurry.

"She sent out a shower of postal cards to many who owed bills to the hospital which they had been unable to pay, asking if they might be willing to work out the bill cleaning and stacking bricks. The answer was quick and generous, and in a short time the 70,000 to 80,000 bricks were cleaned and neatly stacked in the yard.

"In the meantime her study convinced her that it was more practical to continue sending the laundry out. So the hospital laundry did not materialize, but if you want to see those bricks, look at the boiler house in the back yard."

The sisters challenged tax laws, created a hospital from a saloon, and turned slurs into praise. They bent, but were rarely broken.

SISTERS OF ST. FRANCIS
Tiffin, Ohio

Elizabeth Greiveldinger emigrated to America from Luxemburg with her father and brother around the late 1830s or early 1840s. They settled in New Riegel, Ohio, and in 1848, Elizabeth married John Schaefer, a farmer. In 1852, when Elizabeth was pregnant with their second daughter, John died.

Little is known about the life of the family over the next decade and a half. But in 1868, Elizabeth decided to join the pastor of her church in Tiffin in establishing an orphanage and home for the elderly. Despite the fact that her two daughters, elderly father, and an orphan boy whom she was rearing depended on her, Elizabeth sold the family farm to finance the initiative.

Together Elizabeth and Father Joseph Bihn opened St. Francis Home and Orphanage to care for the elderly and orphans.

On June 4, 1869, Elizabeth Schaefer became Mother Francis d'Assisi, superior of the newly formed Sisters of St. Francis of Tiffin, a community founded by Fr. Bihn. Mother Francis led the young community for 24 years until her death in 1893. At that time, 70 sisters cared for 160 orphans and 50 aged persons.

MOTHER MARY BAPTIST RUSSELL
SISTERS OF MERCY
San Francisco, California

Mother Frances Bridgeman, superior of the Sisters of Mercy in Kinsale, Ireland, had nursed with Florence Nightingale in the Crimean War. Hers was not a sheltered life. But when a priest asked her for recruits to go to San Francisco, California, in 1854, she hesitated. "She was afraid they'd get scalped," said Sr. Mary Katherine Doyle, who is writing a book on Mother Mary Baptist Russell.

Resilient and Resourceful

Despite San Francisco's reputation as a lawless city, 29 Irish Sisters of Mercy volunteered to serve there. From that group, Mother Frances chose eight. She selected Sr. Mary Baptist Russell, 26 years old, as the group's leader.

They arrived in San Francisco on December 8, 1854. What the sisters found was jarring. Following the discovery of gold in 1848, "gold fever" had hit San Francisco. Many men went off to seek their fortunes, leaving their wives and children to fend for themselves. The exploitation and sale of women were common practices when the Sisters of Mercy arrived. The aged and infirm fared little better.

Although primarily a teacher, Mother Baptist Russell responded to the needs of the times. She was determined to help the suffering, and one of her first works was to create a safe haven for women. Under her leadership, the Sisters of Mercy began taking in abandoned wives and mothers, prostitutes, and naive young girls. They also took in the elderly and began visiting the sick in their homes.

Less than a month after their arrival, the sisters were asked to visit a woman who had just died. Recounted Doyle: "While kneeling to pray for the woman, they realized she was not dead. After sending for the priest, they revived the woman and sent her to the county hospital. Mary Baptist deliberately rented a house near the hospital. Daily the sisters visited the sick, bringing what comfort they could to the patients."

At that time, "people who went into the hospital rarely left alive," explained Doyle. They "were left all night in the dark, with no water and no one attending them. They had no linen or pillows—they were expected to bring their own if they had any. The nurses were people who were not employable anywhere else."

In September 1855, cholera struck San Francisco. The Sisters of Mercy went to work as nurses in the county hospital. *The Daily News*

RIGHT AND BELOW:
PHOTOS OF THE SAN
FRANCISCO WATERFRONT
PRIOR TO THE 1851
EARTHQUAKE AND FIRES.

INSET:
MOTHER MARY BAPTIST
RUSSELL.

San Francisco Water Front prior to April 1851
From Jenny Lind Theatre, Present Site of Hall of Justice
From April 12, 1849 to year end, 1850, arrived 805 vessels, 62000 Passengers

*O*ftentimes today we have so much strategic planning and long range everything, but Baptist Russell didn't plan what she was going to do. She experienced reality and then began to build. So she didn't necessarily plan to build a home for the aged, but when someone came and asked for shelter and there was no place to put her, that began the whole sheltering of the infirm aged. That was her passion, an absolute passion.

What you see in the early foundresses and certainly in Mother Baptist Russell was a high degree of flexibility, adaptation, creativity, and risk. Her reliance upon the providence of God caused her to respond first and worry about financing the project later, prompting a bishop to comment that 'her heart was bigger than her purse.'

She didn't think in terms of great projects, she thought in terms of people. She wouldn't accept anyone into the community who didn't have a passion for those who were poor. The only thing she would not give an inch on was love for the poor.

SR. MARY KATHERINE DOYLE, WHO IS WRITING A BOOK
ON MOTHER MARY BAPTIST RUSSELL.

described the sisters' labors during the health crisis: "A more horrible and ghastly sight we have seldom witnessed. In the midst of this scene of sorrow, pain, anguish, and danger were ministering angels who disregarded everything to aid their distressed fellow creatures. The Sisters of Mercy…did not stop to inquire whether the poor sufferers were Protestants or Catholics, Americans or foreigners, but with the noblest devotion applied themselves to their relief…. The idea of danger never seems to have occurred to these noble women; they heeded nothing of the kind."

As a result of their nursing during the cholera epidemic, the sisters were asked to take charge of the county hospital. Mother Baptist agreed, but after months of caring for the indigent at the sisters' expense, she told the county it would have to meet its obligation to the sisters. She ended up buying the hospital for $14,000, and when the county built a new hospital, Mother Baptist opened St. Mary's in 1857, the first Catholic hospital on the West Coast.

Not the least of the sisters' challenges was anti-Catholic bigotry. When an ardent anti-Catholic writer waged a campaign accusing the Sisters of Mercy of mismanaging the hospital and abusing patients, Mother Baptist urged a grand jury investigation of his allegations. The grand jury lauded the hospital as one of three outstanding institutions of San Francisco, along with the schools and the fire department.

In 1868, smallpox hit the city. So contagious was the disease that, according to Doyle, "even ministers would not visit their dying parishioners." City officials opened pesthouses for those inflicted with the disease. Nurses worked only during the day, leaving victims of smallpox unattended in the darkness from dusk until dawn.

Sr. Mary Baptist received permission for the sisters to work in the pesthouses, and for

LEFT, TOP:
ST. MARY'S REUNION HILL
WITH 1870 ADDITION, OUR
LADY'S HOME FOR THE
ELDERLY.
BOTTOM:
ST. MARY'S HOSPITAL
IN 1911.

10 months they lived among the smallpox victims. She nursed alongside the sisters until the bishop demanded that she return to the convent. Eventually he gave in, and Mother Baptist went back to the pesthouses. Commented a writer of the period: "Those devoted Sisters of Mercy willingly presented themselves and entered on a mission of charity from which all others shrink in dismay.... Their fearless, self-sacrificing love is an honor to their church and to their order."

Legend has it that Mother Baptist would pull up her petticoat and wrap the hospital bed linens around her waist and stuff them in her sleeves. When she reached the home of a needy family, she would pull the linens out and make the beds. She did this so often that the sisters put locks on the linen closets.

The sisters' acts of mercy helped assuage the anti-Catholic bigotry. According to Doyle, Mother Baptist set the tone for reaching out to persons of all backgrounds and language groups. "She worked with atheists, agnostics, bigots, criminals, murderers. There was no disease too gruesome and no person beyond the realm of transformation." She loved to help people— especially the poor—and in so doing, she became a legend. She provided wedding dresses for brides too poor to purchase them. She visited men in prisons. She stole from the hospital linen supply to give to the poor. Legend has it that Mother Baptist would pull up her petticoat and wrap the hospital bed linens around her waist and stuff them in her sleeves. When she reached the home of a needy family, she would pull the linens out and make the beds. She did this so often that the sisters put locks on the linen closets. One time, she pulled her own mattress down the stairs to give it to a poor man.

When Mother Baptist Russell died in August 1898, thousands came to her funeral. Father R.E. Kenna, a Jesuit priest, summed up her life in a letter to the bereaved sisters: "Gentle as a little child, she was brave and resolute as a crusader. Prudence itself, yet she was fearless in doing good to the needy... All who met her were forced to admire; and those who knew her best loved her most."

ST. BERNARD HOSPITAL
Chicago, Illinois

*I*n November 1903, seven Religious Hospitallers of St. Joseph left Kingston, Ontario, for Chicago to establish a hospital on the city's South Side. They began raising money immediately.

One local merchant, angered by their begging, threw a pork chop to chase them away. They picked up the pork chop, dusted it off, put it in their bag, and thanked him for his gift. The chastened merchant offered them a cash donation.

SANTA ROSA HOSPITAL
San Antonio, Texas

*O*n April 8, 1884, the San Antonio Daily Times ran an editorial questioning why charitable institutions such as Santa Rosa Hospital paid county and state taxes: "The good they are doing for the public is very palpable…. Why an institution of this kind should be required to pay taxes, when churches do not, is a mystery unexplainable….

"No one will ever know of the patient, self-sacrificing administrations of the noble sisters who stood at the bedside and watched over the sufferer. These sisters expect not, nor do they desire to receive any compensation in this life, save the secret consolation and satisfaction of knowing that they have lived for their fellow men; that they have been instrumental in alleviating the suffering of mankind. They are doing in a silent way a grand work."

In July 1897, Mother Madeline Chollet, the leader of the Sisters of Charity of the Incarnate Word, wrote to the mayor of San Antonio protesting the city's failure to pay for care provided by Santa Rosa Hospital to city patients. She demanded credit on taxes owed by the hospital to the city.

"The citizens of San Antonio must be aware that in the fulfillment of the contract, the lives of our sisters were endangered, and the money of the poor spent," her letter read. "Our very leniency towards the city authorities causes us to suffer now. On their part no effort is made to help us, while we have not ceased to care for the poor and destitute and in many other ways advance the interests of the city. Our present request, hon. sir, is that you give us credit on our taxes now due and reduce the debt at least that much."

Mother Madeleine was at least partially successful in her effort. The city eventually deducted some of what it owed from the hospital tax bill.

SISTERS OF MERCY
Aurora, Illinois

In 1884, Aurora, Illinois, became the first city in the United States to light its streets with electricity.

In 1910, six Sisters of Mercy moved from Council Bluffs, Iowa, to Aurora at the invitation of the bishop. They had come to open homes for the aged and for businessmen, they explained to physicians who wanted them to open a maternity hospital. Sometime in the future, they told the doctors, they planned to open a hospital.

On March 16, 1911, St. Joseph Mercy Hospital admitted its first patient, a woman, but not a maternity patient. When this fact was pointed out to one of the physicians, he grinned, prompting one of the founding sisters to comment later "This, we then knew, was the start of a general, not a special, hospital."

SISTERS OF THE SORROWFUL MOTHER
Milwaukee, Wisconsin

Lumber was the industry in Tomahawk, Wisconsin, in the 1880s. Lumber was dangerous, however, and when accidents occurred, the nearest hospital was 100 miles away. When the priest in Tomahawk learned that the Sisters of the Sorrowful Mother were going to start a hospital in Rhinelander, Wisconsin, he asked them to start one in his town. They agreed.

FRANCISCAN SISTERS OF MARY
St. Louis, Missouri

On October 7, 1933, the Franciscan Sisters of Mary opened St. Mary's Infirmary School of Nursing for Negroes, the first Catholic nursing school for African Americans in the United States. The first class had 20 students from seven states. Following the Supreme Court's 1954 decision on segregation, the sisters decided to close the school, and the last class graduated in 1958. During 25 years of existence, the three-year diploma program graduated 380 professional nurses. In 1946, the Franciscan Sisters of Mary were the first white Catholic religious congregation to accept black women as novitiates.

On October 19, 1893, four sisters arrived in Tomahawk. They had their first patient and opened a hospital in an abandoned saloon the day they arrived. A curtain drawn through the middle of the barroom created two rooms. The beds and stove were in the front room, the kitchen in the back. "The old saloon was poorly suited for a hospital," stated a history, so the sisters rented a two-story residence. Still, a larger facility was needed.

To raise money, the sisters hired ticket agents to go to the lumberjack camps. A $5 ticket entitled the holder to medical and surgical treatment in the hospital at any time during one year from the date on the ticket. The sisters also made collection trips, bringing with them medical supplies. They trekked miles across snow-covered woods and lakes or rode in open sleighs and logging trains, enduring sub-zero temperatures.

Work on the new facility began in 1894, although the sisters had no money or credit. Laborers worked a day or week at a time because of the financial uncertainties. People from the community volunteered their services to create the new structure. Sacred Heart Hospital was dedicated on July 20, 1894.

Too poor to hire help, the sisters continued to do all the work themselves. They begged for worn-out sheets and pillowcases so they could pull the threads apart and use the lint instead of purchasing cotton batting. They gathered their own firewood. And all laundry from the hospital was done on washboards and boiled in two large canning kettles, because the sisters could not afford a boiler.

CONGREGATION OF THE SISTERS OF ST. AGNES
ST. AGNES HOSPITAL, *Fond du Lac, Wisconsin*
ST. ANTHONY HOSPITAL, *Hays, Kansas*

*I*n 1896 the Sisters of St. Agnes opened their first hospital, St. Agnes Hospital, in Fond du Lac, Wisconsin.

Earlier in the century, in 1879, they had branched out from Wisconsin to Hays, Kansas, to teach. In 1909, in response to pleas

HOTEL DIEU HOSPITAL
Beaumont, Texas

The opening of Hotel Dieu Hospital, Beaumont, Texas, in 1897 was an event to remember. The Sisters of Charity of the Incarnate Word had arrived in Beaumont in the midst of a downpour. The following day, the four sisters rose early and saw that the rain continued. They decided to open the hospital anyway.

Mother Mechtilde and the three other sisters, enshrouded in voluminous aprons and armed with hammers and other metal devices, began opening crates and cases and setting chairs in the yard. They unpacked bedsteads, tables, chairs, and lockers that held hospital equipment. They worked steadily throughout the day. Someone apparently notified a pastor of the sisters' efforts because at 4 o'clock in the afternoon he sent a cart of groceries to the sisters.

from the community for a hospital, the sisters decided to convert their convent in Hays into a three-story hospital.

St. Anthony Hospital opened on August 25, 1909. From the beginning it was crowded. Often the sisters gave up their own beds to patients, and it was not unusual for the night nurses to sleep in the beds of the day nurses.

The sisters made "collection" trips to local farms. On one such trip, according to one sister's account, "We borrowed a safe gray mare and hitched her to a springless wagon. She didn't move very fast, but we did gather up donations: chickens, a pig—anything the farmers could give us.

"Toward midafternoon we drove into a farmyard which was to be our last stop for the day. Just after we entered the driveway, our horse lay down…and refused to budge. There was nothing we could do except unhitch the horse and accept the invitation to remain at the farmhouse overnight. The next morning we proceeded homeward with our spoils amid the good natured raillery of our host. We were the richer for our embarrassment by a cow securely tied to the back of our wagon." ◌

*The sisters welcomed everyone in need to their healthcare
facilities. Some of the world's great thinkers found creative
inspiration, while others were inspired to give thanks.*

ST. ALEXIUS HOSPITAL
Bismarck, North Dakota

*A*bbot Alexius Edelbrock purchased
the Lamborn Hotel in Bismarck for
$24,000 on April 14, 1885. He immediately
turned the building over to the Benedictine
Sisters.

Less than a month later, five Benedictine
sisters opened Lamborn Hospital, the first
in the Dakota Territory. Among its earliest
clientele were settlers from India, Russia,
Ireland, Sweden, England, Prussia, and
Bavaria.

There were no trained nurses when Lamborn Hospital opened,
so the doctors instructed the sisters on a day-to-day basis.

One of the hospital's early patients was Theodore Roosevelt, who,
according to Sr. Boniface Timmons (one of the first administrators),

On June 1, 1899, the first telephones in North Dakota were installed at St. Alexius Hospital (whose name had been changed from Lamborn in 1887). In her memoirs, Sr. Boniface Timmons recalled the event:

"One day when a man came around with six telephones, I bought all six. Telephone service was established by wire between the hospital and the drug stores and doctors' offices. I remember how hard it was to get the telephones installed. All the doctors agreed to have them, but one said he would do so under the condition that we promise not to call him at night."

"was roughing it in North Dakota and had an attack of pneumonia." In April 1903, in the third year of his presidency, Roosevelt returned to the hospital to pay his respects. Sr. Boniface wrote: "The City Welcome Committee always pinned the famous rabbit tail badges (which were worn when he came to Bismarck) on the sisters whenever Teddy was in town, and we were glad to wear them in his honor."

ST. VINCENT HOSPITAL
Billings, Montana

During the polio epidemic of 1916, St. Vincent Hospital was a haven for children stricken by the disease. Over the next few years, so many children were cared for at St. Vincent that the sisters opened St. Vincent Orthopedic School.

In those days, many parents of children with polio assumed that the disease had inflicted mental damage along with the physical. But Sr. Arcadia Lee, who was among the nurses caring for the children, felt differently. Along with a noted polio physician, she worked at the school to encourage the children to maximize their mental capabilities.

The school provided rehabilitation and education until 1937, when a flood forced the building to be condemned.

•　•　•

In June, 1966, the Billings, Montana, city clerk's office received the following letter:

"Dear Sir:

"In 1920 (maybe about July or August) I was 19 years old. While passing thru Billings, I felt sick, but only had 40 cents in my pocket. I had not been eating regular for two or three days…. I noticed a hospital about two blocks

ABOVE:
SISTER SABINA, CIRCA
1916, MATERNITY NURSE,
ST. ALEXIUS HOSPITAL.

away at the end of the street. I went there, & went inside, entered the office. It was a Catholic hospital because a gracious Lady, Sister (? I have forgotten her name) asked me what she could do for me. I explained that I felt ill, but had no money & of course {was} not too well dressed. She told me to sit down, probably while she looked me over & gave the matter some thought.

"In a few minutes a nurse came in & she told her to put a cot in the hallway. I was given a suit of pyjamas & towel & shown the bathroom. After the bath I was put to bed. A doctor examined me that afternoon. I think he said I had pleurisy. It was probably evident I had gone to {sic} long without food, because that night for supper they gave me a small cup of soup, nothing more… It was about three days before I was given solid food. After five days I felt so much better, I asked for my clothes, since I did not want to impose on them any further. I left that afternoon, with my 40 cents…

"I left Billings the next morning for Seattle on a freight train. (After World War I you couldn't find a job.) That's when war vets were selling apples on the street for five cents apiece…

BELOW:
SRS. AGNES AND EVARISTA
WITH YOUNGSTERS AT
A MONTANA CAMP
(ST. VINCENT HOSPITAL
ARCHIVES, BILLINGS,
MONTANA).

"I have always hoped to get back & pay them for their kindness, but I have never been able to make it. I don't know the name of the hospital, or if it's still there. I could afford to send them $50. Do you suppose you could find out the name? Maybe somebody there still remembers the boy who slept on the cot in the hallway."

Although the writer of that letter was not famous, St. Vincent did have a famous writer as a patient.

From November 1 to December 21, 1930, Ernest Hemingway was hospitalized there. In the early evening of November 1, Hemingway, fellow novelist John Dos Passos, and a cowboy named Floyd Allington were driving to Key West, Florida, when they were involved in an automobile accident 30 miles west of Billings. Hemingway suffered a spiral fracture above the elbow of his right arm.

ABOVE:
ERNEST HEMINGWAY
SPENT SEVEN WEEKS AT
ST. VINCENT HOSPITAL
AFTER BEING INVOLVED
IN A CAR ACCIDENT IN
MONTANA. HE WROTE A
SHORT STORY TITLED "THE
GAMBLER, THE NUN, AND
THE RADIO," BASED ON
SR. FLORENCE CLOONAN,
ABOVE LEFT, WHO SPENT
MUCH TIME WITH
HEMINGWAY DURING HIS
STAY AT ST. VINCENT.

Although he was supposed to stay in St. Vincent for only a
week, his injury did not heal properly, and he spent seven weeks in
the hospital. Dos Passos and Allington were not seriously hurt.

As a result of his stay, he wrote a short story titled "The
Gambler, the Nun, and the Radio." The nun in the story is based on
Sr. Florence Cloonan, who spent much time with Hemingway dur-
ing his stay at St. Vincent.

Sr. Florence enjoyed listening to sports broadcasts on the radio.
"The Gambler, the Nun, and the Radio" focuses on the 1930 nation-
al football championship game between Notre Dame and Southern
California. In the story, Mr. Frazer (Hemingway) invites Sr. Cecilia
(Sr. Florence) to his hospital room to listen to the game on the radio.
"Oh, no," she tells him. "I'd be too excited. I'll be in the chapel
praying."

When Mr. Frazer sends a message to Sr. Cecilia in the chapel
that the score is 14-0, she appears in his room: "What does 14 to
nothing mean?" she asks. "I don't know anything about this game.
That's a nice safe lead in baseball. But I don't know anything about
football. It may not mean a thing. I'm going right back down to the
chapel and pray until it's finished." ✤

Creating Healthcare Options

By opening hospitals in unserved areas, Catholic sisters brought medical services to communities that had long gone without care.

ST. PETER'S HOSPITAL
Albany, New York

It was before dawn in September 1869 when four Sisters of Mercy disembarked from the Hudson River Day Liner in Albany. They had come from New York City with 80 cents among them.

Two days after they arrived in Greenbush, New York, a letter reached them from their superior: "Dear Sisters," it said. "You went according to Gospel fashion without purse. I enclose twenty dollars for first expenses. With love, M.M. Alphonsus."

On November 1, 1869, they opened St. Peter's Hospital. Its first superior was Mother Mary Paula Harris, who had earned a reputation as a talented and caring nurse-healer on the battlefields of the Civil War.

SACRED HEART HOSPITAL
Spokane, Washington

When a Jesuit priest asked Mother Joseph to build a hospital in Spokane, she responded to his call. She arrived in Spokane on April 30, 1886, with Sr. Joseph of Arimathea.

The two lost no time in fulfilling their promise. Within three weeks of their arrival, contractors were busy building.

MERCY REGIONAL MEDICAL CENTER
Laredo, Texas

On October 2, 1894, three Sisters of Mercy arrived in Laredo, Texas, with $445 in their pockets. They had come from a town near Houston to establish Laredo's first hospital. Two weeks later, they opened Mercy Hospital, a six-room facility that accommodated 12 patients.

Mother Joseph, a Sister of Providence and known as the first architect of the Northwest Territory, supervised construction, while Sr. Joseph of Arimathea visited the sick in their homes. The arrival of two additional sisters enabled Sr. Joseph of Arimathea to beg in the nearby railroad camps and at the mines in northern Idaho.

Sacred Heart Hospital opened in January 1887. Within less than a month, the county had awarded a contract to the Sisters of Providence to care for the poor.

SISTERS OF MERCY
Dallas, Pennsylvania

From the 1830s to the 1930s, anthracite was the economic mainstay of Pennsylvania's Wyoming Valley. Mining was a brutal, hazardous profession. Miners had to position the dynamite strategically so the explosion exposed the coal without collapsing the mine.

Mining accidents and disease occurred frequently. Crushed bodies, black lung disease, and dynamite mishaps were business as usual.

While they were establishing schools in Wilkes-Barre, Pennsylvania, the Sisters of Mercy visited the injured miners in their homes, much as their founder Catherine McAuley had visited the sick in Ireland. The sisters cared for many men hurt in mining accidents, as well as persons suffering from tuberculosis and influenza.

The only hospital in Wilkes-Barre in the late 1800s was far north of the mines. Injured miners had to endure a bumpy trip in horse-drawn wagons over cobblestone streets to reach the hospital.

In 1898, at the request of several physicians, the sisters agreed to open a hospital

closer to the mines. A three-story frame house became Mercy Hospital on March 7, 1898. The hospital existed to care for the miners and for the poor.

Records show that by 1899, 500 patients had been cared for at a cost of 87 cents each a day. The hospital existed on donations until 1911, when the sisters began charging fees.

SISTERS OF MARY OF THE PRESENTATION
Fargo, North Dakota

Between 6:30 and 7:00 a.m. on November 13, 1909, 484 men entered the coal mine in Cherry, Illinois. Between 12 and 1 p.m., a kerosene torch ignited some hay bales on a cart near the entrance to the mine, and some men inadvertently pushed the flaming mass into the mineshaft. Although the initial fire was extinguished quickly, the flames had ignited the ceiling timbers in the mine, setting off an underground fire that raged for weeks. The Cherry Mine disaster death toll reached

LEFT:
THE FIRST GROUP OF PRESENTATION SISTERS IN AMERICA, 1902.

BELOW:
HAYMAKING DURING THE SISTERS' EARLY YEARS IN AMERICA.

262. Nearly 500 children were left without fathers and 160 women were widowed.

From Spring Valley, Illinois, came four Presentation Sisters. They had planned to stay for only a few days, but remained for months until all the bodies of the miners were recovered. They consoled the families of the deceased miners and distributed food and clothing to the widows and children. And they helped take care of the injured. As a result of the Cherry Mine disaster, the sisters opened St. Margaret's Hospital in Spring Valley. It exists to this day.

BENEDICTINE SISTERS MONASTERY OF ST. GERTRUDE
Cottonwood, Idaho

The Benedictine Sisters came to Cottonwood, Idaho, from Oregon in 1923 to open a home for the aged. As the sisters prepared the building that was to serve as the home, they were asked to open a hospital instead. They'd had no nurse training, they admitted to the area doctor. "I'll teach you," he replied, bringing two patients with typhoid to the facility. St. Valentine's Home and Hospital was dedicated on August 19, 1923. The home was established "primarily as a place of refuge for those whom the world has buffeted to penniless old age. But no needy one, young or old, poor or rich, will ever be turned from the doors."

SISTERS OF ST. FRANCIS OF PHILADELPHIA
Aston, Pennsylvania

St. Mary Hospital, Philadelphia, is said to have been the first hospital in America to practice Dr. Joseph Lister's antiseptic method of treating wounds and performing surgery. The patient, a 22-year-old man, was admitted on July 6, 1876, after being stepped on by a mule. His laceration was treated with antiseptic dressings, a combination of one part carbolic acid and four parts olive oil. His recovery was complete.

Perseverance

*T*hey never questioned, 'Can you do it?' It was just 'Do it!'

Sr. Thecla McManamon
St. Elizabeth Hospital, Youngstown, Ohio

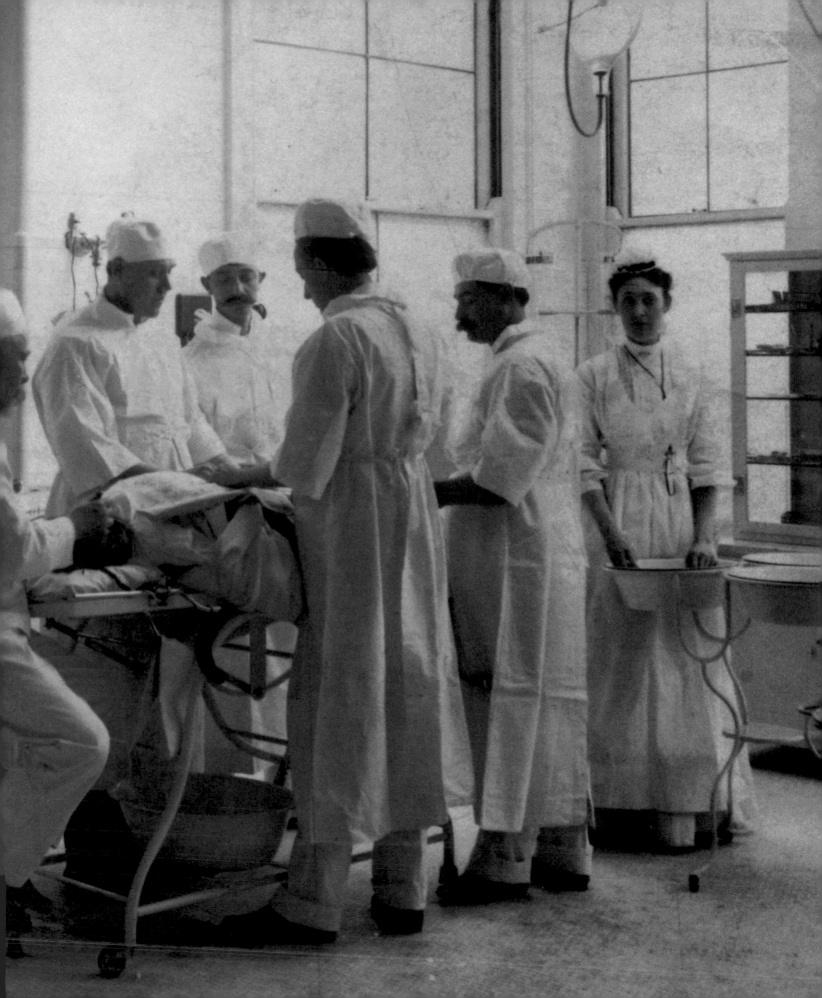

The obstacles often seemed insurmountable. But women religious faced resistance head on, bolstered by their faith and their desire to meet the needs of people.

Below:
As they cared for the elderly cast-off slaves, Henriette and her congregation were so poor that at times their evening meal consisted of sweetened water.

Henriette DeLille

Sisters of the Holy Family
New Orleans, Louisiana

Six weeks before President Abraham Lincoln signed the Emancipation Proclamation, the following obituary appeared in a New Orleans newspaper:

> *"Last Monday died one of these women whose obscure and retired life was nothing remarkable in the eyes of the world but is full of merit before God... Without ever having heard speak of philanthropy, this poor maid had done more good than the great philanthropists with their systems so brilliant yet so vain.*
>
> *"Worn out by work, she died at the age of 50 years after a long and painful illness borne with the most edifying resignation."*

Henriette DeLille was born a to a well-to-do New Orleans family in 1813. While still a girl, she began visiting the sick and the aging of her race, slave and free.

Henriette was a light-skinned woman of color. Although the laws changed to offer her an opportunity to be listed as a white

person, she refused to deny her heritage —
even though her action caused numerous
difficulties as she attempted to pursue life
in a religious community.

Barred by law from joining a white
religious community, Henriette sought to
establish one for women of color. At first the
bishop denied her request. Eventually he
became convinced of her determination to
serve God and neighbor.

Along with two other free women of
color, Henriette DeLille, on November 21,
1842, founded the Sisters of the Holy
Family, a religious community for women of color. The end of
slavery was still more than 20 years away.

When Henriette and a second sister moved into a small rented
convent, they took with them five elderly women from the
neighborhood. The sisters did not charge for their services and
subsisted by begging.

In addition to caring for the elderly and visiting ailing slaves in
their quarters, the sisters held classes for free and slave children and
adults. Many nights the sisters went to bed hungry. They were
known to give their own meals to those poorer than they and to
simply drink sweetened water.

At the time of Henriette DeLille's death on November 17,
1862, her sisters numbered 12. Henriette never wore a habit.
It was not until 1872 that the right was granted to women
religious of color.

The legacy of Henriette DeLille continues to this day. Lafon
Nursing Home of the Holy Family is 153 years old, possibly the
oldest nursing home in the United States. The Sisters of the Holy
Family number 250. ☙

*L*ong before the first women's rights convention in 1848, these women of color had gone into the streets, homes, and churches of their city to alleviate the suffering of people of their race.

From a letter from Susan B. Anthony to the Sisters of the Holy Family (Corbis-Bettmann).

With their call, sisters gave up creature comforts and financial recompense. They endured great poverty, and the battle to meet their financial obligations was sometimes their greatest struggle.

SISTERS OF CHARITY OF THE INCARNATE WORD
San Antonio, Texas

In their early years in the United States, the Sisters of Charity of the Incarnate Word in San Antonio were hard pressed to raise funds. Despite begging trips, the sisters constantly needed money to keep their orphanage running.

Mother Saint Pierre Cinquin, leader of the congregation from 1872 to 1891, always turned to St. Joseph, the protector of the Holy Family, in times of great need. The letter below was most likely written in the 1880s.

> *"St. Joseph, we need 60 piastres to pay for that horse which Sr. Mary of Jesus bought; 155 piastres to pay Mr. Grenett; 110 piastres to pay Mr. Woolfson; 60 piastres to pay Mr. Thalteyer. We need this money at once, my good Father. These debts are contracted by you who are the owner, father, and protector of your orphanage St. Joseph's, San Antonio, Texas.*

> *"The servants of your house, those who have charge of it, are the spouses of the Incarnate Word, your Son on earth and your God in time and eternity.*

LEFT:
AMONG THE HOSPITALS BEGUN BY THE SISTERS OF CHARITY OF THE INCARNATE WORD WAS ST. JOSEPH'S HOSPITAL, PARIS, TEXAS.

We are not asking you for this money in our name; we, especially I, do not deserve to be heard....

"I am going to have a candle burned for you today and, having given you this missive, I hope you will reply immediately. For you there is no difficulty; what you want you can do. If you answer this appeal, I shall have a mass in your honor offered in thanksgiving. If you do not reply, I will punish you in some way, my good Father. You have always spared me this latter pain. Please do not deceive our confidence in you. I am displeased for I have reminded you during the month about these debts and asked you to send us the money to pay them. You have not done so yet and the day of payment is approaching. Hurry! Hurry! Your honor is at stake.

"P.S. In heaven there cannot be any bankruptcy; its funds and treasures are inexhaustible. Pay your debts, St. Joseph. We are asking for nothing superfluous but only for what is just and necessary."

Did Mother Saint Pierre get her money? "If she said she needed it, I'm sure she got it," said Sr. Francisca Eiken, archivist for the congregation.

FRANCISCAN SISTERS OF PERPETUAL ADORATION
La Crosse, Wisconsin

In 1883, La Crosse, Wisconsin, was a thriving port on the Mississippi River. For mariners who were injured or became ill, La Crosse offered only hotel rooms.

The Franciscan Sisters of Perpetual Adoration had come to La Crosse in 1871 to teach. When physicians and community leaders asked them to build a hospital, Mother M. Ludovica, the superior general, worried that her community was not prepared, since none of the sisters had been trained in nursing. She wondered, too,

ABOVE, LEFT:
HORSE DRAWN
AMBULANCE AT ST.
JOSEPH'S INFIRMARY,
FT. WORTH, TEXAS,
BEGUN BY THE SISTERS
OF CHARITY OF THE
INCARNATE WORD.
RIGHT:
MOTHER ST. PIERRE
CINQUIN

whether a town of 15,000 could support a hospital. But eventually the congregation agreed to build a 35-bed hospital and train the nursing staff.

St. Francis Hospital opened on January 1, 1884. Diary entries from that year reveal days fraught with anxiety, financial hardship, and setbacks. Patients were few. The hospital was often used by individuals seeking rooms for the night, with little or no payment. A few older persons took up residence there.

An agreement with the city to set aside a special ward as a Marine Hospital provided at least some regular income.

As the shipping industry declined, the railroad industry grew. Eventually, it, too declined. St. Francis has adapted as the needs and times changed. Among the services it offers today is the Clare Mission specifically for people without insurance and for the Hmong population of La Crosse.

ST. JOSEPH HOSPITAL
Fort Worth, Texas

*I*n 1885, 16 years after the Sisters of Charity of the Incarnate Word arrived in the United States from France, they were asked to take charge of the Missouri Pacific Hospital on the outskirts of Fort Worth.

BELOW:
THE MEN WHO BUILT THE
RAILROADS, CIRCA 1890
(CORBIS-BETTMANN).

Mother Pierre, the superior, was at first reluctant because the area was rife with cowboys and rough, hard, railroad men — not to mention the saloons. However, the railroad had agreed to pay the sisters. What finally convinced Mother Pierre was the fact that the would-be patients were poor, immigrant workers separated from their families.

Mother Pierre accompanied the first group of sisters to Fort Worth. Later, when she wrote about the experience, she said it was not possible to describe the disorder and filth they found.

Four weeks after their arrival, fire broke out in the hospital building. The sisters who had stayed home from mass were able to prevent loss of life. One of the workers came running out of the burning building carrying what he thought was something very sacred that he had risked his life to save—a starched linen guimpe and bandeau (part of the sisters' habit). They were the only items of clothing left for the sisters.

The sisters worked up to 20 hours a day. They not only cared for patients, they scrubbed floors, cooked all the food, and raised fruit and vegetables behind the hospital. They tended chickens and cows to provide additional food. They did the hospital laundry by hand in gigantic tubs and hung it up to dry in the chicken yard.

From its beginnings, St. Joseph's admitted black as well as white patients, despite opposition from some physicians and city officials.

MERCY HOSPITAL
Big Rapids, Michigan

*T*he following is a recollection from a Sister of Mercy, Big Rapids, Michigan.

"In 1893 we left…to solicit funds to enable us to get a new furnace under the men's ward… A team of horses and two-seated sleigh was given us with a one-arm driver to drive thirty-five miles.

"Entering a side camp, our rig was broken, and upon asking to stay long enough to fix it, and also to ask campmen for a donation, we were told it would not be worth while, so we continued a little farther until we came to the main camp of one hundred men.

"We were warmly welcomed there for the men had not seen a woman for a year, and they said it was worth five dollars to see one. They were all in the shanty preparing for the next day's hard work, drying their socks and mackinaws 'round a huge stove in the center of the shanty.

BELOW:
TICKETS FROM MERCY
HOSPITAL SOLD TO RAISE
MONEY.

For 43 years, Sr. Oswalda Stark blazed a "begging" trail in eastern Washington state. Twice yearly, she was loaned a railroad car, which she used to gather supplies donated by farmers and businessmen.

Sr. Oswalda would fill the car with wheat (what she didn't feed to the chickens, she sold), potatoes, cabbage, eggs, bacon, ham, and chickens.

The farmers grew to expect her visits. One day the Druffel family returned from the fields chagrined that they had missed Sr. Oswalda. Not to worry. A note on the smokehouse door informed them, "I took a slab of bacon and a schinken [ham]." Another note, where the eggs were kept, said, "I took 15 dozen eggs. —Sister Oswalda."

"At first entering, it was not very pleasant, but such a life of hardship did not mean much to the men. One of us took one side of the shanty, and the foreman taking my companion on the other, we continued to present our cause; stating our reason for begging this way. Some of the boys were trying to sew up the holes in their socks and clothing, others were lying on their bunks, writing. One would have to be quite tired to rest on boards with a little hay and horse blanket....

"The boys were very generous that evening. Then the foreman took us to his office, a small building large enough to keep books and a few shelves where a few mittens, mackinaws, felt shoes, to accommodate the men, were kept. There were two bunks there which were given us to rest on 'til morning. The foreman then went out and left us alone. Locking the door we proceeded to examine the bunks. Which would it be—the top one or the bottom? We chose the top as it would give us more air, and, as the pigs were sleeping under the floor, we would be farther from them."

ABOVE:
RULES OF MERCY
HOSPITAL, BIG RAPIDS,
MICHIGAN.

BENEDICTINE SISTERS
Watertown, South Dakota

After numerous congregations had turned down a request from the bishop of Pierre, South Dakota, to start a school, the Benedictine Sisters arrived from Vermillion, South Dakota, on August 31, 1899. They brought with them $20.

The very morning after their arrival, the physicians came to call. They insisted that what the town really needed was a hospital.

When they showed the sisters the abandoned hotel that they wanted to turn into a hospital, the sisters were aghast. The building had been vacant for seven years. Wrote one of the sisters: "What a sight!.... Nothing was in the house, no beds, no dishes, no furniture. Dust, dirt, and spiderwebs were the decorations."

Nevertheless, the sisters "started to scrub and clean to have a few rooms ready.... The people brought cots from town. From a pile of rubbish in the backyard we salvaged spoons, forks, knives, pitchers, and plates. These we scoured and used."

ABOVE, LEFT:
A GROUND-BREAKING
CEREMONY AT ST. MARY'S
IN THE 1930S.
RIGHT:
THE BENEDICTINE SISTERS
ON A LAKE IN SOUTH
DAKOTA EARLIER THIS
CENTURY.

The very next day, even as the sisters scrubbed, the doctors brought the first patient.

By late September, they had named the hospital St. Mary's.

SISTERS OF ST. JOSEPH
Concordia, Kansas

*F*rom an account by Sr. Frances Joanne Bonfield, who died in 1995:

> *"We hear much today about the changes in our hospitals and the care of the sick…. I will tell about some of the changes that I remember in the hospital since the 1930s.*

> *"I had been a teacher for years and was in the classroom Friday. Monday morning I reported to the St. Joseph Hospital {Concordia, Kansas} office to take charge, as the sister there had been sick for some time. My orientation— the administrator spent about 20 minutes showing me where the books, etc., were and then disappeared. I just stared unbelievingly, not remembering a thing she had said.*

> *"My hours were 7:30 am until 9:30 pm seven days a week, with time off for meals and prayers. My duties were switchboard, meeting ambulances, placing of patients, discharging, collections, payroll, payment of all bills, all the bookkeeping, etc.*

> *"The early 1930s were still a result of the Depression and no one had any money. It was the time when the hobos rode the freight trains looking for work. Those were the days when charity was a virtue instead of a deduction."* ❧

Women religious faced prejudice and disapproval in many forms. Sometimes it was skin color or national origin. Often it was anger over their courage to challenge the status quo. Despite the resistance, the sisters remained firm in the face of adversity.

SISTERS OF ST. JOSEPH
Tipton, Indiana

Imprisoned in 1794 during the Reign of Terror that followed the French Revolution, 36-year-old Mother St. John Fontbonne refused to sign an oath of allegiance to the government. Her refusal meant that she would die by guillotine.

Although seven Sisters of St. Joseph were executed during the Reign of Terror, the day before Mother St. John and other Sisters of St. Joseph were to die, Robespierre fell from power. The lives of the women were spared.

Even after the prisons were opened, years passed before the Sisters of St. Joseph could wear habits and live communally. But the women's faith was strong. And in 1836, when Mother St. John was 78 years old, she sent six sisters to a new land. The travelers bade goodbye to women they would never see again and boarded the

Heidelberg in LeHavre, France. In St. Louis, Missouri, the sisters opened a school for the deaf.

On a bleak, chilly March day in 1888, three Sisters of St. Joseph left their convent and headed to Tipton, Ohio, a small, farming community. The pastor had requested they come to teach children.

The first year in Tipton was especially difficult. The work never ended, and the group's leader, Mother Gertrude, demanded perfection. It was said that she tried so hard to be divine that she sometimes forgot to be human. The sisters wondered if indeed they were accomplishing anything.

As with many other congregations, it took years for the Sisters of St. Joseph of Tipton to establish their first hospital. Good Samaritan Hospital opened in 1913 in Kokomo, Indiana, a part of the country where the Ku Klux Klan was especially strong. Eventually the hospital's name was changed to Saint Joseph.

In the 1920s, the Klan held fund-raising events to raise money to open a second hospital in Kokomo to drive out the sisters. They raised enough money to open Howard County Hospital and ran it successfully for several years.

But a twist of fate sealed the doom of Howard County Hospital. One day, J. Henry Fisse, Jr., a Kokomo real estate mogul, sought admission at the Klan hospital. However, because of his somewhat shoddy appearance and the fact that he could not pay cash in advance, the physicians refused to admit him and sent him to Saint Joseph.

The sisters did not question his ability to pay and admitted him immediately. Fisse spent a month at Saint Joseph Hospital. When he recovered, his business manager reminded him that he had named the Howard County Hospital as his primary beneficiary in his will. Fisse called his lawyer and changed his will. When he died in 1935, the sisters were able to purchase Howard County Hospital through his beneficence. Says Sr. Martin McEntee, Saint Joseph president, "We're the only Catholic hospital founded by the Ku Klux Klan."

During the Civil War, the [Daughters of Charity] cared for more than 5,000 soldiers at St. Mary's Hospital. It was not unusual for soldiers to go on leave from police duty at the hospital and go into town to get drunk. When one soldier arrived at the hospital drunk, a young lieutenant ordered the man tied up by his thumbs. When Sr. Hieronymo learned of the incident, she had the man untied and took him to the guard house herself and locked him in. When the lieutenant learned what she had done, he demanded the key. Sr. Hieronymo refused and told him her house was a place of refuge for the sick and wounded, not a house of torture. The lieutenant wrote out his resignation, thinking his superior would support him. Instead, the man accepted the

lieutenant's resignation, in support of Sr. Hieronymo.

St. Mary's Hospital
Rochester, New York

From September through Christmas 1857, three Daughters of Charity slept on pallets of straw in a tiny stone building in Rochester, New York, with little more than their habits for cover. Rats scampered over their bodies at night. Winter winds blew through a broken window, but when the sisters sought to build a door in its place, they abandoned the plan when they learned the price would be $15.

The sisters' diet consisted primarily of water thickened with flour. The same pot that was used for their morning coffee was used to boil potatoes for dinner. A tin bucket did triple duty as soup tureen, dishpan, and water bucket.

This was the beginning of St. Mary's Hospital in Rochester. Mother Hieronymo, leader of the group that established the hospital, refused to give in to the prejudices rampant in society at the time. She insisted from the start that St. Mary's would welcome "the sick of all denominations, or of none."

Saint Cloud Hospital
St. Cloud, Minnesota

Patients did not flock to St. Benedict Hospital (now Saint Cloud Hospital) when the Benedictine Sisters opened it in 1886. Legend has it that the sisters decided to pray for nine days, asking for a sign as to whether they should keep the hospital open. The fifth day, April 14, 1886, dawned bright and sunny. But by afternoon, the weather had changed. A cyclone swept through St. Cloud, killing and injuring many. Although buildings around

St. Benedict Hospital were destroyed, the hospital remained untouched. It became the center of rescue efforts, with the sisters working 48 hours without rest to care for the injured until relief came from nearby Minneapolis and St. Paul. The cyclone was a sign all right. Saint Cloud Hospital exists to this day, still sponsored by the Benedictine Sisters, St. Joseph, Minnesota.

FRANCISCAN SISTERS OF THE POOR
Cincinnati, Ohio

The German congregation Sisters of the Poor of St. Francis (now Franciscan Sisters of the Poor) was a mere 13 years old when, in 1858, Mother Frances Schervier, its founder, sent six sisters to America to care for poor, sick German immigrants in Cincinnati. Their service had been requested by the archbishop.

Leaving Germany for a land across the ocean was emotional for the six pioneering sisters. The congregation's annals reported: "We shall not endeavor to describe the feelings and emotions which filled the hearts of the travelers, caused by the grief of parting, combined with their wish to comply with the sacred duty of obedience."

When they arrived in Cincinnati on September 11, 1858, the sisters learned that

BELOW, LEFT:
THE *SUPERIOR* WAS A
FLOATING HOSPITAL ON
WHICH THE SISTERS
SERVED DURING THE CIVIL
WAR (COURTESY OF THE
CINCINNATI HISTORICAL
SOCIETY).
RIGHT:
MOTHER FRANCES IN NEW
YORK, AUGUST 28, 1863.

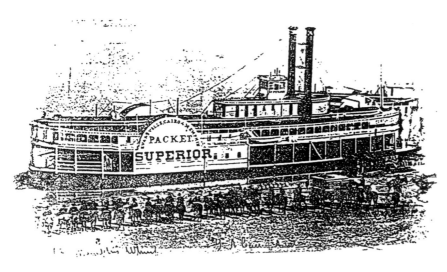

the archbishop no longer wanted them there. It would be wise for them to seek an opportunity elsewhere, they were told. The local pastor said they were superfluous in Cincinnati and ordered them to return home.

Far from their native land and their congregation, in a country whose customs they did not understand, the sisters were devastated. Yet their obedience was to Mother Frances. When the sisters received the offer of a three-story brick building from the Catholic Orphan Society, they accepted. They told the archbishop they could not return until they were called back to Germany by Mother Frances.

In the end, their persistence prevailed, and the archbishop changed his mind. On September 21, 1858, only 10 days after arriving in Cincinnati, the sisters accepted their first patient in their new 40-bed hospital, Maria Hilf (Mary Help, later Saint Mary's).

ABOVE:
"MARIA HILF", THE FIRST U.S. HOSPITAL OF THE FRANCISCAN SISTERS OF THE POOR.

SISTERS OF SAINT FRANCIS OF PERPETUAL ADORATION
Mishawaka, Indiana

It was dark when the Sisters of St. Francis reached Lafayette, Indiana, in December 1875. They had come all the way from Germany at the request of the bishop and spent their first night in Lafayette at a hotel across from the depot.

They had come to be in charge of a new hospital, St. Elizabeth's. Within 3 weeks of their arrival, the sisters had opened the facility.

It was a time, according to the sisters' history, when "people looked with suspicion on brown- robed nuns who spoke German."

Despite prejudice, the sisters began immediately to minister to the sick and poor outside the hospital as well as within. They visited the homebound sick, using lanterns

The Sisters of Saint Francis begged for money wherever they opened hospitals. They opened St. Joseph's Hospital in Omaha in 1886.

Patients who paid were the exception to the rule, but one day a man hospitalizing his sick wife told the sisters in a rough German accent: "I always bay gash—I bay noddings but gash." Sister waited, but no money was forthcoming. When he turned to leave, she mentioned the cash. He told her. "Vy, I bay cash next year ven I zell mine oats."

to light their way at night. They collected food, clothing, and funds.

In running the hospital, the sisters depended on the charity of local citizens. If the patients ate all the food, the sisters went to bed with no supper and then rose at 2 a.m. to do the washing.

Says the history: "Their ambition was to build a hospital, yet during those weary days they must often have questioned whether the expense was not too great, and whether it was not a mistake to try to harmonize a foreign way of living with the pioneer independence of the Hoosier. Of one thing we are certain, their serenity was often broken, their hopes were often dashed."

LITTLE FRANCISCANS OF MARY
SAINT FRANCIS HOME
Worcester, Massachusetts

In 1888, Father Joseph Brouillet, a French-Canadian priest in Worcester, Massachusetts, sought the help of two secular Franciscans to open an orphanage. The women had been given permission to wear the Franciscan habit and pronounce simple vows for one year.

Once the orphanage opened, Father Brouillet decided he would also accept the elderly. He soon realized that more than two women would be needed to care for the growing numbers. When he promised to start a new religious community devoted to the care of orphans and the elderly, a number of women were eager to share that dream. The community rapidly grew.

After they had served the orphans and the elderly for a year, the women began asking Father Brouillet when they would take vows. At first he was elusive; later he became hostile. (The theory is that Father Brouillet had not received permission from the bishop to

On August 27, 1890, the women drew up bylaws for the Oblate Sisters of Saint Francis of Assisi. Its ministry would be orphans and the elderly.

But when the sisters approached the bishop of Springfield, Massachusetts, for his permission, he said he did not want the responsibility of a new religious community. The bishop gave them three options: go back into the world, join an already-existing Franciscan congregation, or establish their motherhouse in Canada.

found a religious community, and he had hoped the women would agree to join an already-existing order.)

In exasperation, the women sought to create a corporation to enable them to run the orphanage themselves. They knew Father Brouillet would oppose them and were unaware of how to incorporate without assistance. On August 27, 1890, the women drew up bylaws for the Oblate Sisters of Saint Francis of Assisi. Its ministry would be orphans and the elderly.

But when the sisters approached the bishop of Springfield, Massachusetts, for his permission, he said he did not want the responsibility of a new religious community. The bishop gave them three options: go back into the world, join an already-existing Franciscan congregation, or establish their motherhouse in Canada.

But, he told them, they could live and work together and incorporate as a civil organization.

Father Brouillet was irate. Not only did he disagree with their desire to incorporate, he was extremely displeased that they had visited the bishop without his authorization.

The sisters decided to move the orphanage to a new site, and on January 12, 1891, the moving vans arrived at the back door of the orphanage. Only a few trips had been made when Father Brouillet arrived with the deputy sheriff, who locked the house in the name of the law! Some sisters were outside and others were trapped inside the orphanage. Father Brouillet insisted they remove their religious habits before he would allow them to leave. They refused.

Several sisters escaped and called the sheriff, who ordered the doors unlocked and declared the sisters free to leave. Fifteen of the 17 sisters found refuge in the homes of locals. The other two remained at the orphanage. The orphans and elderly inhabitants found refuge with families in Worcester.

Quickly the sisters rented a vacant, run-down house for $10 a month. On January 22, 15 sisters and four orphans moved in. The next indignity was a letter from the bishop ordering the women to remove their religious habits. Again, two of the sisters, dressed as laywomen, traveled to Springfield to talk to him in person. Amazed at their tenacity and their obvious desire to serve the Lord, he granted them permission to wear a modified habit temporarily.

In April 1891, 12 sisters, 21 orphans, and one old woman moved into a new residence. In October, they moved to a still larger residence. And in November, at the request of a priest who was willing to let them open a motherhouse, four of the sisters moved to Quebec, Canada, to care for the elderly. With the motherhouse established in Canada, eight of the women pronounced their vows on August 12, 1892. Two others professed their vows the following January. The new congregation was called the Little Franciscans of Mary.

It was not until July 28, 1897, that the congregation was officially recognized by the Diocese of Springfield. And recognition came only after the sisters agreed to turn over the care of the orphans to the Grey Nuns and to accept for themselves the care of the aged.

It took several months to work out the details, but in December 1897, Father Brouillet mounted the pulpit of his church in Worcester and announced that the Little Franciscans of Mary were officially recognized as religious in the Diocese of Springfield.

In January 1898, the sisters welcomed the elderly of Worcester into Saint Francis Home. To this day, the motherhouse remains in Baie-Saint-Paul, Canada.

FRANCISCAN SISTERS
Little Falls, Minnesota

*I*n the late 1880s, the Franciscan Sisters ran a small boarding school in Belle Prairie, Minnesota. When they ran into difficulties with the pastor, they wrote to their superior in Rome, Italy, asking what to do. But time passed, and they received no response.

Meanwhile, the pastor spread ill will toward the sisters in the community. On April 25, 1889, the children and sisters retired for

an... ...was
and... ...arc...
po... ...on...
th... ...sp...
I... ...pu...
hos... ...re...
ni... ...pe...
a... ...t...
th... ...t
muc...
help and felt bad. That was all she needed and it...
seeing an angel come in the door when she came in...
a few words and cheer me up. It was not that she...
pect me to do anything for her. She did it just f...
God, and people who will do things for the love o...
not found often. She was religious, but she was...
that; she did the things which have to be done if...
to have real Christian charity.

        I have been reading a book which I r...
help me learn the language-- The Bible. About thr...
ago I read about a man who lived in a town called...
He was just an ordinary sort of a man who didn't...
anyone to admire him, but his heart was in the ri...
One time he was out for a walk and he came across...
man who was all beat up and bleeding. Some robber...
him up and took his money and his clothes. Well,...
from Samaria washed him up and doctored his wound...
then let him ride on his horse to get into the ne...
where he stopped at a hotel and paid in advance f...
and room and said to the manager, "You keep him h...
he is all-right again. If he is not all right whe...
money is used up you stand him off and I'll be ba...
a while and pay you."

        If that man was a woman she would be...
Sr. Rose (and the other sisters too). I hear she...
derful business woman but she was also a wonderfu...
with a soft heart and a good word for only a plai...
who could never do half so much for her as she di...
If you never have been sick and unable to get up...
for a long time you can not know how much it mean...
every morning-- those few words she found time to say out...
of a busy day's work. But no matter how busy she was or...
how much other things she had to to, she would put them...
aside for a minute or two.

        Not everybody writes letters about it, but...
from every part of the country short, deep prayers must be...
going up for her. "She did for others the things that...
Christ would have done if he had been there."

                Your friend,

                Gust S. Kaponis
            Boston Cafe, Mgr.

*A*mong the hospitals founded by the Franciscan Sisters was St. Francis Hospital, Breckenridge, Minnesota. On October 18, 1921, a railroad laborer learned of the death of a sister who had nursed him during a stay at St. Francis. In a letter to the sisters, he wrote:

Dear Sisters:

I was hurt in an accident by falling off a moving hand-car March 11, 1915, and brought to the St. Francis Hospital… My home was thousands of miles away and I did not have a friend in this country.

I was put in the hospital, and what a heaven it was! Everybody treated me nice, and Mother Rose and the other sisters helped me to learn a few words of the American language so I could talk to them. It did not make any difference to her that I wasn't much… I needed help and felt bad. That was all she needed and it was like seeing an angel come in the door when she came in to say a few words and cheer me up. It was not that she could expect me to do anything for her. She did it just for love of God, and people who will do things for the love of God are not found often. She was religious, but she was more than that; she did the things which have to be done if we want to have real Christian charity.

THE LETTER IS SIGNED "GUST D. KAPONIS, BOSTON CAFE, MGR."

the night. Two girls who were having trouble sleeping noticed a flash of light. The older child knew it was fire and notified the sisters, who evacuated everyone within minutes. The building burned to the ground, and an investigation found traces of kerosene at the site.

Although everyone survived, the sisters lost everything they owned. The children and women were homeless. All they had were the clothes on their backs.

With no response to their letters to Rome, the group of 16 sisters had nowhere to turn. They asked permission from the bishop of St. Cloud, Minnesota, to stay together as a religious community. He gave his consent and advised them to break all ties with their foundress and elect a new leader.

In 1891 Mother Francis Beauchamp was elected superior of the Franciscan Sisters of Little Falls.

Since the new congregation had lost everything in the fire, the sisters had to beg to raise money for even the most basic goods. But by summer, they had built a convent. Over the years, a hospital, a nursing home, an orphanage, and a girls high school each got its start in the building.

Among the Franciscan Sisters' contributions to the health of society is their presence in one of the poorest counties in Mississippi. In the 1970s, sisters went to Holmes County and opened a clinic. It was not unusual for eggs and okra to be exchanged for medical care.

The sisters' involvement with the poorest of the poor led them to become advocates to break the cycle of poverty. They stood up for the rights of African Americans, only to have the windows of their house shot out, nails scattered in their driveway, and threatening phone calls made to their house.

On five occasions, sisters were jailed. In one instance, the sisters protested, on behalf of all inmates, the food and filth at the jail—such things as cockroaches in the grits. They fought for the rights of inmates to exercise and to receive medical care. When the jailers refused to remove weeks-old garbage from the sisters' cell, they moved the garbage out themselves, piece by piece through the jail bars. For that, the sisters were sprayed with mace.

Among their works today is a home for babies with HIV in Mississippi.

SISTERS OF MERCY OF THE HOLY CROSS
Merrill, Wisconsin

*B*ishop Vincent Wehrle from Bismarck, North Dakota, asked at least six European congregations before the Sisters of Mercy of the Holy Cross in Ingenbohl, Switzerland, agreed to go to America to open a hospital in Dickinson, North Dakota.

Six women were selected. A history of the congregation in the United States points out, "They were under no illusions and were ready to sacrifice personal home contact for the rest of their lives."

Spring was coming to Switzerland when the sisters left it in 1912. When they reached New York, they took the northern route to Dickinson. They thought they'd arrived in Siberia by mistake. Snow and ice were everywhere. They reached Dickinson on March 22.

The hospital Bishop Wehrle had built was a virtual shell. There was no electricity, no bells, no elevator, and nothing in the operating room. Outside, building material and rubbish lay everywhere.

The first step was to clean up the place. The sisters scrubbed from the basement to the third floor. St. Joseph's Hospital opened on March 31.

The Russian-German immigrants had no trouble trusting the sisters. But the English-speaking citizens were not so easily won over. Although the sisters were learning English, they were far from proficient.

When the United States entered World War I, the number of patients dropped noticeably. When a sister asked one of the physicians why, he told her, "The people know that some of your sisters are German and so they don't want to come here anymore."

The woman, a native of Switzerland, replied, "Until now I considered the Americans broad-minded, but now I can only believe that they are pitifully narrow. The sisters can't help that they were born in Germany and that the U.S. has declared war on their Fatherland. Those very sisters fulfill their duties most conscientiously. They shun no sacrifice for the Americans. No doubt they do more for the country than that type of fanatic."

Eventually, the hospital filled up again, and the sisters' response during the influenza epidemic helped restore the community's faith in them.

The Sisters of Mercy of the Holy Cross weathered the fierce North Dakota winters and the devastating windstorms.

A strange event in their history occurred in 1926. On the evening of Saturday, February 13, two of the sisters complained of being terribly sleepy. The following morning, two other sisters felt ill, but all four got up to attend Mass. On their way there, one of the sisters collapsed. All four went immediately to bed. The physicians who examined them thought they had gotten sick from the paint fumes in the new section of the hospital.

The four sisters worsened, and doctors stayed by their side. One by one all four died, two on Monday, February 15, one on Tuesday, and the fourth on Saturday. The following Monday a fifth sister died.

At first doctors thought they had died of gas fumes from the wood stain in the new building. But eventually their deaths were attributed to encephalitis. ☙

> *U*ntil now I considered the Americans broad-minded, but now I can only believe that they are pitifully narrow. The sisters can't help that they were born in Germany and that the U.S. has declared war on their Fatherland. Those very sisters fulfill their duties most conscientiously. They shun no sacrifice for the Americans. No doubt they do more for the country than that type of fanatic.
>
> A SISTER OF MERCY OF THE HOLY CROSS, A NATIVE OF SWITZERLAND, COMMENTING ON THE ANTI-GERMAN SENTIMENT TOWARD THE SISTERS AT ST. JOSEPH HOSPITAL DURING WORLD WAR I.

BELOW:
LIBERTY LOAN POSTER FROM WORLD WAR I EXPRESSING THE ANTI-GERMAN SENTIMENT COMMON IN THE UNITED STATES AT THAT TIME (CORBIS-BETTMANN).

THIS is Prussianism!

"By their deeds ye shall know them!" Ruin, Destruction, Desolation mark the pathway of the Hun. Rheims and Louvain! Their shattered towers and crumbling walls cry to Heaven for Vengeance! Remember the fire, the sword, the axe that laid waste the whole countrysides with no other purpose than ruin.

Now, crush this THING that is base and vile and shameful, and crush it forever. This is AMERICANISM! Buy Bonds with cash and buy them on installments! And do it now!

LIBERTY LOAN COMMITTEE, THIRD FEDERAL RESERVE DISTRICT
LINCOLN BUILDING, PHILADELPHIA

THE TIME TO ACT IS NOW

Women religious traveled many routes to minister to the needy. Although land and sea were formidable obstacles, the roadblocks caused by worldly decision makers could be just as difficult to overcome.

SISTERS OF CHARITY OF OUR LADY OF MERCY
Charleston, South Carolina

One of the first eight permanent congregations founded in the United States, the Sisters of Charity of Our Lady of Mercy was established in Charleston in 1829. By the 1840s, the sisters numbered 19. They ran an orphanage, an academy for girls, a free school for girls from poor families, and a school for free black children. When yellow fever and cholera epidemics occurred, their schools were closed and the sister teachers became sister nurses.

The sisters' nursing abilities won the respect of both Northern and Southern troops during the Civil War. Although shelling had destroyed their convent and orphanage, with much of Charleston in ruins, the bishop could not help them raise funds to rebuild. Instead the sisters turned to the U.S. Government.

Getting the convent repaired was easy. In 1866, President Andrew Johnson ordered the government to pay $4,000 for the repairs. But repairing the orphanage was an entirely different matter. The sisters rented a house for the orphans, while they figured out how to ask Congress for funding.

On March 25, 1867, Congressman Benjamin Butler, a representative from Massachusetts, introduced a bill asking for $20,000 "in consideration of the services rendered by the Sisters of Our Lady of Mercy of Charleston, S.C., to the sick and wounded Union officers and soldiers while said city was under the bombardment during the war…in rebuilding their Orphan Asylum." A similar bill was introduced in the Senate.

The sisters expected speedy action. But the first session of the Fortieth Congress drew to a close with their bill still in committee.

Difficult Journeys and Surprise Directions

RIGHT:

SR. XAVIER DUNN

During the second session, the sisters tried to hasten the bill's passage to no avail.

On February 24, 1868, the House of Representatives voted to impeach the President of the United States. The sisters continued to wait throughout the trial. Their bill was not acted on. In the meantime, the sisters suffered a serious setback when the U.S. government cut off rations to the girls orphanage. With as many as 70 children to feed, clothe, and educate, the sisters went to Washington to plead their case. They were granted rations through January 1869. Pleas to the Charleston government yielded a grant of $6,000 for the orphans.

During the winter of 1869, Sr. Xavier Dunn apparently decided enough was enough. She traveled to Washington, DC, and wrote to the men she had helped in the Charleston prisons during the war, asking them to contact their members of Congress on the sisters' behalf. She lobbied members of the South Carolina legislature until 20 state senators and 50 state representatives signed a petition in support of the sisters' bill. She obtained the support of the governor, who, in turn, lobbied the U.S. senators from South Carolina.

On March 21, 1870, the House of Representatives passed the sisters' bill, and it was sent to the Senate. The Senate delayed action until December.

The sisters were not idle. They purchased a house for the orphans for $19,000, borrowing money from friends to meet the first installment.

Back in Washington, the third session of Congress convened in December 1870. The sisters' bill reached the Senate floor on the last day of the lame duck session, March 3, 1871. Despite a last-minute effort to pass the bill, the session ended without action on it.

The bill reappeared as part of a catch-all measure in the first session of the 42nd Congress. On April 19, 1871, the Senate passed the measure. It was signed by the President the following day. Although the funding had been cut from $20,000 to $12,000, the sisters' years of efforts had finally yielded some payment.

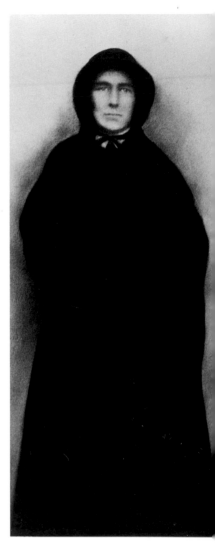

St. Joseph's Hospital
Chicago, Illinois

*I*n 1868, three Daughters of Charity arrived in Chicago to care for victims of a cholera epidemic. They had come from Emmitsburg, Maryland, at the request of the bishop to establish the first hospital on the city's north side. He provided furniture and bedding and promised much more, but soon after the sisters arrived, he was committed to an insane asylum. After six months of sewing pillows and bedding, the sister in charge begged for money to open the hospital.

On June 30, 1869, they opened a tiny hospital. As the number of patients increased, the sisters began building a new facility at another location. Sr. Walburga, who had served in the Civil War, kept a diary. In the early morning hours of October 9, 1871, the sisters were abruptly awakened. Wrote Sr. Walburga: "A wagon loaded with children and all kinds of furniture drove into our yard. The children told us the city was on fire. We could see the great light; the sky was red with it…"

The sisters headed for the city to "see if we could do anything. As we advanced, we found the heat so great and the wind so high that we were obliged to stop" and turn back. All that day, people flocked to the little hospital seeking water, since the Water Works had been destroyed by fire.

Toward evening, as the Chicago fire came closer and closer to the hospital, the sisters evacuated the patients, hiring a carriage to transport them to the prairie. The tiny hospital did not burn.

ABOVE, LEFT:
A PATIENT IS CARED
FOR BY A DAUGHTER
OF CHARITY.
ABOVE, RIGHT:
SR. WALBURGA

At midnight, with the fire still half a mile away, the wind changed and soon after, the rain came. But the new building did not fare so well. In the midst of caring for hundreds of patients in the days that followed the fire, the sisters learned that their new, unfinished building had burned.

With no money to rebuild, Sr. Walburga took out a five-year loan of $30,000. When the city of Chicago set up barracks hospitals in the fire's aftermath, several of the sisters went to work there. They slept on the icy floors with blankets but no sheets, awakening to find themselves covered with thick frost. They kept warm by working.

Before the new hospital—St. Joseph's—was completed, money ran out. They sought an additional $2,000 loan at every bank and money house they knew, to no avail. In desperation, they called on the bishop, who refused to give them any money. "He grieved us to the soul," wrote Sr. Walburga, "and we could not keep our tears back walking along the street... It gave us a lesson to rely on God alone."

Finally the sisters got money from the Chicago Relief and Aid Society. Over the next decade the society continued to generously

fund St. Joseph's Hospital, prompting Sr. Walburga to write: "We owe our success in Chicago, under God, to the Relief and Aid Society."

SISTERS OF THE PRESENTATION
Fargo, North Dakota

On March 7, 1880, at the request of a bishop who worked with Indians in the Dakota Territory, six Irish women left their homeland to come to the United States. Three were Presentation Sisters, two were seeking to enter that congregation, and one was a servant.

So rough was the sea voyage that the lifeboats washed away. The ship docked in New York City on March 18, and the sisters boarded a train to Yankton, in the Dakota Territory. From there they journeyed up the Missouri River to St. Anne's Mission to establish a school for Native Americans and white settlers. Among their pupils was Sitting Bull.

The sisters lived and taught school in a two-story structure of fieldstone and sod. The winter of 1880 was one of the coldest in pioneer history. The snow began on October 15 and covered the ground through May.

Mother M. John Hughes wrote to a friend in January 1881:

> *"You cannot even have an idea of what frost means at home. We have got no milk direct from the cow since October for nobody milks a cow in winter here... We had a great number of fowl, but nearly all have frozen to death. We shall be more experienced next year."*

There was no next year at the St. Anne's Mission. The structure in which they lived crumbled with the thaw, and they made the long and difficult journey to Deadwood, where they hoped to start a school. But things did not work out in Deadwood, and the sisters returned briefly to St. Anne's where they lived in an abandoned log cabin. Wrote Sr. Magdalen: "At night we made our beds by spreading a blanket on the rough logs."

The sisters wondered if they would have a ministry of their own in the United States, or whether it would be better to return to Ireland. For a year, the Presentation Sisters stayed with the Sisters of Mercy in Yankton while awaiting word from the bishop about their next assignment. Of the original group of six, three sisters arrived in Fargo on July 22, 1882, where a priest was looking for sisters to open a school. There is no record of the other three women. Fargo became the first permanent settlement of the Presentation Sisters in the United States.

From the convent, as far as the eye could reach, only three log cabins could be seen. The view was never monotonous to me, the extensive prairie extending to the Missouri and sunsets were fresh marvels to me every day after the New York sunsets behind miles of walls.

We had many other privations, but we were happy at St. Anne's. We received no salary, but were supplied with food. Salt pork was the only meat, except when the Indians sent some venison in the fall. We had no butter, eggs, or fresh vegetables. Sometimes we had condensed milk and boiled rice was substituted for potatoes...

We suffered most from the cold.

Years later, Sr. M. Magdalen Menahan would comment on the conditions at St. Anne's.

As did countless congregations, the Presentation Sisters went on begging trips to raise money to keep the school open. It was not unusual to collect money, produce, and livestock. But sometimes these trips yielded children who were either orphans or whose parents could not support them.

In 1882, in response to the needs of the times, the Presentation Sisters opened St. John's Orphanage and Free School. The orphanage remained open until 1961.

SISTERS OF SAINT JOSEPH OF PEACE
Bellevue, Washington

On August 3, 1890, Srs. Teresa Moran and Stanislaus bade a tearful farewell to the other sisters in their congregation and left Jersey City, New Jersey, on a 3,000-mile journey to Tacoma, Washington.

When the two sisters reached Tacoma, they learned that their final destination would be the town of Fairhaven 100 miles north. The hospital being built there, a two-story frame building, would accommodate 30 patients.

Srs. Teresa and Stanislaus begged for funds. Lumber was the big industry, and the two women spent much time seeking money from the lumberjacks.

One means of soliciting, according to a history written later by Mother Teresa, was the sale of hospital tickets at $10 each. "This ticket entitled the holder to one year's hospital care, including doctors' services. They were a good investment in case of sickness or injury, and were in use for several years until the various Lumber Companies established a sick fund for their men by deducting one dollar per month from their payroll. These deductions were given to the hospital and served instead of the ten dollar ticket."

As work proceeded on the new hospital—including the local women sewing quilts—four more sisters were dispatched from Jersey City. They arrived on January 6, 1891, to serve as the hospital staff. St. Joseph's Hospital opened on January 9.

One of the first patients was Daniel Riordan, a seriously ill rancher. Riordan willed all of his possessions to St. Joseph's Hospital: 160 acres of land, with all its crops and stock, including several tons of hay, two tons of potatoes, one ton of onions with a quantity of other vegetables, plus three cows, some pigs, and some chickens. The hospital also got a tomato can hidden in a tree stump containing $200 in gold and silver coins tied in a red handkerchief.

From Fairview, the sisters' reputation spread. On November 4, 1896, the Sisters of Saint Joseph of Peace opened a hospital in Rossland, British Columbia, a silver, gold, and copper mining town. They went on to open hospitals in Seward, Alaska; Longview, Washington; Eugene, Oregon; Greenwood, British Columbia; and Ketchikan, Alaska.

SR. THECLA
ST. ELIZABETH HOSPITAL
Youngstown, Ohio

*I*n a 1984 interview, at age 93, Sr. Thecla McManamon recalled how she began her career at St. Elizabeth Hospital, Youngstown, Ohio.

In February 1912, when the hospital was a mere two months old, Sr. Thecla, a Sister of the Humility of Mary, was a teacher in Shelby, Ohio. When she developed an ear infection, her physician sent her to St. Elizabeth's Hospital in Youngstown.

Sr. Thecla knocked on the hospital door and told the sister who answered it that the doctor had sent her. The sister threw up her arms and exclaimed that her prayers had been answered.

She brought the bewildered Sr. Thecla inside, put an apron on her, and told her to begin passing food trays to the patients. Sr. Thecla left St. Elizabeth Hospital 30 years later to move on to other institutions where her services were needed.

Her ear infection was treated at St. Elizabeth, and she was one of four sisters in the first graduating class at St. Elizabeth's School of Nursing in 1914. She worked

ABOVE, LEFT:
SR. THECLA IN 1914.
RIGHT:
ST. JOSEPH HOSPITAL
OPENED IN 1881 AND
LATER WAS TORN DOWN
WHEN THE SISTERS OPENED
ST. ELIZABETH HOSPITAL,
YOUNGSTOWN, OHIO.

wherever she was needed at the hospital: the ER, the pharmacy, and radiology. "They never questioned, 'Can you do it?' It was just 'Do it!'" she told an interviewer years later. Sr. Thecla lived to age 102.

SR. ELIZABETH CORRY
OUR LADY OF LOURDES MEDICAL CENTER
Camden, New Jersey

When asked how she had gotten involved in hospital administration, Sr. M. Elizabeth Corry, administrator of Our Lady of Lourdes Medical Center from 1969 to 1983 and from 1987 to the present, replied:

> "Well, it's like the Army. You are not always 'asked.' You say you want something and you get something else. That was what the convent was like. I always wanted to teach. I always thought I'd like to be a teacher ever since I was little, but when I entered the convent I was assigned to St. Elizabeth's Hospital in New York City.

> "I was amazed at how many people in the world were sick, how hard it was on families, how much distress there was out there in the world. It made a tremendous impression on me. I was in the hospital awhile, and then I went on to school and got my degree in hospital administration." ✑

Even when the obstacles seemed overwhelming, women religious did what needed to be done. In meeting the needs, they won the hearts of many.

Sr. Nolasco McCohn
Sisters of Mercy
Silver Spring, Maryland

Defying the Odds

During the Spanish-American War, the Sisters of Mercy of Baltimore, Maryland, offered their services nursing wounded and sick soldiers. At first the War Department felt the presence of "ladies in the field hospitals would embarrass the men," according to a diary kept by Sr. Nolasco McCohn, then 43. But when they saw "how brutally the sick were treated by the male nurses, then they agreed to engage the 'Red Cross' and other trained nurses; finding that these were not able to cope with difficulties, the offers of the various religious were accepted; finally orders were issued that no nurses were to be sent to any camp unless under the supervision of the sisters."

On August 20, 1898, the Baltimore Sisters of Mercy received a telegram ordering them to proceed to Chickamauga, Georgia, where 50,000 troops were encamped. The sisters traveled by train

Below:
Two Sisters of Mercy during the Spanish-American War.

At the time, all the newspapers were teeming with the horrors of Chickamauga, and it seemed like going to certain death to go there, yet no one hesitated.

We found one waiting room in the depot filled with sick soldiers on cots and stretchers attended by members of the Hospital Corps… Tired as we were, we at once gave our attention to them, and with much difficulty persuaded the nurses (all men) to get them some milk.

FROM THE DIARY OF SR. NOLASCO McCOHN, THE SISTERS OF MERCY OF BALTIMORE, MARYLAND.

for 27 hours before reaching their destination.

"At the time," Sr. Nolasco wrote, "all the newspapers were teeming with the horrors of Chickamauga, and it seemed like going to certain death to go there, yet no one hesitated."

Over the next several days, the sisters set about caring for the soldiers. The hospital "consisted of rows of tents to which were added wooden barracks or wards, capable of holding about twenty-five patients," wrote Sr. Nolasco. The sisters slept on cots in tents.

Sr. Nolasco described some of the conditions faced by the sisters:

"The washing for this great hospital of over 400 patients was done by hand by a few Negroes who lived in filthy quarters not far from the hospital. No care was taken of the clothes, no disinfecting; they were taken from the patients and thrown on a pile, those covered with filth with those slightly soiled, out on the ground in the dust and mud, and sometimes left there for several days though they were supposed to be taken away every day.

"There was plenty of whisky, brandy & alcohol; in fact though there was little system or order about getting medical supplies, we always got what we wanted both quality & quantity. Whatever the cause of lack of medical supplies before we took charge, certain it is 'Uncle Sam' gave us plentifully of the best. The diet was good enough, but wretchedly served; for instance, each man had a tin cup; into that was poured water, milk, beef tea, broth, oatmeal, etc., whatever was served at the time; he drank it and set the cup on the floor under his bed; it was never washed….

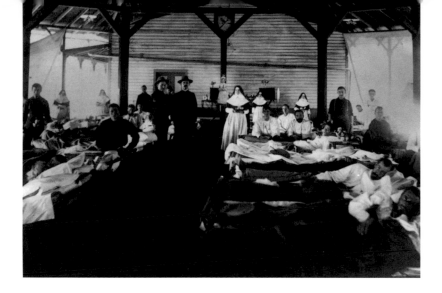

ABOVE:
HOSPITAL WARD DURING
THE SPANISH-AMERICAN
WAR.

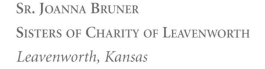

"It must be born in mind that the members of the hospital corps were for the most part rude rough ignorant men who had either enlisted…or were detailed from their regiments."

On September 6, the sisters' patients were moved to new tents and the old ones torn down. The Sisters of Mercy nursed alongside other religious communities during the Spanish-American War. Sr. Nolasco's group remained at Chickamauga through September and then moved on to camps in Knoxville, Tennessee, and later in Columbus, Georgia. They returned to Baltimore in December. Sr. Nolasco died in 1936 at age 81.

BELOW:
IN 1971 THE TOWN OF
LARAMIE, WYOMING,
NAMED A STREET IN THE
NAME OF SR. JOANNA
BRUNER.

SR. JOANNA BRUNER
SISTERS OF CHARITY OF LEAVENWORTH
Leavenworth, Kansas

Sr. Joanna Bruner weighed 300 pounds and opened hospitals throughout the West. Born in 1820, she became a Sister of Charity of Nazareth, Kentucky, in 1839. In 1848, while Sr. Joanna was teaching in Nashville, Tennessee, cholera struck the city. She quickly volunteered to help and realized that the love of her life was caring for the sick.

In Nashville Sr. Joanna and several other sisters became convinced that the work of the sisters was in the West. After nearly 20 years with the Nazareth Charities, she and Mother Xavier Ross began a new religious community in the late 1850s. The first members of the new group arrived in Leavenworth,

Kansas, on November 11, 1858. Mother Xavier and Sr. Joanna arrived on February 21, 1859.

Sr. Joanna was the first administrator of St. John's Hospital in Leavenworth, the first hospital in Kansas. She helped open St. Joseph's Hospital in Denver in 1873, and in 1876 opened another St. Joseph's Hospital in Laramie, Wyoming. Where the needs were, Sr. Joanna would go, despite failing health and huge girth. At age 68, she was sent to Wind River, Wyoming, to open a school for Arapaho Indian children. Chief Black Coal drove a wagon in which Sr. Joanna rode. At the end of the drive, he placed one hand on his heart and pointed toward her with the other: "She all good," he declared.

The following was said about her:

"She loved sauerkraut with a lump of lard."

"The Indians danced at her jubilee."

"She was so big she had a rope woven bed to hold her up. She took the bed with her when she went to Wyoming to the Indians."

Sr. Joanna spent her final years in a wheelchair. She died on February 2, 1903. In 1971, the town of Laramie, Wyoming, named a street in her honor. "Joanna Bruner Drive" was the first Laramie street named for a woman.

FRANCISCAN SISTERS OF MARY
St. Louis, Missouri

When the yellow fever epidemic occurred in 1878, the Sisters of Mary of the Third Order of St. Francis (now the Franciscan Sisters of Mary) was a mere six years old and numbered 31 sisters. Yet Mother Odilia Berger sent 13 sisters to nurse those stricken during the epidemic.

Five sisters were dispatched to Memphis on August 30. By September 12, four were dead. Mother Odilia then sent three additional sisters to Memphis and five to Canton, Mississippi. ❧

BELOW:
MOTHER ODILIA BERGER SENT 13 SISTERS TO NURSE THOSE STRICKEN DURING THE YELLOW FEVER EPIDEMIC.

RIGHT:
PAGE FROM THE BOOK, *STRONGER THAN DEATH: YELLOW FEVER HEROES.*
FAR RIGHT:
INSET FEATURES THE COVER FROM A YELLOW FEVER PAMPHLET, MEMPHIS, 1878.

CHAPTER I

THE RAVAGES OF YELLOW FEVER

The year 1929 marks the fiftieth anniversary of the dreadful scourge of yellow fever which visited Memphis in 1879, the last of the three epidemics which struck the city in the seventies, the other visitations occurring in 1873 and 1878.

Those were terrible days, recalling graphic pages from Manzoni's great masterpiece, *The Betrothed,* and the awful ravages of the plague of Milan in the days

ST. ROCH, *Tertiary*
Patron of Contagious Diseases

of the heroic Cardinal Frederick Borromeo. For Memphis, too, had its heroe[s] the midst of the panic that prevailed, and it is well that the memory of the pr[iests] and sisters who risked life and health in those soul-trying days should be [ ] recalled.

Before relating what has immediate reference to the heroes of the yellow fe[ver] it will be interesting to form an idea of conditions which prevailed at each re[cur]rence of the dread visitation. One description is that of Father Quinn, a surv[ivor] of the three epidemics of the seventies, which he sent to the *Providence Vi*[sitor] when the yellow fever put in an appearance in Alabama, Mississippi and Louis[iana]

*O*ctober 2, 1878...

I am homesick,

Reverend Mother, and every day I wish

I could see you, even if only for a moment.

Then everything would be all right. Since that

is not possible, I must be prepared to live my

vocation as best as possible.

The yellow fever is really horrible and

the other sisters are still quite weak and can't

be left alone. I feel so lonely during the days

and nights being 500 miles away from you

and unable to listen to your words. It seems

an eternity to me, and I hope that God will let

us come home soon... Only four nights have

I been able to take off my clothes when I went

to bed; all the other nights I was always caring

for the sick. However, I am happy to be

of service...

SR. ROSE GUBRY, A FRANCISCAN SISTER OF MARY,
WROTE OF HER LONELINESS WHILE NURSING IN CANTON
DURING THE YELLOW FEVER EPIDEMIC OF 1878.

Compassion

*F*or these sisters, compassion meant more than caring deeply. Compassion meant self-sacrifice and personal risk. These sisters willingly involved themselves to make life better for others.

ABOVE:
CHAPEL OF ST. ROSE'S
FREE HOME FOR
INCURABLE CANCER.

LEFT:
NEW YORK'S LOWER EAST
SIDE, WHERE ROSE CHOSE
TO LIVE AND WORK
(LIBRARY OF CONGRESS).

RIGHT:
ROSE HAWTHORNE
LATHROP IN PROBABLY
THE LAST PORTRAIT THAT
WAS TAKEN OF HER
BEFORE SHE BECAME
SR. ALPHONSA.

ROSE HAWTHORNE LATHROP

DOMINICAN SISTERS, THE SERVANTS
OF RELIEF FOR INCURABLE CANCER
New York, New York

Born in 1851, Rose Hawthorne was "Rosebud" to her father, the famous American author Nathaniel Hawthorne. She married George Lathrop, a young, aspiring writer, when she was 20. After the death of their young son in 1881, the couple moved to New York City. They converted to Catholicism in 1891, and Rose became involved in helping the needy. When the marriage failed a few years later, she took a three-month course at the New York Cancer Hospital.

Rose's interest in cancer was prompted by her friendship with the poet Emma Lazarus, author of the inscription on the base of the Statue of Liberty. During a conversation, Rose learned that Emma was suffering from a dreaded disease: cancer. In the late 1800s, cancer carried a fierce stigma and was believed to be contagious. Although Lazarus was well cared for until she died, others who contracted the disease were not so lucky. People with

*Caring
for the
Terminally Ill*

ABOVE:
THE SECOND LOCATION OF
ST. ROSE'S FREE HOME
FOR INCURABLE CANCER
WAS AT 71 JACKSON
STREET, NEW YORK CITY.

cancer who had no economic resources were sent to the grim Blackwell's Island, New York City's last resort for the penniless.

At 44, the socially well-connected Rose Hawthorne Lathrop took a flat in the poorest section of New York City, the Lower East Side. To work among the poor, she reasoned, she would have to live among the poor. She had her first patient before her bags were unpacked: a seven-year-old boy. Many more quickly followed. Rose turned down no one. Going from tenement to tenement, she cared for the poor, the downtrodden, and the dying in their own homes.

She began taking into her home poor people with cancer who had no place to go. Soon she had to move to larger quarters.

To support her efforts, the daughter of Nathaniel Hawthorne begged. In her diary, she described how painful begging was for her:

"Fifth Avenue {where the wealthy lived} seems as far and as frozen as the road to Alaska. It seems so when I stand in my little rooms very nearly at the end of my money and ask myself if I have the courage to enter the homes of the well-to-do and the rich and beg for the destitute."

To enlist the aid of the public, Rose began writing newspaper articles about her work. One day a woman who had read her articles stopped outside Rose's home. Alice Huber, an art student from a well-to-do family, wanted to join Rose Hawthorne in her efforts to help the sick. The two became lifetime companions. In May 1899, they opened St. Rose's Free Home for Incurable Cancer. The following year, the two women founded a religious congregation: the Dominican Sisters, the Servants of Relief for Incurable Cancer, now known as the Hawthorne Dominican Sisters. Rose Hawthorne

ABOVE, TOP:
PORTRAIT OF ROSE
AS A CHILD.
MIDDLE:
ROSE'S FATHER,
NATHANIEL HAWTHORNE
(BERG COLLECTION, NEW
YORK PUBLIC LIBRARY).
BOTTOM:
ALICE HUBER

ABOVE AND RIGHT:
PATIENTS AT ST. ROSE'S
FREE HOME FOR
INCURABLE CANCER.

Lathrop became Sr. Alphonsa, and Alice Huber became Sr. Mary Rose.

Sr. Alphonsa had three rules: the sisters were never to show disgust at disfigurement brought about by cancer, no patient could be a guinea pig for medical research, and no money would be accepted from patients or their relatives.

In 1900, Sr. Alphonsa purchased a house 30 miles north of New York City as the site for a second home for her patients. Today the town where it is situated is named Hawthorne.

She remained at Rosary Hill, the new site, while Sr. Mary Rose returned to St. Rose's Home in New York City. The two corresponded regularly, and Sr. Mary Rose often sent Sr. Alphonsa patients whom she felt the country air would do good.

Today both homes continue Rose Hawthorne's mission. They are among seven homes in the United States operated by the congregation for the sole purpose of caring for people with terminal cancer who cannot pay for their care. Every year, the Hawthorne Dominican Sisters care for more than 1,000 people whose stays average six to eight weeks.

To this day, the sisters do not charge their patients. Nor do they rely on government support, accepting neither Medicare nor Medicaid. What they rely on is "what the mailman brings us every day," according to Sr. M. Joseph, administrator of St. Rose's Home today.

"Rose Hawthorne depended on God, and she promised never to charge her patients. We've upheld our part of that promise, and He's upheld His." ☙

And certainly if there is an unassailably good cause in the world, it is this one undertaken by the Dominican Sisters, of housing, nourishing, and nursing the most pathetically unfortunate of all the afflicted among us— men and women sentenced to a painful and lingering death by incurable disease.

I have seen [this lofty work of yours] rise from seedling to tree with no endowment but the voluntary aid which your patient labor and faith have drawn from the purses of grateful and compassionate men; and I am glad… to know that this prosperity will continue and be permanent… It cannot fail until pity fails in the hearts of men, and that will never be.

EXCERPT FROM A LETTER FROM MARK TWAIN TO ROSE HAWTHORNE LATHROP.

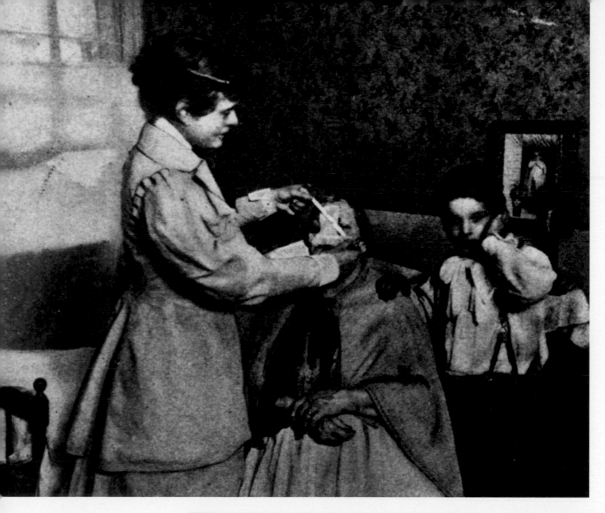

ABOVE:
ROSE HAWTHORNE
BANDAGING THE WOUNDS
OF A CANCER PATIENT.

LEFT:
MARK TWAIN (NATIONAL
ARCHIVES).

RIGHT:
THE FIRST ROSARY HILL
HOME IN HAWTHORNE,
NEW YORK.

ABOVE:
PLANTATION MANSION
THAT HOUSED THE SISTERS
AT THE LOUISIANA LEPER
HOME IN CARVILLE,
LOUISIANA. PHOTO TAKEN
IN 1896.

A Commitment Stronger Than the Fear of Disease

*Undaunted by the severity of the illness or the danger
to themselves, women religious stepped forward to give
care and love to the needy.*

MERCY HOSPITAL,
Pittsburgh, Pennsylvania

When Mother Frances Warde arrived in Pittsburgh on December 21, 1843, the Sisters of Mercy were a mere 12 years old. The day after her arrival, Mother Frances opened the first Mercy convent in the United States. In 1847, the convent became the site of Mercy Hospital.

In January 1848, the sisters admitted a sick boatman to the hospital. When they realized he had typhus, their first thought was of the devastating epidemics they had seen in Ireland. Despite their fear, they let him stay at the hospital and opened a special ward for victims of the disease. Soon 18 more typhus victims were admitted to Mercy. The sisters nursed the sick patients night and day, exhausting themselves. By the time the epidemic ended less than a month later, all but four of the patients had recovered, but the entire nursing staff—four Sisters of Mercy—had died. All of them were under 30.

Daughters of Charity
Carville, Louisiana

*T*he Louisiana Leper Home was two years old when four Daughters of Charity arrived in 1896. In taking positions as nurses, the sisters accepted exile and isolation from society for the rest of their lives.

At Carville, the sisters found 20 societal outcasts, despised because of their disease. In a letter home, the leader of the group, Sr. Beatrice Hart, wrote: "The word 'leper' we will not use if possible. We went to each one separately and tried to make them feel we were come to be one with them, to care for them, and make them happy, to look into their wants and supply them."

Life was hard for the exiled sisters. Water moccasins nested in walls and climbed their bedposts at night. The swampy Louisiana land bred mosquitoes and malaria.

The sisters worked every day to exhaustion. Attacks of malaria were so regular that the sisters came to expect them. So no one was alarmed when Sr. Beatrice remained ill for several weeks in the summer of 1901. She carried on as usual, spending the night at the bedside of a dying patient.

She left his bedside for her own death bed. Sr. Beatrice Hart died on September 6, 1901.

Ninety-five years later, 10 Daughters of Charity still serve at Carville. Although Hansen's Disease, as leprosy is now known, can be controlled by drugs, Carville remains home to individuals with the disease who have nowhere else to go. The sisters have opted to stay with them.

Poor Handmaids of Jesus Christ
Donaldson, Indiana

*F*rom 1881 to 1950, the Poor Handmaids of Jesus Christ cared for patients at the Chicago Municipal Isolation Hospital. In 1882, they nursed 1,055 smallpox patients. In 1893,

ABOVE, TOP:
THE FIRST FOUR SISTERS TO
SERVE AT CARVILLE.
SR. BEATRICE IS AT LEFT.
MIDDLE:
RAISING THE U.S. FLAG
IN 1921 WHEN THE HOME
BECAME THE NATIONAL
LEPROSARIUM.
BOTTOM:
SISTERS READING TO
PATIENTS, 1896.

LEFT:
POSTCARDS FROM THE
LOUISIANA LEPER HOME.

On February 16 [we] admitted a young man that just arrived at the Union Station. He journeyed all the way from Lithuania through Russia, Germany, and over the ocean to Chicago, still 99 miles from his destination which was Cherryville, Illinois. God only knows what would have been his lot.

"His passport and all were written in German, so we notified his brother what had happened, and to come here as soon as he could. A rosary around his neck showed he must be a Catholic, but could only speak Lithuanian. The brother came to visit him and was told to see if he could get a Lithuanian priest, but this was impossible because none would take the risk to come here. Well, our priest, the Benedictine who comes here, did what he could to hear his confession, and gave him the Last Sacrament and three days later he died.

"It was a pitiful sight, to see him taken away to be buried, a trip of 2,000 miles and still miles from his destination...."

JOURNAL ENTRY BY
A SISTER OF THE POOR
HANDMAIDS OF JESUS
CHRIST, 1911.

LEFT:
JOURNAL ENTRY FROM
A SISTER OF THE POOR
HANDMAIDS OF JESUS
CHRIST.

BELOW:
IMMIGRANTS LOADING
THEIR BAGS ONTO HORSE-
DRAWN CARRIAGES
(CORBIS-BETTMANN).

an even more severe epidemic swept the city. A history of the sisters described the event:

> "Daily and hourly new patients were brought in and the few sisters could scarcely manage. A call was sent to the Motherhouse for more help. When the epidemic was at its height, twenty-four sisters were on duty.

> "The work at this time was well-nigh above the strength of the average nurse. The sisters were on duty night and day and frequently sought out a bed in the wee hours of the night only. It was utterly impossible for the sister on night duty to look after all the patients. Moreover, it was difficult to get hired or outside help, for the lay nurse generally feared contagion...."

SERVANTS OF THE IMMACULATE HEART OF MARY
Saco, Maine

During the influenza epidemic of 1918, the Servants of the Immaculate Heart of Mary cared for the sick at a tent hospital in Lawrence, Massachusetts. More than 200 tents were erected to shelter people who could not be cared for in their homes. Military personnel picked up the sisters at their convent each morning and returned them to their home in the evening. Sr. Jeanne d'Arc Duperry, 100 years old in 1995, was a young sister when she was called to the tent hospital.

> "In August 1916 I was assigned to Lawrence, my first mission. October 1918 found the cities of Lawrence and Methuen in the midst of the worst of epidemics, that of INFLUENZA (grippe Espagñol). The site of what is now St. Ann's Orphanage was occupied by hundreds of victims with the dreadful sickness. Tents, doctors, nurses, and volunteer workers were seen day and night on the immense area. When a tent was closed that person had breathed her last. How often I saw dead people in baskets waiting to be buried."

SISTERS OF ST. FRANCIS OF PHILADELPHIA
Aston, Pennsylvania

On September 1, 1904, St. Joseph's Tuberculosis Hospital opened in Hillsgrove, Rhode Island. The hospital was originally two tents, one for patients and one for the Sisters of

RIGHT, TOP:
A SISTER OF THE SERVANTS
OF THE IMMACULATE
HEART OF MARY AT
A TENT HOSPITAL DURING
THE 1918 INFLUENZA
EPIDEMIC.
BOTTOM:
SISTERS AT WORK
IN THE TENT HOSPITALS
AT LAWRENCE,
MASSACHUSETTS.

St. Francis of Philadelphia. When storms blew the tents down, the outcasts found shelter in a nearby farmhouse.

In a September 6, 1915 address to the Rhode Island Medical Society, Jay Perkins, a physician who had worked with the sisters at the hospital, offered the following comments:

> "During the past year there has been an average of 70+ patients a day, and to care for these there have been five sisters, three nurses, two orderlies.... Because of the fear in the public mind in reference to tuberculosis, the isolation of the hospital and the depression caused by so much sickness, it is extremely hard to secure help, in fact, almost impossible, for what this hospital can pay...."

SISTERS OF CHARITY OF NAZARETH
Nazareth, Kentucky

In 1918, Sr. Mary Jane Henning was among the four Sisters of Charity of Nazareth who nursed influenza patients in the Kentucky mountains. She wrote of the experience in a letter to the sisters back home.

> "We got an urgent call to send aid to the 'Flu' stricken of the mountain region. I, among others, answered that Call of Humanity and was one of the four selected for the dreaded service.

> "Sr. Mary Amelia and I were sent 40 miles further in the remote fastness of the mountains and told to get off at Wallin's Creek.... After walking some distance over stones, ridges, and gullies and crossing a hanging bridge, we came to a small boxcar which we entered and set out for where e'er Providence called us.

> "We followed Wallin's Creek up a narrow valley, with the Cumberland Mountains shutting us in on one side and the Black River on the other.... We were conducted to a large boarding-house for miners. We were still under the impression that we were going to a hospital, when we were informed that we were to start a hospital here and that patients would be in on the next train, which was due at 2 p.m. It was then 10 a.m. You never saw a hospital gotten ready so quickly in your life...." ✎

Such accomplishment is possible only by those whose motives are something higher than worldly gain. . . . The ordinary working women will not do for money what these women do for love of the sick and destitute, for the love of relieving others.

Jay Perkins, physician, on the Sisters of St. Francis of Philadelphia, in a 1915 address to the Rhode Island Medical Society.

St. Joseph's Hospital, Tuberculosis Department,
Hills Grove, R. I.
1904 – 1937

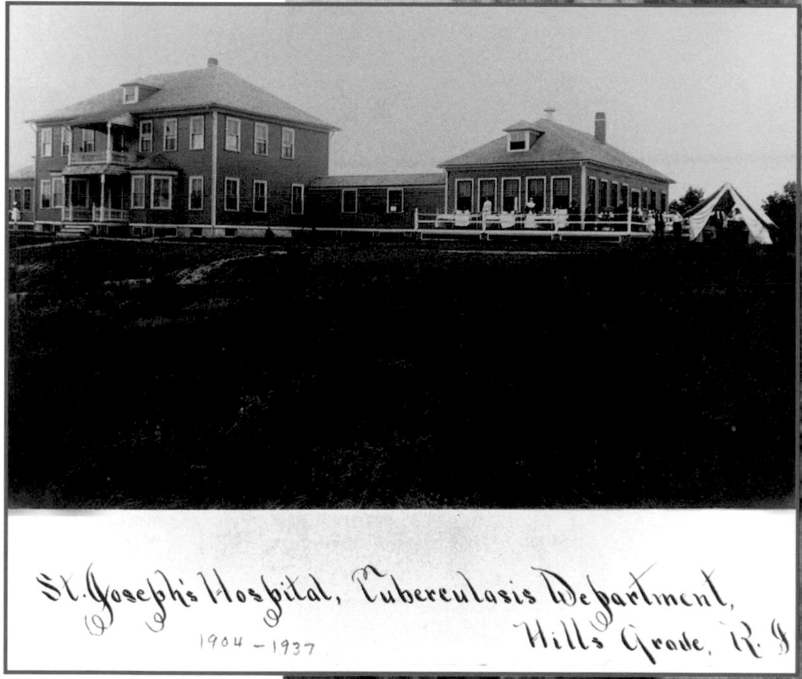

Above:
St. Joseph's Hospital, Hillsgrove, Rhode Island, circa 1935.

Right:
The original St. Joseph's Hospital consisted of two tents, one for patients and one for the Sisters of St. Francis.

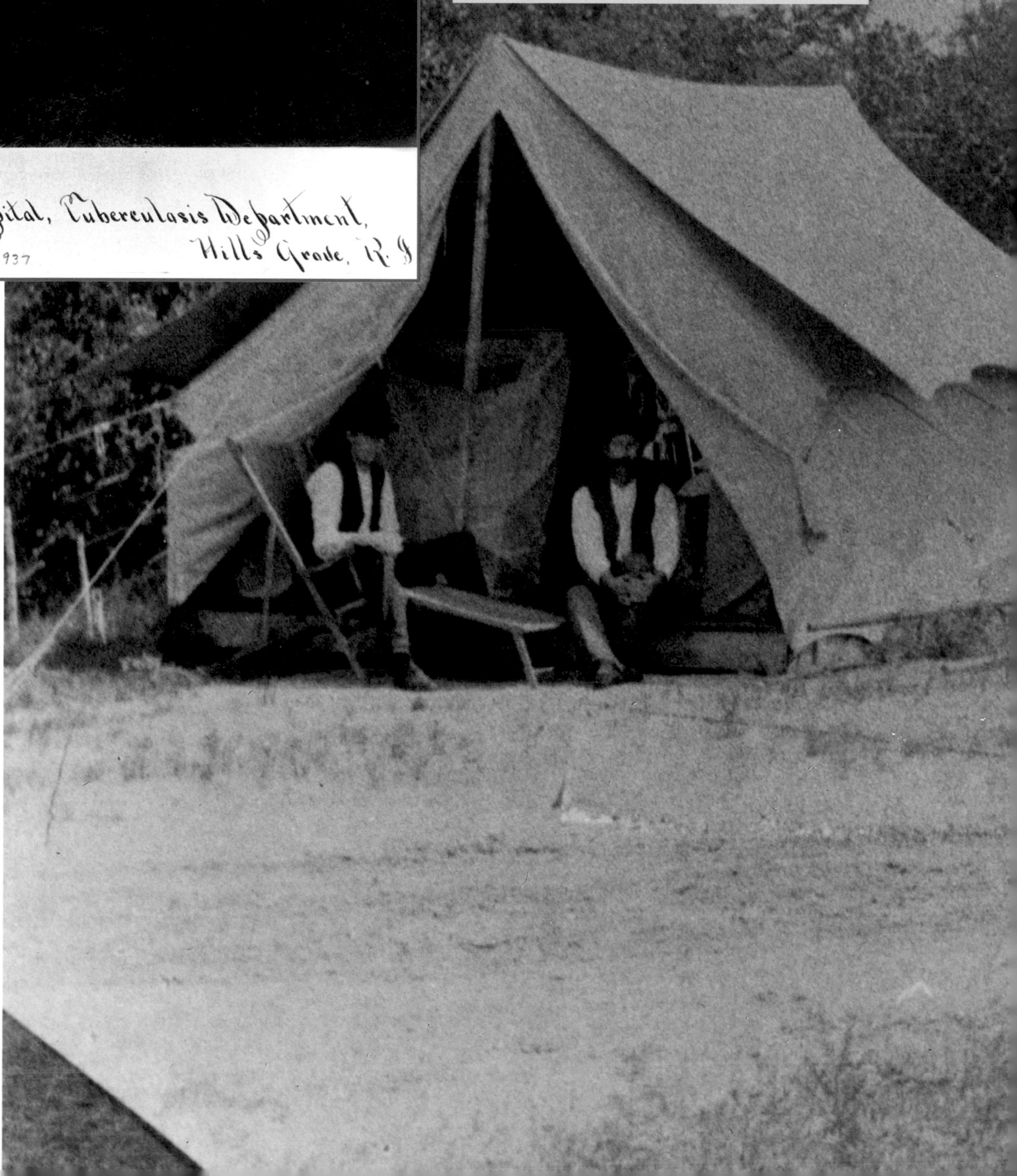

FELICIAN SISTERS

Mother of Good Counsel Province Chicago, Illinois

FAR LEFT:
CALLED THE "BROWN SISTERS" BECAUSE OF THE COLOR OF THEIR HABITS, THE FELICIAN SISTERS WENT TO MANITOWOC, WISCONSIN, IN 1887 AT THE REQUEST OF A POLISH PRIEST WHO HAD OPENED AN ORPHANAGE FOR BOYS. DURING THE 47 YEARS THE SISTERS RAN THE HOME, THEY CARED FOR A TOTAL OF 633 ORPHAN BOYS. THEY CLOSED ST. MARY'S HOME IN 1934.

LEFT:
FELICIAN SISTER MARY ELEKTA TEACHING ORPHANS HOW TO PACK BOXES FOR THE POOR OF MANITOWOC, 1913.

Embracing the Lonely and the Troubled

When the need was there, so were the sisters. They lovingly answered the call to care for those ravaged by birth, infirmity, or old age.

DAUGHTERS OF CHARITY
Baltimore, Maryland

*I*n October 1840, the Sisters of Charity (now known as the Daughters of Charity) established a mental hospital on a site west of Baltimore. The following year, a state investigator visited the facility, known as Mount St. Vincent's, and offered the following comments on the care there:

> *"Solitary confinement and precautionary restraints used elsewhere the sisters say causes the mind to prey upon itself; they prefer, as far as possible, the restraint of their own presence and companionship to actual bonds....*
>
> *"Treat them as rational beings, converse with them as such, endeavor to conceal every symptom of distrust. Occasionally lead them to converse upon the theme of their derangement, rather than leave this sorrow uncommunicated. Gradually gaining their confidence, endeavor to insinuate more rational ideas. Sometimes let two communicate with each other freely...sympathy is thus excited instead of the morbid selfishness of the insane."*

THE LITTLE SISTERS OF THE POOR
Baltimore, Maryland

On August 31, 1868, seven Little Sisters of the Poor sailed from Brest, France, to New York City to open a home for the aged. Six days after they reached New York, they welcomed their first resident at the house they had rented in Brooklyn. The priest who had invited the sisters to New York described one sister's reaction to the elderly gentleman's arrival: "I have never seen sister so animated or enthusiastic before."

Money collection began immediately, since begging was the way the sisters financed care of the elderly.

The Little Sisters of the Poor established other homes for the aged across the United States. The following account came from an unknown sister in Evansville, Indiana, in 1882.

ABOVE:
HORSE-DRAWN AMBULANCE OF THE LITTLE SISTERS OF THE POOR.

RIGHT:
A LITTLE SISTER OF THE POOR WITH A BASKET.

FAR RIGHT:
A MEMBER OF THE CONGREGATION WITH THE COMMUNITY'S DONKEY.

"On Wednesday…an old person presented himself asking that we keep him. We already had 11 men and no more beds or quilts. This old person begged us to take him in. We started gathering pieces to make a quilt. Seeing herself with the impossibility of providing a bed for the newcomer, the good mother gave up her own and placed her straw mattress on the floor, when charity came to her aid.

"The good God did not want her to be deprived of her place of repose. People came bringing pillows, three warm quilts, and all that was necessary to make a good bed. The next day we received three wooden beds and several quilts. Providence sent not only the poor, but what was needed for their care as well. How much these little attentions touch the Little Sisters and strengthen their faith."

RIGHT:
SOME OF THE ELDERLY
WHO SOUGHT SHELTER
WITH THE FRANCISCAN
SISTERS.

BELOW:
MOTHER CLARA

FRANCISCAN SISTERS OF ST. JOSEPH
Hamburg, New York

When homeless and hungry elderly citizens repeatedly sought shelter at the gates of the Franciscan Sisters convent in Buffalo, New York, the sisters felt compelled to do something. In 1925, Mother Clara purchased a brick farmhouse and several acres of land. The house was renovated and opened in February 1926 as a home for the aged.

Ten elderly individuals immediately sought admittance, and the sisters' work with the aged had begun. Throughout the 1920s and 1930s, the sisters cared for the destitute elderly. The number of residents increased, and the facility grew overcrowded. On June 13, 1939, the sisters broke ground for a new home. ❧

Cast out by an unforgiving society, unwed mothers and their children found shelter and encouragement from the Catholic sisters.

SISTERS OF MISERICORDE
Misericordia Hospital, New York City

Love Stronger Than Scorn

*I*t was not medicine but mercy that brought five French-Canadian sisters to New York City in the late 1800s. They were summoned by the Archbishop of New York from Canada to care for unmarried pregnant women.

The Sisters of Misericorde had been caring for unmarried, pregnant women in Montreal for more than 30 years. On September 1, 1887, five sisters and a nurse arrived in New York from Canada. Their "baggage" consisted of $1 and the clothes on their backs.

New York City in the late 1800s was the entry point to the United States for millions of immigrants seeking better lives in a new land. The city's Lower East Side, a haven for immigrants, quickly became seriously overcrowded as tenement buildings sprang up to house the new arrivals. Of every 1,000 babies born in the 1880s, an average of 125 died soon after birth. In 1886, the leading cause of death among infants was tuberculosis, followed by infant diarrhea. Unmarried pregnant women were social outcasts. Poor women who were unmarried and pregnant had no place to go.

The sisters settled in a large wooden farmhouse in extreme disrepair. The rooms were "too many to maintain" and "unfit to live in," according to a report from one sister. Nevertheless, they were not deterred from opening the doors to needy pregnant women. The Great Blizzard of 1888 only compounded the dire living conditions. On March 11, rain poured through the roof.

BELOW:
THE SISTERS OF MISERICORDE HAD BEEN CARING FOR UNMARRIED, PREGNANT WOMEN IN MONTREAL FOR MORE THAN 30 YEARS BEFORE THEY ARRIVED IN THE U.S. IN 1887.

The next day the temperature fell and the rain turned to sleet. On the night of March 12, more than 16 inches of snow fell on the city. The snow kept up for two days, bringing the city to a halt.

In the spring, the sisters and the women moved to a better site. In their first year in New York, the sisters cared for 86 women and recorded 57 births. Thirty-three babies and two mothers died. They moved again in their second year, increasing the number of women they cared for to 243.

Besides begging for money, the sisters sold garden produce to raise funds to run the home. One sister, a carpenter, raised money by selling her handmade furniture.

Even as the sisters continued to serve women, their home evolved into a hospital. In 1905, the Mother's Home was renamed Misericordia Hospital.

SISTERS OF THE HOLY FAMILY OF NAZARETH
Altoona, Pennsylvania

Sr. Seraphim was one of the first Sisters of the Holy Family of Nazareth to work at Altoona Mercy Hospital when the sisters took over the hospital in 1935. Small of stature, with red bangs protruding from her veil, she spent 43 years as supervisor of the nursery and maternity. Hers was a quiet contribution.

She told of a stillborn baby whom she placed gently on a table. As she straightened the baby's legs, he began to breathe. Sr. Seraphim held that baby through the night until he died the next morning. Her act was small in the sweep of human history, but, because of her, one frail and dying baby knew love during his brief existence.

Sr. Seraphim died on February 19, 1995 at 83, in her sixty-seventh year of religious life.

> *W*e struggled to keep everyone warm and to provide one warm meal each day. Everyone suffered. ...there was no heat... no outside help.
>
> EXCERPT FROM WRITINGS OF A SISTER OF MISERICORDE.

BELOW:
SR. SERAPHIM WAS ONE OF THE FIRST SISTERS OF THE HOLY FAMILY OF NAZARETH TO WORK AT ALTOONA MERCY HOSPITAL WHEN THE SISTERS TOOK OVER THE HOSPITAL IN 1935.

SR. MARY STELLA SIMPSON AND THE DAUGHTERS OF CHARITY
Evansville, Indiana

*I*n 1967, at the request of the American Nurses Association, Sr. Mary Stella Simpson moved to Mound Bayou, an African-American community in Mississippi. As a nurse midwife, Sr. Mary Stella cared for pregnant women and provided education to the young mothers. Her work was part of a comprehensive health center established to serve a 500-square-mile area. When she arrived in Mound Bayou, she learned that when their children got sick, the women had to choose between a visit to the doctor and feeding the rest of the family.

While in Mound Bayou, Sr. Mary Stella wrote letters to her religious community at the motherhouse in Evansville describing her experiences.

MONDAY, NOVEMBER 27

"Today was my day for home visits…. On the very first one I had to come back to town to get milk for a baby. He had finished his last bottle. It has gotten really cold, and the 14 people in that family all congregate in one room around a small wood-burning stove. I had to go through a front room which was like a deep-freeze. The floor was slick with ice where water had been tracked in and then froze. The children were all barefoot, therefore could not go to school. The parents have no way of getting shoes for them since they have no income…."

THURSDAY, NOVEMBER 30

"Today I went to the clinic. We saw about 55 patients by 5 pm. Such an ill, sordid day. The numbers get bigger and the children sicker. So many badly

BELOW:
SIGN FOR MOUND BAYOU,
MISSISSIPPI. PHOTO, ALEN
MACWEENEY.

I went to visit an expectant mother who lives in Duncan today…. She is the mother of 12, all at home. They live in three small rooms. The children were all in school, except the baby — a two-year-old. The house was cold. One gas heater in the middle room made very little heat. I was cold as I talked to the mother, and I had on boots and my all-weather coat with a heavy lining…. The baby was whining, trying to cry. I picked her up, and it was like holding a frozen fish. The poor little darling had on a dress—period. So I had to go get something to keep her warm.

How can a country as rich as ours have so much poverty? I keep asking myself that question day after day. I could see daylight in places right through the roof and could see anything I chose through the holes in the walls. The mother is so lovely, very intelligent, and loves her children and husband….

From a letter from Sr. Mary Stella Simpson to her motherhouse, the Daughters of Charity, Evansville, Indiana, February 23, 1968.

infected ears! ...To end the day, an elderly man came in and asked to see 'that nurse that wears a Catholic dress.' He was the grandfather of some new twins that I have been going out to see. He just wanted to thank me for all I did for them."

FRIDAY, JANUARY 26
"It is in the upper 60s. I sat out in the backyard on a large stump of an oak tree and ate my lunch. The robins came to join me, and there were several beautiful cardinals there also. I tried to concentrate on the birds since just below me, about 20 feet, flowed the very necessary drainage ditch and across it are many hovels which house some of our poorest people...

ABOVE AND AT LEFT:
SR. MARY STELLA SIMPSON
AT WORK WITH THE POOR
IN MOUND BAYOU,
MISSISSIPPI. PHOTOS, ALEN
MACWEENEY.

"A year-old baby with a terrible hand was brought to the clinic by his mother today. A month ago he stuck his hand in a pan of boiling grease, and his burns were second- and third-degree. They took him to a neighborhood doctor. The burn healed fine, but his hand is positioned into a fist and cannot be straightened. Of course, you and I know that such a thing is neglect in the worst sense...."

WEDNESDAY, JANUARY 31
"It has been raining for two days straight. Home visits had to be made, so the mud was part of the bargain. You know, after today I really have respect for the mini skirt and wish I had one to wear...."

THURSDAY, APRIL 4
"I saw an 11-month-old baby who was almost dead from starvation at the clinic yesterday. I have seen pictures of these little starved ones from India and Viet Nam, but the actual face-to-face encounter is really an experience...."

WEDNESDAY, JUNE 19
"Remember that postmistress we reported for holding back welfare checks from black people? She is now enjoying retirement. Poor Mississippi will never be the same with all these health center people occupying the Delta area. Things are really a-changing!"

SUNDAY, OCTOBER 5
"Tonight it is pouring rain, and the lightning is quite lively.... There are a few home visits to make tomorrow, so I'll have to get out my boots, raincoat, and other mud gear again. Good old Mississippi! Rain and all, I love her magnolias and her poor."

Today Sr. Mary Stella Simpson is 86, retired, and lives in Evansville with her community. ❧

With the spiritual power of their faith and their own physical labor, sisters built hospitals where there were none and brought hope to those who might have been forgotten.

SISTERS OF ST. DOMINIC
ADRIAN, MICHIGAN

> *"The old elm house was a bleak spot, set off by itself in the fields…. Sister Villana and Sister Adelaide, two of the hospital pioneers who labored all their long lives in the 'peninsula of promise,' remembered the site as so dismal that 'not even a stray dog or cat would come near it'."*

That old elm house served as the original St. Joseph's Hospital in Adrian, Michigan, according to *Amid the Alien Corn,* a history of the community. Although the Adrian Dominicans were a teaching order, they responded to the needs of the community and in 1844 opened St. Joseph's as a hospital and home for the elderly with nowhere else to go.

Sr. Mary Philip Ryan, author of *Amid the Alien Corn,* offered an interesting observation about the begging the sisters carried out to raise funds for the hospital. The black-garbed sisters became familiar faces as they traveled the countryside surrounding Adrian in a horse-drawn buggy. Collection trips could yield a side of beef, a slab of bacon, an apron of apples, or a live chicken. But, contends Sr. Mary Philip, the sisters' greatest achievement may have been establishing friendly relations with the community. "Limited by enclosure, the nuns would have been doomed to immobility had not the lay sisters gone out among the people. To the demeaning task of begging they brought dignity and radiance. Families were attracted through them to the hospital…."

THE LITTLE SISTERS OF THE ASSUMPTION
New York, New York

On April 20, 1941, the fiftieth anniversary of the arrival of the Little Sisters of the Assumption in New York City,

---

Building Hospitals: Laying Foundations for Healing

I have seen the Sisters of St. Francis working hard to aid the sick, and I know from my own observation they are sadly in need of financial aid. The hospital is filled with poor patients and the sisters give their time and kind attention without financial remuneration. The number of pay patients is less at St. Francis Hospital than in any other institution, and therefore it needs more financial aid.

QUOTE FROM A DONOR OF AN UNSOLICITED $20,000 TO ST. FRANCIS HOSPITAL, TRENTON, NEW JERSEY, 1905.

Msgr. William Cashin offered the following comments:

"So quietly and modestly has this {work} been done that I dare say that not one in a hundred know of them or their work. They appear daily on the streets of our city, bent on their errands of mercy, and but few outside of those who have been the recipients of their kindly ministrations know of their purpose or their mission. They are God's angels of mercy. They enter into the homes of the sick poor and bring cheer, consolation, encouragement, and blessing. Healing is in their hands; prayer in their hearts and on their lips…. They minister to bodily illness in order that they may cure also, the sickness of the souls. Their mission in life is to establish the kingdom of God in the minds and souls of their charges…."

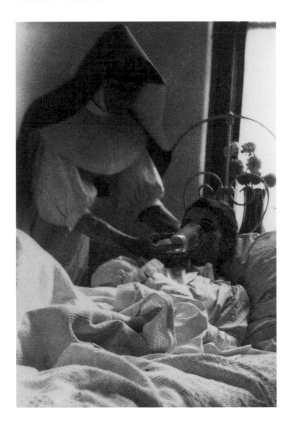

FRANCISCAN SISTERS OF CHRISTIAN CHARITY
Manitowoc, Wisconsin

From a chronicle by Sr. Clarence Hennessey at Holy Family Hospital, Manitowoc, Wisconsin:

"Sr. M. Victima came here in the spring of 1900 and took charge of the second floor. At that time she had a spell of headaches and stomach trouble. Everybody thought she would die. All said: 'Why does she want to be a nurse? She can't live very long. She's half dead now and her whole mind and heart is fixed on being a nurse. That's all she talks about and all the good she will do when she gets started.'

"'I will do all in my power to give good hospital service to every patient that I have in my charge. I will do my very best for all.' That was her whole cry for about two weeks. Then she got up and started to work. She put her whole dream in action, and did just what she had said. She gave good service. Everybody said that about her, so it must be true. They all said that she did her work so perfect that nobody else could please the patient after she had a hand in the work. Nobody will try to please all like she did.

"Her name went out far and wide. Although she suffered much, still she worked on. Many a night she suffered pain, and then got up at the sound of

the bell…. With all her sufferings she wanted to live and work for the hospital and do all she could for the sick. That was her whole aim in the world.

"Sr. Victima had many experiences during her lifetime. One time an old Irishman's record was needed and sister asked him how old he was, but he said he couldn't count. She told him to tell her the year he was born and she would do the counting. He replied, 'I was born the same year that our white cow had the black calf in Ireland.'

"Sr. Victima died of a throat infection on April 1, 1930…. The whole city honored her."

A newspaper account at the time of her death offered the following:

"Many the small watches of the night, many the lonely vigil, many the kindliest offices are attributed to her and at times when the institution had insufficient nurses, it was Sr. Victima who denied herself sleep and rest so that her patients would not suffer from inattention.

"She gave her life that others might live and she will be remembered as Manitowoc's outstanding angel of mercy."

RIGHT:
RELIGIOUS HOSPITALLERS
OF ST. JOSEPH IN THE
MEN'S WARD.

ST. JOSEPH HOSPITAL
Polson, Montana

Three Religious Hospitallers of St. Joseph arrived in Polson, Montana, on September 20, 1916. All bore the last name of Leahy, although only two were blood sisters. They had come to this undeveloped area of the Blackfeet Indians to run a hospital. When they discovered that no hospital existed there, they wired the sisters back home in Kingston, Ontario. The reply, "We cannot help you further. If you decide to stay with your $150 in funds, we will pray for you. If you choose to return home, you will be very welcome."

The sisters prayed and then rolled up their sleeves to turn a small boarding house into their first hospital. The first patient, admitted on November 6, 1916, was a Native American from the Flathead Reservation.

St. Joseph Hospital in Polson is said to be the first U.S. hospital to integrate Native Americans with other patients.

LEFT:
EARLY PHOTO OF
ST. JOSEPH HOSPITAL,
POLSON, MONTANA.

ST. CHARLES HOSPITAL
Bend, Oregon

Five Sisters of St. Joseph of Tipton, Indiana, arrived in Bend, Oregon, in 1917 to open a hospital at the request of a priest. Within a week, they had opened Bend's first hospital in a former mill clinic. When the owners of the mill told the sisters the hospital was only for the use of mill employees, the sisters said, "We will care for everyone who needs us or we will care for no one at all." And so it was.

ABOVE:
SR. MARY ANTHONY WAS
THE CHIEF FUND-RAISER
FOR THE FRANCISCAN
SISTERS OF LITTLE FALLS.

FRANCISCAN SISTERS
Little Falls, Minnesota

*I*n 1899 Sr. Mary Anthony Lyons was known in every logging camp, business place, office, railroad yard, farm, and home in central and west central Minnesota. Sr. Mary Anthony was the chief fund-raiser for the Franciscan Sisters of Little Falls, who delivered healthcare in homes and hospitals. One evening, she got off the train with a cargo of wheat, geese, and pigs. It had been a wild trip, with the geese and pigs tearing up and down the aisle of the train, sister in pursuit, but she managed to corral them and give them to patients at the sisters' hospital.

When townsfolk asked the sisters to open a hospital in Breckenridge, Minnesota, Sr. Mary Anthony raised the money. When St. Francis Hospital needed to expand in 1904, Sr. Mary Anthony returned to the logging camps, railroad yards, farms, and homes to sell tickets. A $7 donation offered free hospital care for a year. The new hospital opened in 1905.

One story about Sr. Mary Anthony recalls the time when St. Francis Hospital had a foot-high stack of unpaid bills. She agreed to try her hand at bill collecting. Sr. Mary Anthony stopped at the house of a family whose name was on top of the stack. After 10 minutes she came out of the house with tears streaming down her cheeks. She said the people didn't even have enough to eat, so how could anyone ask them for money? That was the end of her bill collection duties. Sr. Mary Anthony returned to fund-raising, which she did successfully for many years. She died in 1950 at age 90. ❧

Little Old
NEW YORK

By ED SULLIVAN

Mother Alice in Wonderland

FRANCISCAN SISTERS OF ALLEGANY
Allegany, New York

Between Ninth and Tenth Avenues, on New York's West Side, there was a section so noted for toughness, in the old days, that it acquired the nickname of 'Hell's Kitchen' ….

Into Hell's Kitchen, in 1934, came Mother Mary Alice, of the Third Order of St. Francis, and five nuns. Today, St. Clare's Hospital, on W. 51st, between Ninth and Tenth, testifies to the work which she and her five nuns have accomplished. Then they had 35 beds; now there are 450 beds and a regional emergency ambulance service….

"Don't write about me," she tells newspaper men. "I'd hate to get into the same boots with those politicians I read about."

FROM THE "LITTLE OLD NEW YORK" COLUMN, *THE NEW YORK DAILY NEWS*, SUNDAY, OCTOBER 9, 1949.

The Work Continues…

**Walking with
the Poor**

SR. MICHAELEEN FRIEDERS
SR. GLADYS MARIE MARTIN

SISTERS OF THE HOLY CROSS
Southern Maryland

When the Navy came to Southern Maryland in 1942, it built wooden barracks to house sailors. Most of the young men who lived there during World War II are old men now and long gone from the area.

But the barracks have survived. Drafty, leaky, rundown, they are home to poor people who can't afford to live anywhere else. The area is known as Flat Tops.

Few homeless people get into Flat Tops because there are not many openings. Some go in desperation to the Skip Jack Motel in Lexington Park, Maryland, which is also home to prostitutes and drug traffickers.

When African Americans asked the police to rid the area of drug dealers, the police did nothing.

"There's a lot of discrimination here," says Sr. Michaeleen Frieders, a Holy Cross Sister. Sr. Michaeleen and her friend

LEFT:
SR. MICHAELEEN AND
SR. GLADYS.
BELOW:
SR. GLADYS AT WORK IN
THE SOUP KITCHEN.

226

LEFT:
SR. MICHAELEEN
VISITING AN ELDERLY
WOMAN IN SOUTHERN
MARYLAND.

Sr. Gladys Marie Martin, also a Sister of the Holy Cross, know the
people of Flat Tops and the Skip Jack Motel, as well as other poor
people in the area.

A few years ago, Sr. Michaeleen enjoyed a powerful position as
CEO of Mercy Health System in Cincinnati. Sr. Gladys, likewise a
career CEO, was ending her term as provincial of her community's
eastern province. The two Holy Cross Sisters had for some time
felt a need to get back to what had called them to become
religious sisters in the first place. Something told them that in
their top management positions, they were not listening to their
innermost voice, a voice that called them to walk with the poor.

So in the very prime of their careers, at a time when they
were at the very top, they gave it all away. They came to southern
Maryland and formed Mary's Song, an initiative that has aided
not only the poor, but has engendered spiritual renewal for
Sr. Michaeleen and Sr. Gladys.

These women who used to run corporate board meetings
now get up at dawn to prepare lunch for up to 100 hungry people.
After serving the hungry crowd, they wash all the dishes at the

ABOVE:
THE MARY'S SONG SOUP
KITCHEN AT LUNCHTIME.
RIGHT:
SR. GLADYS WITH A YOUNG
DINER AT THE SOUP
KITCHEN.

soup kitchen, work at a clinic they founded, and help young
African American girls find alternatives to lives of poverty.

The poor are plentiful in southern Maryland, but they are
hard to find. You have to know where to look. In their Jeep,
Sr. Michaeleen and Sr. Gladys find them at the end of long dirt lanes
in tired trailers and tiny houses beaten down by time and poverty.

"We knock on doors and introduce ourselves," says
Sr. Michaeleen. "We ask people what they need and how we can
help them."

"My life as a woman religious is about helping those less fortunate," she adds. "Sr. Gladys and I have chosen to return to the people for a one-on-one ministry."

The change from CEO to "just a person" requires patience. "When you walk with the poor, you stand in line a lot," Sr. Michaeleen explains. "I see things I never saw when I was at the top."

She admits that the perks were great as a CEO. She had a car, nice clothes, and three secretaries. But even as the two sisters lived lives of corporate plenty, they were haunted by the thought that they had strayed from their calling.

Says Sr. Gladys: "In the Old Testament, to convert means to be again who you really are and to remember to whom you really belong.

"The New Testament stresses the necessity of a radical turnaround and invites us to pursue an entirely different course of life."

So, despite the physical hardships they've endured since coming to southern Maryland in 1991, the two women relish their new lives. And they regularly invite other sisters to walk with the poor.

"I would have to say that this has been a gift," says Sr. Michaeleen. "God has given us the strength to take the pain and move into the joy of serving the poor. We couldn't ask for more." ✆

ALL PHOTOS FOR THIS SECTION, ROMAN SAPECKI

We knock on doors and introduce ourselves. We ask people what they need and how we can help them....

When you walk with the poor, you stand in line a lot. I see things I never saw when I was at the top.

SR. MICHAELEEN FRIEDERS, SISTERS OF THE HOLY CROSS.

Contributors

*T*he stories in this book represent only a few of the wonderful contributions women religious have made to healthcare in America. They were selected from hundreds of stories submitted by members of the Catholic Health Association. Our thanks to everyone who contributed to this project.

Jeanette Jabour, OP
Bayley Place
Cincinnati, OH

Janis Kivela Hooey
Benedictine Health System
Duluth, MN

Sr. Mary Lucille Nachtsheim, OSB
Benedictine Sisters
Cottonwood, ID

Sr. Aelred Roehl, OSB
Benedictine Sisters
Duluth, MN

Sr. Antoinette Tramp, OSB
Benedictine Sisters
Watertown, SD

Tracey P. Lafferty
Bon Secours Hospital
Baltimore, MD

Geraldine Travali
Cabrini Medical Center
New York, NY

Sr. M. Bernadette de Lourdes,
    OCarm
Carmelite Sisters for the Aged
    and Infirm
Germantown, NY

Sr. Mary Louise Kelly, CIJ
Congregation of the Infant Jesus
Brooklyn, NY

Sr. Jeremy Quinn, CSA
Congregation of the Sisters of
    Saint Agnes
Fond du Lac, WI

Mary Ellen Brown
Daniel Freeman Hospitals
Inglewood, CA

Sr. Elaine Wheeler, DC
Daughters of Charity of St. Vincent
    de Paul
Albany, NY

Sr. Aloysia, DC
Daughters of Charity of St. Vincent
    de Paul
Emmitsburg, MD

Sr. Margaret Flynn, DC
Daughters of Charity of St. Vincent
    de Paul
Evansville, IN

Sr. Genevieve, DC
Daughters of Charity of St. Vincent
    de Paul
St. Louis, MO

Jane Hamilton
DePaul Health Center
St. Louis, MO

Mike Lee
Dominican Santa Cruz Hospital
Santa Cruz, CA

Sr. Marie Edward, OP
Dominican Sisters of Hawthorne
Hawthorne, NY

Dominican Sisters of Spokane
Spokane, WA

Sr. M. Linda Tonellato, OP
Dominican Sisters of Springfield
Springfield, IL

Susan Melanson
Fanny Allen Hospital
Colchester, VT

Sr. Mary Andrea Chudzik, CSSF
Felician Sisters
Chicago, IL

Sr. Mary Amelia, CSSF
Felician Sisters
Lodi, NJ

Sr. Mary Charles Rydzewski, SCSC
Franciscan Missionaries of Our Lady
    Health System, Inc.
Baton Rouge, LA

Sr. Sabina Collins, OSF
Franciscan Sisters
Little Falls, MN

Sr. Ann Kelly, OSF
Franciscan Sisters of Allegany
Allegany, NY

Sr. Martin Flavin, OSF
Sr. Donna Marie Kessler, OSF
Franciscan Sisters of Christian
    Charity HealthCare Ministry Inc.
Manitowoc, WI

Sr. Marylu Stueber, FSM
Franciscan Sisters of Mary
St. Louis, MO

Sr. Jolyce Greteman, FSPA
Franciscan Sisters of Perpetual
    Adoration
LaCrosse, WI

Sr. Mary Louise Sahm, SFP
Franciscan Sisters of the Poor
Cincinnati, OH

Sr. Kathleen Moseley, OSF
Franciscan Sisters of the Sacred Heart
Frankfort, IL

Sr. M. Marvina Kupiszewski, FSSJ
Franciscan Sisters of St. Joseph
Hamburg, NY

Beckie Reeves
Good Samaritan Medical Center
Zanesville, OH

Jodi Garrett
Holy Cross Health System
South Bend, IN

Carole Cufone
Holy Name Hospital
Teaneck, NJ

Sr. Ann Bailey, OSF
Hospital Sisters of the Third Order
    of St. Francis
Springfield, IL

Judi Neubecker
Incarnate Word Hospital
St. Louis, MO

Sr. Annette Allain, LSA
Little Sisters of the Assumption
New York, NY

Sr. Constance Carolyn, FSP
Little Sisters of the Poor
Baltimore, MD

Cheryl A. Frazier
Sr. Mary Linus Bax, SC
The Maria Joseph Living Care Center
Dayton, OH

Sr. Madeleine Sophie Hebert, MSC
Marianites of Holy Cross
New Orleans, LA

Sr. Lucy Hennessy, SMG
Maryfield Nursing Home
High Point, NC

Ellen Pierce
Maryknoll Mission Archives
Maryknoll, NY

Nancy S. Hopp
Mercy Center for Health Care
  Services
Aurora, IL

Jill Fraim
Mercy Health Center
Oklahoma City, OK

Michael Scahill
Mercy Healthcare San Diego
San Diego, CA

Lin Welling
Mercy Hospital
Charlotte, NC

June Bayh
Mercy Hospital
Devils Lake, ND

Denice R. Connell
Mercy Hospital
Iowa City, IA

Kathleen M. Washy
Mercy Hospital
Pittsburgh, PA

Kim Toppi
Mercy Hospital
Portland, ME

Sr. M. Seraphia McMahon, RSM
Mark R. Baldwin
Loretta Greiner
Mercy Hospital Medical Center
Des Moines, IA

Sr. Ann Louise Willman, RSM
Mercy Hospital of Tiffin
Tiffin, OH

Ruth Larson
Mercy Hospital of Valley City
Valley City, ND

Sr. Patricia Smith, RSM
Mercy Medical Center
Baltimore, MD

Sr. M. Augustine Roth, RSM
Sr. Marilyn Ward, RSM
Mercy Medical Center
Cedar Rapids, IA

Kelly S. Buechler
Mercy Medical Foundation
Williston, ND

C. David Kimmel
David Cuzzolina
Sr. Evelyn Marie Augustyn, RSM
Mercy Regional Health System
Altoona, PA

Susan Swinney
Mercy Regional Medical Center
Laredo, TX

Joanne Stiles
April Benedict
Mercycare Corporation
Albany, NY

Robert Poole
Mt. Carmel Medical Center
Pittsburg, KS

Sr. M. Helena Naviaux, RSM
Mt. St. Joseph's Residence and
  Extended Care Center
Portland, OR

Karen M. Kennelly
Mount St. Mary's College
Los Angeles, CA

Michelle M. Stewart
Nazareth Hospital
Philadelphia, PA

Lori Lippert
North Iowa Mercy Health Center
Mason City, IA

Laura Shaw
Our Lady of the Lake Regional
  Medical Center
Baton Rouge, LA

Jennifer S. Graves
Our Lady of Lourdes Health Center
Pasco, WA

Michele Chierici Fritz
Our Lady of Lourdes Medical Center
Camden, NJ

Maria Parker
Our Lady of Mercy Medical Center
Bronx, NY

Sr. Elizabeth Roberts, PHJC
Poor Handmaids of Jesus Christ
Donaldson, IN

Kathy McGreevy
Presentation Health System
Sioux Falls, SD

Janet Oates
Providence Hospital
Anchorage, AK

Liz Maillard
Providence Hospital
Sandusky, OH

Carol Johnson
Providence Hospital
Southfield, MI

G. W. Meredith
Providence Hospital
Washington, DC

Jane Underhill
Providence St. Vincent
  Medical Center
Portland, OR

Sr. Georgette Bayless, SP
Providence Yakima Medical Center
Yakima, WA

Sr. Mary Philip La Palme, SCMM
Regina Medical Center
Hastings, MN

Sr. Marion Chaloux, RHSJ
Religious Hospitallers of St. Joseph
Colchester, VT

Sr. Loretta Gaffney, RHSJ
Religious Hospitallers of St. Joseph
Kingston, Ontario, Canada

Martha A. Tully
Resurrection Medical Center
Chicago, IL

Christopher Brown
Sacred Heart Health System
Eugene, OR

Peggy Allen Weber
Sacred Heart Rehabilitation Hospital
Milwaukee, WI

Sr. Audrey Martin, OSB
St. Alexius Medical Center
Bismarck, ND

Sr. Mary Richard, LSP
St. Anne's Novitiate
Queen's Village, NY

Mary Jane Hughes
St. Anthony Hospital
Oklahoma City, OK

Carolyn J. Hager
Joe Dejanovic
St. Anthony Medical Center, Inc.
Crown Point, IN

Fr. Cassian Miles, OFM
St. Anthony's Guild
Paterson, NJ

Sr. M. Ancilla, OSF
Saint Anthony's Hospital
Alton, IL

Linda Behrens
St. Anthony's Medical Center
St. Louis, MO

Sr. Genevieve Karels, DSMP
St. Bernard's Providence Hospital
Milbank, SD

Dixie Scovel
St. Charles Hospital & Rehabilitation
  Center
Port Jefferson, NY

Carol Dixon
St. Edward Mercy Medical Network
Fort Smith, AR

Cindy Black Bouchie
St. Francis Cabrini Hospital
Alexandria, LA

Sr. Jacquelyn Alix, PFM
Saint Francis Home
Worcester, MA

Kathy White
St. Francis Hospital & Health Center
Blue Island, IL

Susan A. Lewis
Saint Francis Hospital and
  Medical Center
Hartford, CT

Saint Francis Medical Center
Grand Island, NE

Angie C. Wyss
St. Francis Medical Center
Honolulu, HI

Sr. Mary Joseph Trimbur, OSF
St. Francis Medical Center
Pittsburgh, PA

Larry Baker
St. Francis Regional Medical Center
Wichita, KS

Sr. Pat Prinzing, RSM
St. James Mercy Hospital
Hornell, NY

Avonelle Chitwood
St. John Medical Center
Tulsa, OK

Retha Porter
St. John's Medical Center
Longview, WA

Vincentian Studies Institute
St. John's University
Jamaica, NY

Deborah White
Saint Joseph Health Center
Kansas City, MO

Anita Kepley
Saint Joseph Health Centers &
Hospital
Chicago, IL

St. Joseph Healthcare System
Albuquerque, NM

Melanie Griffis
St. Joseph Hospital
Cheektowaga, NY

Pat Barker
Saint Joseph Hospital
Denver, CO

St. Joseph Hospital and Health
Care Center
Tacoma, WA

Melissa Spelsburg Loder
St. Joseph's Hospital
Buckhannon, WV

Carla David
St. Joseph's Hospital
Marshfield, WI

Tamara Perdue
St. Joseph's Hospital
Parkersburg, WV

Patty Anderson
St. Joseph's Hospital and
Medical Center
Paterson, NJ

St. Joseph's Hospital and
Medical Center
Phoenix, AZ

Sr. Helen Jacobson, OSF
Saint Joseph Medical Center
Baltimore, MD

Sue Wyninegar
Saint Joseph Medical Center
Burbank, CA

Tracy Piette
Saint Joseph Medical Center
Joliet, IL

St. Joseph Medical Center
Stamford, CT

Maureen Kolaczenko
Sue Lewis
Saint Mary Home
West Hartford, CT

Sr. M. Cynthia Ann Machlik, CSSF
St. Mary Hospital
Livonia, MI

Trish Spaulding
Saint Mary's Health Services
Grand Rapids, MI

Linda Macdonald
St. Mary's Hospital
Galveston, TX

Sr. Lauren Weinandt, OSF
Saint Marys Hospital
Rochester, MN

Sr. Geraldine Coleman, DC
St. Mary's Hospital
Rochester, NY

Phyllis Pavese
Saint Mary of Nazareth
Hospital Center
Chicago, IL

Sharon Houghton
St. Mary's Hospital
Huntington, WV

Sr. M. Bede Heinen, OP
Saint Mary's Regional Medical
Center
Reno, NV

Sr. Mary Lu Slowey, SSM
Saint Michael's Hospital
Stevens Point, WI

Shari Laist
Saint Raphael Healthcare System
New Haven, CT

Robert C. Howden
Saint Vincent Health Center
Erie, PA

Michael Wronski
Saint Vincent Hospital
Worcester, MA

Cindy Astle Lyle
Saint Vincent Hospital and
Health Center
Billings, MT

Beverly Owens
St. Vincent Hospitals and
Health Services
Indianapolis, IN

Shirley Jackson
St. Vincent Medical Center
Los Angeles, CA

Debora Maclay
St. Vincent's Health System
Jacksonville, FL

Barbara Traylor
St. Vincent's Hospital
Birmingham, AL

Fred Feiner
St. Vincent's Hospital and
Medical Center of New York
New York, NY

Tim Burchill
St. Vincent's Nursing Home
Bismarck, ND

Sr. Mary Louise Sullivan, MSC
Scalabrini Pastoral Institute
Staten Island, NY

Sr. Carol Karnitsky, SSCM
ServantCor
Kankakee, IL

Sr. Claire Pelletier, SCIM
Servants of the Immaculate
Heart of Mary
Bay View, Saco, ME

Sr. Alice M. Henke, OSM
Servants of Mary
Ladysmith, WI

Kathi Beard
Sisters of Bon Secours USA
Marriottsville, MD

Karen Hurley
Sisters of Charity of Cincinnati
Mount St. Joseph, OH

Sr. Monica LaFleur, CCVI
Sisters of Charity of the
Incarnate Word
Houston, TX

Sr. Francisca Eiken, CCVI
Sisters of Charity of the
Incarnate Word
San Antonio, TX

Sisters of Charity of the Incarnate
Word Health System
Houston, TX

Sr. Paulette Krick, SCL
Sisters of Charity of Leavenworth
Health Services Corporation
Leavenworth, KS

Sr. Mary Collette Crone, SCN
Sisters of Charity of Nazareth
Nazareth, KY

Sr. Claire Cayer, SCO
Sisters of Charity at Ottawa
Lowell, MA

Sr. M. Anne Francis Campbell, OLM
Sisters of Charity of Our Lady
of Mercy
Charleston, SC

Sr. Mary Denis Maher, CSA
Sisters of Charity of Saint Augustine
Richfield, OH

Sr. Elizabeth McLoughlin, SC
Sisters of Charity of Saint Elizabeth
Convent Station, NJ

Sr. Rita King, SC
Sisters of Charity of St. Vincent de
Paul of New York
Bronx, NY

Sr. Mary Philip Hampton, CDP
Sisters of Divine Providence
St. Louis, MO

Sr. Monica Lietz, SDS
Sisters of the Divine Savior
Milwaukee, WI

Sr. M. Boniface Adams, SSF
Sisters of the Holy Family
Motherhouse and Novitiate
New Orleans, LA

Sr. M. Gemma, CSFN
Sisters of the Holy Family
of Nazareth
Des Plaines, IL

Sr. Margaret Mary, CSFN
Sisters of the Holy Family
of Nazareth
Grand Prairie, TX

Sr. Evelyn Marie Augustyn, CSFN
Sisters of the Holy Family of
Nazareth
Pittsburgh, PA

Sr. Mary-Joanna Huegle, HM
Sisters of the Humility of Mary
Villa Maria, PA

Sr. Marguerite Guarneri, SMP
Sisters of Mary of the Presentation
Valley City, ND

Sr. Kevin Stroh, SMP
Sisters of Mary of the Presentation
  Health Corporation
Fargo, ND

Sr. Marilyn Gouailhardou, RSM
Sisters of Mercy
Burlingame, CA

Sr. Mary Prisca, RSM
Sisters of Mercy
Louisville, KY

Sr. Mary Paul, RSM
Sisters of Mercy
Merion Station, PA

Sr. Helen Sigrist, RSM
Sisters of Mercy of the Americas
Baltimore, MD

Sr. Pat Illing, RSM
Sisters of Mercy of the Americas
Chicago, IL

Sr. Mary Berding, RSM
Sr. Margaret Molitor, RSM
Sisters of Mercy of the Americas
Cincinnati, OH

Sr. Sylvia Connell, RSM
Sisters of Mercy of the Americas
Dallas, PA

Sr. Edna Maria LeRoux, RSM
Sisters of Mercy of the Americas
Farmington Hills, MI

Sr. Mary Kenneth Mullen, RSM
Sisters of Mercy of the Americas
Orchard Park, NY

Mollie McMahon
Sisters of Mercy of the Americas
Silver Spring, MD

Gwen Mauntel
Sisters of Mercy Health System
St. Louis, MO

Sr. Barbara Misner, SCSC
Sisters of Mercy of the Holy Cross
Merrill, WI

Deb Newcomer
Sisters of Mercy Provincialate
Omaha, NE

Sr. Louanna Orth, SNDdeN
Sisters of Notre Dame de Namur
Cincinnati, OH

Sr. Mary Jo Hasey, PBVM
Sisters of the Presentation
Fargo, ND

Tracy A. Russman
Sisters of the Presentation of
  the Blessed Virgin Mary
Aberdeen, SD

Grace R. Bennett
Sisters of Providence
Holyoke, MA

Loretta Zwolak Greene
Sisters of Providence
Seattle, WA

Sr. Claire Bouffard, SP
Sisters of Providence
Spokane, WA

Sr. Virginia Ann Wanzek, CR
Sisters of the Resurrection
Chicago, IL

Sr. Ruth Boedigheimer, OSB
Sisters of Saint Benedict
Saint Joseph, MN

Laura Rowe
Sisters of St. Francis
Clinton, IA

Sr. M. Joella Revers, OSF
Sisters of St. Francis
Colorado Springs, CO

Sr. Elvira Kelley, OSF
Sisters of St. Francis
Dubuque, IA

Sr. Marian Voelker, OSF
Sisters of Saint Francis
Joliet, IL

Sr. M. Severina Caron, OSF
Sisters of St. Francis
Rochester, MN

Sr. Mary Serbacki, OSF
Sisters of St. Francis
Stella Niagara, NY

Sr. Nora Klewicki, OSF
Sisters of St. Francis
Sylvania, OH

Sr. Mary Laurence Hanley, OSF
Sisters of St. Francis
Syracuse, NY

Sr. Helen Linder, OSF
Sisters of St. Francis
Tiffin, OH

Sr. Patricia Burkard, OSF
Sisters of St. Francis
Williamsville, NY

Sr. M. Thomasita Heller, OSF
Sisters of St. Francis of Millvale
Pittsburgh, PA

Sr. M. Corita Last, OSF
Sisters of Saint Francis of
  Perpetual Adoration
Mishawaka, IN

Sr. Andrew Persing, OSF
Sisters of St. Francis of Philadelphia
Aston, PA

Sr. Lawrence J. Murphy, SSJ
Sisters of Saint Joseph
Chestnut Hill, Philadelphia, PA

Sr. Liberata Pellerin, CSJ
Sisters of Saint Joseph
Concordia, KS

Sr. Marilyn Sullivan, SSJ
Sisters of St. Joseph
Nazareth, MI

Sr. Ruth Whalen, CSJ
Sisters of St. Joseph
Tipton, IN

Sr. Mary Thomas Camilletti, SSJ
Sr. Christine Riley
Sisters of Saint Joseph
Wheeling, WV

Sr. Charline Sullivane, CSJ
Sisters of St. Joseph of Carondelet
St. Louis, MO

Sr. Mary E. Kraft, CSJ
Sisters of St. Joseph of Carondelet
St. Paul, MN

Jude Langhurst
Sisters of St. Joseph of Wichita
Wichita, KS

Sr. Irene Waldman, SSJ
Sisters of St. Joseph Health System
Ann Arbor, MI

Sr. Annette Bachand, CSJ
Sisters of St. Joseph of Orange
Orange, CA

Sr. Joanna Vogelsang, CSJP
Sisters of Saint Joseph of Peace
Bellevue, WA

Sr. Thereserte Hunting, CSJP
Sisters of St. Joseph of Peace
Englewood Cliffs, NJ

Sr. Josephine Marie Peplinski,
  SSJ-TOSF
Sisters of St. Joseph of the Third
  Order of St. Francis
South Bend, IN

Sr. M. Clotilda, SSCM
Sisters of SS. Cyril and Methodius
Danville, PA

Sr. M. Bona Ney, SSM
Sisters of the Sorrowful Mother
Broken Arrow, OK

Sisters of the Sorrowful Mother
  Ministry Corporation
Milwaukee, WI

Sr. Maria Elena, OSF
Sisters of the Third Order
  of St. Francis
East Peoria, IL

Laura Popp
Spohn Health System
Corpus Christi, TX

Sr. M. Anne Angelcyk, SDR
Villa St. Teresa
Darby, PA

Tom Schroeder
Wheaton Franciscan Services, Inc.
Wheaton, IL

Sr. Jean Louise Forkin, CSC
Wheeling Hospital
Wheeling, WV

Sr. M. Paulinus
Jackson, MS

George Craig Stewart, Jr.
Fayetteville, NC

Index